Legislation and the Regulatory State

Legislation and the Regulatory State

SECOND EDITION

Document Supplement

Samuel Estreicher
Dwight D. Opperman Professor of Law
Director, Center for Labor and Employment Law
Co-Director, Institute of Judicial Administration
New York University School of Law

David L. Noll
Associate Professor of Law
Rutgers Law School

Carolina Academic Press
Durham, North Carolina

Print ISBN 978-1-5310-0565-8
e-ISBN 978-1-53100-566-5

Carolina Academic Press, LLC
700 Kent Street
Durham, North Carolina 27701
Telephone (919) 489-7486
Fax (919) 493-5668
www.cap-press.com

Printed in the United States of America

Contents

Organization of the Federal Government

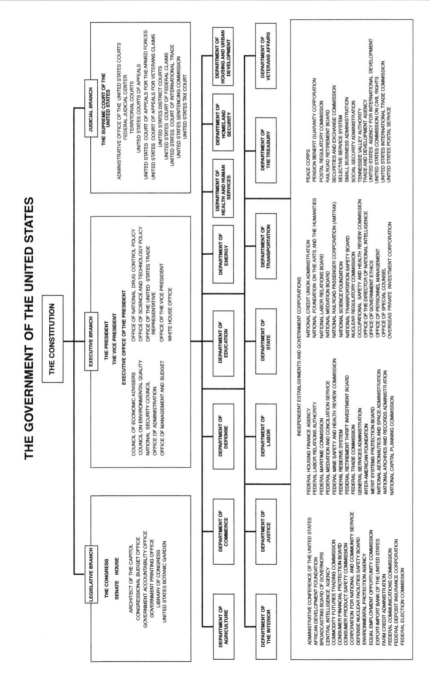

THE GOVERNMENT OF THE UNITED STATES

THE CONSTITUTION

LEGISLATIVE BRANCH

THE CONGRESS
SENATE   HOUSE

ARCHITECT OF THE CAPITOL
CONGRESSIONAL BUDGET OFFICE
GOVERNMENT ACCOUNTABILITY OFFICE
GOVERNMENT PRINTING OFFICE
LIBRARY OF CONGRESS
UNITED STATES BOTANIC GARDEN

EXECUTIVE BRANCH

THE PRESIDENT
THE VICE PRESIDENT

EXECUTIVE OFFICE OF THE PRESIDENT

COUNCIL OF ECONOMIC ADVISERS
COUNCIL ON ENVIRONMENTAL QUALITY
NATIONAL SECURITY COUNCIL
OFFICE OF ADMINISTRATION
OFFICE OF MANAGEMENT AND BUDGET
OFFICE OF NATIONAL DRUG CONTROL POLICY
OFFICE OF SCIENCE AND TECHNOLOGY POLICY
OFFICE OF THE UNITED STATES TRADE REPRESENTATIVE
OFFICE OF THE VICE PRESIDENT
WHITE HOUSE OFFICE

JUDICIAL BRANCH

THE SUPREME COURT OF THE UNITED STATES

ADMINISTRATIVE OFFICE OF THE UNITED STATES COURTS
FEDERAL JUDICIAL CENTER
TERRITORIAL COURTS
UNITED STATES COURTS OF APPEALS
UNITED STATES COURT OF APPEALS FOR THE ARMED FORCES
UNITED STATES COURT OF APPEALS FOR VETERANS CLAIMS
UNITED STATES DISTRICT COURTS
UNITED STATES COURT OF FEDERAL CLAIMS
UNITED STATES COURT OF INTERNATIONAL TRADE
UNITED STATES SENTENCING COMMISSION
UNITED STATES TAX COURT

DEPARTMENT OF AGRICULTURE

DEPARTMENT OF COMMERCE

DEPARTMENT OF DEFENSE

DEPARTMENT OF EDUCATION

DEPARTMENT OF ENERGY

DEPARTMENT OF HEALTH AND HUMAN SERVICES

DEPARTMENT OF HOMELAND SECURITY

DEPARTMENT OF HOUSING AND URBAN DEVELOPMENT

DEPARTMENT OF THE INTERIOR

DEPARTMENT OF JUSTICE

DEPARTMENT OF LABOR

DEPARTMENT OF STATE

DEPARTMENT OF TRANSPORTATION

DEPARTMENT OF THE TREASURY

DEPARTMENT OF VETERANS AFFAIRS

INDEPENDENT ESTABLISHMENTS AND GOVERNMENT CORPORATIONS

ADMINISTRATIVE CONFERENCE OF THE UNITED STATES
AFRICAN DEVELOPMENT FOUNDATION
BROADCASTING BOARD OF GOVERNORS
CENTRAL INTELLIGENCE AGENCY
COMMODITY FUTURES TRADING COMMISSION
CONSUMER FINANCIAL PROTECTION BOARD
CONSUMER PRODUCT SAFETY COMMISSION
CORPORATION FOR NATIONAL AND COMMUNITY SERVICE
DEFENSE NUCLEAR FACILITIES SAFETY BOARD
ENVIRONMENTAL PROTECTION AGENCY
EQUAL EMPLOYMENT OPPORTUNITY COMMISSION
EXPORT-IMPORT BANK OF THE UNITED STATES
FARM CREDIT ADMINISTRATION
FEDERAL COMMUNICATIONS COMMISSION
FEDERAL DEPOSIT INSURANCE CORPORATION
FEDERAL ELECTION COMMISSION

FEDERAL HOUSING FINANCE AGENCY
FEDERAL LABOR RELATIONS AUTHORITY
FEDERAL MARITIME COMMISSION
FEDERAL MEDIATION AND CONCILIATION SERVICE
FEDERAL MINE SAFETY AND HEALTH REVIEW COMMISSION
FEDERAL RESERVE SYSTEM
FEDERAL RETIREMENT THRIFT INVESTMENT BOARD
FEDERAL TRADE COMMISSION
GENERAL SERVICES ADMINISTRATION
INTER-AMERICAN FOUNDATION
MERIT SYSTEMS PROTECTION BOARD
NATIONAL AERONAUTICS AND SPACE ADMINISTRATION
NATIONAL ARCHIVES AND RECORDS ADMINISTRATION
NATIONAL CAPITAL PLANNING COMMISSION

NATIONAL CREDIT UNION ADMINISTRATION
NATIONAL FOUNDATION ON THE ARTS AND THE HUMANITIES
NATIONAL LABOR RELATIONS BOARD
NATIONAL MEDIATION BOARD
NATIONAL RAILROAD PASSENGER CORPORATION (AMTRAK)
NATIONAL SCIENCE FOUNDATION
NATIONAL TRANSPORTATION SAFETY BOARD
NUCLEAR REGULATORY COMMISSION
OCCUPATIONAL SAFETY AND HEALTH REVIEW COMMISSION
OFFICE OF THE DIRECTOR OF NATIONAL INTELLIGENCE
OFFICE OF GOVERNMENT ETHICS
OFFICE OF PERSONNEL MANAGEMENT
OFFICE OF SPECIAL COUNSEL
OVERSEAS PRIVATE INVESTMENT CORPORATION

PEACE CORPS
PENSION BENEFIT GUARANTY CORPORATION
POSTAL REGULATORY COMMISSION
RAILROAD RETIREMENT BOARD
SECURITIES AND EXCHANGE COMMISSION
SELECTIVE SERVICE SYSTEM
SMALL BUSINESS ADMINISTRATION
SOCIAL SECURITY ADMINISTRATION
TENNESSEE VALLEY AUTHORITY
TRADE AND DEVELOPMENT AGENCY
UNITED STATES AGENCY FOR INTERNATIONAL DEVELOPMENT
UNITED STATES COMMISSION ON CIVIL RIGHTS
UNITED STATES INTERNATIONAL TRADE COMMISSION
UNITED STATES POSTAL SERVICE

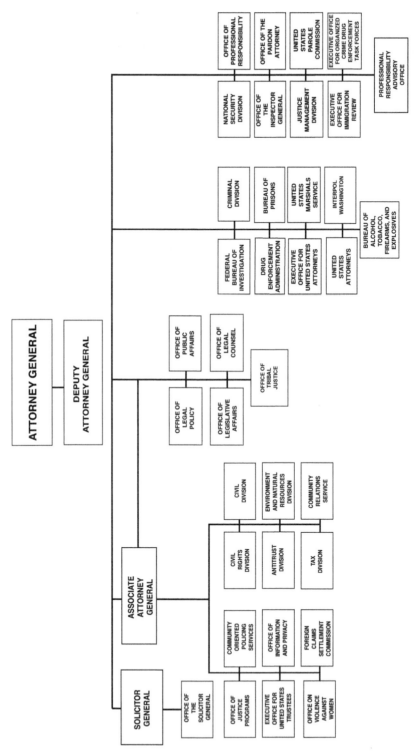

SOCIAL SECURITY ADMINISTRATION

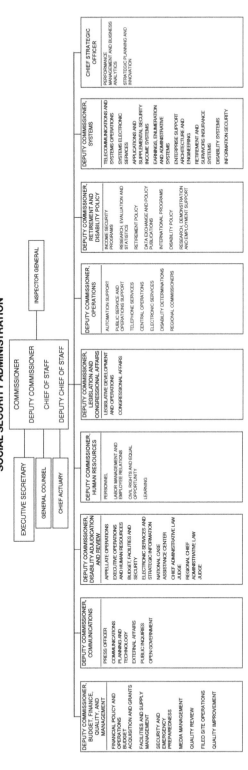

The Constitution of the United States of America

This text of the Constitution is reproduced from the U.S. Code (2016). It follows the engrossed copy signed by Gen. Washington and the deputies from twelve states.

We the People of the United States, in Order to form a more perfect Union, establish Justice, insure domestic Tranquility, provide for the common defence, promote the general Welfare, and secure the Blessings of Liberty to ourselves and our Posterity, do ordain and establish this Constitution for the United States of America.

Article. I.

Section. 1.

All legislative Powers herein granted shall be vested in a Congress of the United States, which shall consist of a Senate and House of Representatives.

Section. 2.

Clause 1: The House of Representatives shall be composed of Members chosen every second Year by the People of the several States, and the Electors in each State shall have the Qualifications requisite for Electors of the most numerous Branch of the State Legislature.

Clause 2: No Person shall be a Representative who shall not have attained to the Age of twenty five Years, and been seven Years a Citizen of the United States, and who shall not, when elected, be an Inhabitant of that State in which he shall be chosen.

Clause 3: Representatives and direct Taxes shall be apportioned among the several States which may be included within this Union, according to their respective Numbers, which shall be determined by adding to the whole Number of free Persons, including those bound to Service for a Term of Years, and excluding Indians not taxed, three fifths of all other Persons. (See Note 2) The actual Enumeration shall be made within three Years after the first Meeting of the Congress of the United States, and within every subsequent Term of ten Years, in such Manner as they shall by Law direct. The Number of Representatives shall not exceed one for every thirty Thousand, but each State shall have at Least one Representative; and until such enumeration shall be made, the State of New Hampshire shall be entitled to chuse three, Massachusetts eight,

Rhode-Island and Providence Plantations one, Connecticut five, New-York six, New Jersey four, Pennsylvania eight, Delaware one, Maryland six, Virginia ten, North Carolina five, South Carolina five, and Georgia three.

Clause 4: When vacancies happen in the Representation from any State, the Executive Authority thereof shall issue Writs of Election to fill such Vacancies.

Clause 5: The House of Representatives shall chuse their Speaker and other Officers; and shall have the sole Power of Impeachment.

Section. 3.

Clause 1: The Senate of the United States shall be composed of two Senators from each State, chosen by the Legislature thereof, (See Note 3) for six Years; and each Senator shall have one Vote.

Clause 2: Immediately after they shall be assembled in Consequence of the first Election, they shall be divided as equally as may be into three Classes. The Seats of the Senators of the first Class shall be vacated at the Expiration of the second Year, of the second Class at the Expiration of the fourth Year, and of the third Class at the Expiration of the sixth Year, so that one third may be chosen every second Year; and if Vacancies happen by Resignation, or otherwise, during the Recess of the Legislature of any State, the Executive thereof may make temporary Appointments until the next Meeting of the Legislature, which shall then fill such Vacancies. (See Note 4)

Clause 3: No Person shall be a Senator who shall not have attained to the Age of thirty Years, and been nine Years a Citizen of the United States, and who shall not, when elected, be an Inhabitant of that State for which he shall be chosen.

Clause 4: The Vice President of the United States shall be President of the Senate, but shall have no Vote, unless they be equally divided.

Clause 5: The Senate shall chuse their other Officers, and also a President pro tempore, in the Absence of the Vice President, or when he shall exercise the Office of President of the United States.

Clause 6: The Senate shall have the sole Power to try all Impeachments. When sitting for that Purpose, they shall be on Oath or Affirmation. When the President of the United States is tried, the Chief Justice shall preside: And no Person shall be convicted without the Concurrence of two thirds of the Members present.

Clause 7: Judgment in Cases of Impeachment shall not extend further than to removal from Office, and disqualification to hold and enjoy any Office of honor, Trust or Profit under the United States: but the Party convicted shall nevertheless be liable and subject to Indictment, Trial, Judgment and Punishment, according to Law.

Section. 4.

Clause 1: The Times, Places and Manner of holding Elections for Senators and Representatives, shall be prescribed in each State by the Legislature thereof; but the Congress may at any time by Law make or alter such Regulations, except as to the Places of chusing Senators.

Clause 2: The Congress shall assemble at least once in every Year, and such Meeting shall be on the first Monday in December, (See Note 5) unless they shall by Law appoint a different Day.

Section. 5.

Clause 1: Each House shall be the Judge of the Elections, Returns and Qualifications of its own Members, and a Majority of each shall constitute a Quorum to do Business; but a smaller Number may adjourn from day to day, and may be authorized to compel the Attendance of absent Members, in such Manner, and under such Penalties as each House may provide.

Clause 2: Each House may determine the Rules of its Proceedings, punish its Members for disorderly Behaviour, and, with the Concurrence of two thirds, expel a Member.

Clause 3: Each House shall keep a Journal of its Proceedings, and from time to time publish the same, excepting such Parts as may in their Judgment require Secrecy; and the Yeas and Nays of the Members of either House on any question shall, at the Desire of one fifth of those Present, be entered on the Journal.

Clause 4: Neither House, during the Session of Congress, shall, without the Consent of the other, adjourn for more than three days, nor to any other Place than that in which the two Houses shall be sitting.

Section. 6.

Clause 1: The Senators and Representatives shall receive a Compensation for their Services, to be ascertained by Law, and paid out of the Treasury of the United States. (See Note 6) They shall in all Cases, except Treason, Felony and Breach of the Peace, be privileged from Arrest during their Attendance at the Session of their respective Houses, and in going to and returning from the same; and for any Speech or Debate in either House, they shall not be questioned in any other Place.

Clause 2: No Senator or Representative shall, during the Time for which he was elected, be appointed to any civil Office under the Authority of the United States, which shall have been created, or the Emoluments whereof shall have been increased during such time; and no Person holding any Office under the United States, shall be a Member of either House during his Continuance in Office.

Section. 7.

Clause 1: All Bills for raising Revenue shall originate in the House of Representatives; but the Senate may propose or concur with Amendments as on other Bills.

Clause 2: Every Bill which shall have passed the House of Representatives and the Senate, shall, before it become a Law, be presented to the President of the United States; If he approve he shall sign it, but if not he shall return it, with his Objections to that House in which it shall have originated, who shall enter the Objections at large on their Journal, and proceed to reconsider it. If after such Reconsideration two thirds of that House shall agree to pass the Bill, it shall be sent, together with the Objections, to the other House, by which it shall likewise be reconsidered, and if approved by two thirds of that House, it shall become a Law. But in all such Cases the Votes of both Houses shall be determined by yeas and Nays, and the Names of the Persons voting for and against the Bill shall be entered on the Journal of each House respectively. If any Bill shall not be returned by the President within ten Days (Sundays excepted) after it shall have been presented to him, the Same shall be a Law, in like Manner as if he had signed it, unless the Congress by their Adjournment prevent its Return, in which Case it shall not be a Law.

Clause 3: Every Order, Resolution, or Vote to which the Concurrence of the Senate and House of Representatives may be necessary (except on a question of Adjournment) shall be presented to the President of the United States; and before the Same shall take Effect, shall be approved by him, or being disapproved by him, shall be repassed by two thirds of the Senate and House of Representatives, according to the Rules and Limitations prescribed in the Case of a Bill.

Section. 8.

Clause 1: The Congress shall have Power To lay and collect Taxes, Duties, Imposts and Excises, to pay the Debts and provide for the common Defence and general Welfare of the United States; but all Duties, Imposts and Excises shall be uniform throughout the United States;

Clause 2: To borrow Money on the credit of the United States;

Clause 3: To regulate Commerce with foreign Nations, and among the several States, and with the Indian Tribes;

Clause 4: To establish an uniform Rule of Naturalization, and uniform Laws on the subject of Bankruptcies throughout the United States;

Clause 5: To coin Money, regulate the Value thereof, and of foreign Coin, and fix the Standard of Weights and Measures;

Clause 6: To provide for the Punishment of counterfeiting the Securities and current Coin of the United States;

Clause 7: To establish Post Offices and post Roads;

Clause 8: To promote the Progress of Science and useful Arts, by securing for limited Times to Authors and Inventors the exclusive Right to their respective Writings and Discoveries;

Clause 9: To constitute Tribunals inferior to the supreme Court;

Clause 10: To define and punish Piracies and Felonies committed on the high Seas, and Offences against the Law of Nations;

Clause 11: To declare War, grant Letters of Marque and Reprisal, and make Rules concerning Captures on Land and Water;

Clause 12: To raise and support Armies, but no Appropriation of Money to that Use shall be for a longer Term than two Years;

Clause 13: To provide and maintain a Navy;

Clause 14: To make Rules for the Government and Regulation of the land and naval Forces;

Clause 15: To provide for calling forth the Militia to execute the Laws of the Union, suppress Insurrections and repel Invasions;

Clause 16: To provide for organizing, arming, and disciplining, the Militia, and for governing such Part of them as may be employed in the Service of the United States, reserving to the States respectively, the Appointment of the Officers, and the Authority of training the Militia according to the discipline prescribed by Congress;

Clause 17: To exercise exclusive Legislation in all Cases whatsoever, over such District (not exceeding ten Miles square) as may, by Cession of particular States, and the Acceptance of Congress, become the Seat of the Government of the United States, and to exercise like Authority over all Places purchased by the Consent of the Legislature of the State in which the Same shall be, for the Erection of Forts, Magazines, Arsenals, dock-Yards, and other needful Buildings;—And

Clause 18: To make all Laws which shall be necessary and proper for carrying into Execution the foregoing Powers, and all other Powers vested by this Constitution in the Government of the United States, or in any Department or Officer thereof.

Section. 9.

Clause 1: The Migration or Importation of such Persons as any of the States now existing shall think proper to admit, shall not be prohibited by the Congress prior to the Year one thousand eight hundred and eight, but a Tax or duty may be imposed on such Importation, not exceeding ten dollars for each Person.

Clause 2: The Privilege of the Writ of Habeas Corpus shall not be suspended, unless when in Cases of Rebellion or Invasion the public Safety may require it.

Clause 3: No Bill of Attainder or ex post facto Law shall be passed.

Clause 4: No Capitation, or other direct, Tax shall be laid, unless in Proportion to the Census or Enumeration herein before directed to be taken. (See Note 7)

Clause 5: No Tax or Duty shall be laid on Articles exported from any State.

Clause 6: No Preference shall be given by any Regulation of Commerce or Revenue to the Ports of one State over those of another: nor shall Vessels bound to, or from, one State, be obliged to enter, clear, or pay Duties in another.

Clause 7: No Money shall be drawn from the Treasury, but in Consequence of Appropriations made by Law; and a regular Statement and Account of the Receipts and Expenditures of all public Money shall be published from time to time.

Clause 8: No Title of Nobility shall be granted by the United States: And no Person holding any Office of Profit or Trust under them, shall, without the Consent of the Congress, accept of any present, Emolument, Office, or Title, of any kind whatever, from any King, Prince, or foreign State.

Section. 10.

Clause 1: No State shall enter into any Treaty, Alliance, or Confederation; grant Letters of Marque and Reprisal; coin Money; emit Bills of Credit; make any Thing but gold and silver Coin a Tender in Payment of Debts; pass any Bill of Attainder, ex post facto Law, or Law impairing the Obligation of Contracts, or grant any Title of Nobility.

Clause 2: No State shall, without the Consent of the Congress, lay any Imposts or Duties on Imports or Exports, except what may be absolutely necessary for executing it's inspection Laws: and the net Produce of all Duties and Imposts, laid by any State on Imports or Exports, shall be for the Use of the Treasury of the United States; and all such Laws shall be subject to the Revision and Controul of the Congress.

Clause 3: No State shall, without the Consent of Congress, lay any Duty of Tonnage, keep Troops, or Ships of War in time of Peace, enter into any Agreement or Compact with another State, or with a foreign Power, or engage in War, unless actually invaded, or in such imminent Danger as will not admit of delay.

Article. II.

Section. 1.

Clause 1: The executive Power shall be vested in a President of the United States of America. He shall hold his Office during the Term of four Years, and, together with the Vice President, chosen for the same Term, be elected, as follows:

Clause 2: Each State shall appoint, in such Manner as the Legislature thereof may direct, a Number of Electors, equal to the whole Number of Senators and Representatives to which the State may be entitled in the Congress: but no Senator or

Representative, or Person holding an Office of Trust or Profit under the United States, shall be appointed an Elector.

Clause 3: The Electors shall meet in their respective States, and vote by Ballot for two Persons, of whom one at least shall not be an Inhabitant of the same State with themselves. And they shall make a List of all the Persons voted for, and of the Number of Votes for each; which List they shall sign and certify, and transmit sealed to the Seat of the Government of the United States, directed to the President of the Senate. The President of the Senate shall, in the Presence of the Senate and House of Representatives, open all the Certificates, and the Votes shall then be counted. The Person having the greatest Number of Votes shall be the President, if such Number be a Majority of the whole Number of Electors appointed; and if there be more than one who have such Majority, and have an equal Number of Votes, then the House of Representatives shall immediately chuse by Ballot one of them for President; and if no Person have a Majority, then from the five highest on the List the said House shall in like Manner chuse the President. But in choosing the President, the Votes shall be taken by States, the Representation from each State having one Vote; A quorum for this Purpose shall consist of a Member or Members from two thirds of the States, and a Majority of all the States shall be necessary to a Choice. In every Case, after the Choice of the President, the Person having the greatest Number of Votes of the Electors shall be the Vice President. But if there should remain two or more who have equal Votes, the Senate shall chuse from them by Ballot the Vice President. (See Note 8)

Clause 4: The Congress may determine the Time of chusing the Electors, and the Day on which they shall give their Votes; which Day shall be the same throughout the United States.

Clause 5: No Person except a natural born Citizen, or a Citizen of the United States, at the time of the Adoption of this Constitution, shall be eligible to the Office of President; neither shall any Person be eligible to that Office who shall not have attained to the Age of thirty five Years, and been fourteen Years a Resident within the United States.

Clause 6: In Case of the Removal of the President from Office, or of his Death, Resignation, or Inability to discharge the Powers and Duties of the said Office, (See Note 9) the Same shall devolve on the Vice President, and the Congress may by Law provide for the Case of Removal, Death, Resignation or Inability, both of the President and Vice President, declaring what Officer shall then act as President, and such Officer shall act accordingly, until the Disability be removed, or a President shall be elected.

Clause 7: The President shall, at stated Times, receive for his Services, a Compensation, which shall neither be encreased nor diminished during the Period for which he shall have been elected, and he shall not receive within that Period any other Emolument from the United States, or any of them.

Clause 8: Before he enter on the Execution of his Office, he shall take the following Oath or Affirmation: — "I do solemnly swear (or affirm) that I will faithfully execute the Office of President of the United States, and will to the best of my Ability, preserve, protect and defend the Constitution of the United States."

Section. 2.

Clause 1: The President shall be Commander in Chief of the Army and Navy of the United States, and of the Militia of the several States, when called into the actual Service of the United States; he may require the Opinion, in writing, of the principal Officer in each of the executive Departments, upon any Subject relating to the Duties of their respective Offices, and he shall have Power to grant Reprieves and Pardons for Offences against the United States, except in Cases of Impeachment.

Clause 2: He shall have Power, by and with the Advice and Consent of the Senate, to make Treaties, provided two thirds of the Senators present concur; and he shall nominate, and by and with the Advice and Consent of the Senate, shall appoint Ambassadors, other public Ministers and Consuls, Judges of the supreme Court, and all other Officers of the United States, whose Appointments are not herein otherwise provided for, and which shall be established by Law: but the Congress may by Law vest the Appointment of such inferior Officers, as they think proper, in the President alone, in the Courts of Law, or in the Heads of Departments.

Clause 3: The President shall have Power to fill up all Vacancies that may happen during the Recess of the Senate, by granting Commissions which shall expire at the End of their next Session.

Section. 3.

He shall from time to time give to the Congress Information of the State of the Union, and recommend to their Consideration such Measures as he shall judge necessary and expedient; he may, on extraordinary Occasions, convene both Houses, or either of them, and in Case of Disagreement between them, with Respect to the Time of Adjournment, he may adjourn them to such Time as he shall think proper; he shall receive Ambassadors and other public Ministers; he shall take Care that the Laws be faithfully executed, and shall Commission all the Officers of the United States.

Section. 4.

The President, Vice President and all civil Officers of the United States, shall be removed from Office on Impeachment for, and Conviction of, Treason, Bribery, or other high Crimes and Misdemeanors.

Article. III.

Section. 1.

The judicial Power of the United States, shall be vested in one supreme Court, and in such inferior Courts as the Congress may from time to time ordain and establish. The Judges, both of the supreme and inferior Courts, shall hold their Offices during good Behaviour, and shall, at stated Times, receive for their Services, a Compensation, which shall not be diminished during their Continuance in Office.

Section. 2.

Clause 1: The judicial Power shall extend to all Cases, in Law and Equity, arising under this Constitution, the Laws of the United States, and Treaties made, or which shall be made, under their Authority;—to all Cases affecting Ambassadors, other public Ministers and Consuls;—to all Cases of admiralty and maritime Jurisdiction;—to Controversies to which the United States shall be a Party;—to Controversies between two or more States;—between a State and Citizens of another State; (See Note 10)—between Citizens of different States,—between Citizens of the same State claiming Lands under Grants of different States, and between a State, or the Citizens thereof, and foreign States, Citizens or Subjects.

Clause 2: In all Cases affecting Ambassadors, other public Ministers and Consuls, and those in which a State shall be Party, the supreme Court shall have original Jurisdiction. In all the other Cases before mentioned, the supreme Court shall have appellate Jurisdiction, both as to Law and Fact, with such Exceptions, and under such Regulations as the Congress shall make.

Clause 3: The Trial of all Crimes, except in Cases of Impeachment, shall be by Jury; and such Trial shall be held in the State where the said Crimes shall have been committed; but when not committed within any State, the Trial shall be at such Place or Places as the Congress may by Law have directed.

Section. 3.

Clause 1: Treason against the United States, shall consist only in levying War against them, or in adhering to their Enemies, giving them Aid and Comfort.

No Person shall be convicted of Treason unless on the Testimony of two Witnesses to the same overt Act, or on Confession in open Court.

Clause 2: The Congress shall have Power to declare the Punishment of Treason, but no Attainder of Treason shall work Corruption of Blood, or Forfeiture except during the Life of the Person attainted.

Article. IV.

Section. 1.

Full Faith and Credit shall be given in each State to the public Acts, Records, and judicial Proceedings of every other State. And the Congress may by general Laws prescribe the Manner in which such Acts, Records and Proceedings shall be proved, and the Effect thereof.

Section. 2.

Clause 1: The Citizens of each State shall be entitled to all Privileges and Immunities of Citizens in the several States.

Clause 2: A Person charged in any State with Treason, Felony, or other Crime, who shall flee from Justice, and be found in another State, shall on Demand of the executive Authority of the State from which he fled, be delivered up, to be removed to the State having Jurisdiction of the Crime.

Clause 3: No Person held to Service or Labour in one State, under the Laws thereof, escaping into another, shall, in Consequence of any Law or Regulation therein, be discharged from such Service or Labour, but shall be delivered up on Claim of the Party to whom such Service or Labour may be due. (See Note 11)

Section. 3.

Clause 1: New States may be admitted by the Congress into this Union; but no new State shall be formed or erected within the Jurisdiction of any other State; nor any State be formed by the Junction of two or more States, or Parts of States, without the Consent of the Legislatures of the States concerned as well as of the Congress.

Clause 2: The Congress shall have Power to dispose of and make all needful Rules and Regulations respecting the Territory or other Property belonging to the United States; and nothing in this Constitution shall be so construed as to Prejudice any Claims of the United States, or of any particular State.

Section. 4.

The United States shall guarantee to every State in this Union a Republican Form of Government, and shall protect each of them against Invasion; and on Application of the Legislature, or of the Executive (when the Legislature cannot be convened) against domestic Violence.

Article. V.

The Congress, whenever two thirds of both Houses shall deem it necessary, shall propose Amendments to this Constitution, or, on the Application of the Legislatures of two thirds of the several States, shall call a Convention for proposing Amendments, which, in either Case, shall be valid to all Intents and Purposes, as Part of this Constitution, when ratified by the Legislatures of three fourths of the several States, or by Conventions in three fourths thereof, as the one or the other Mode of Ratification may be proposed by the Congress; Provided hat no Amendment which may be made prior to the Year One thousand eight hundred and eight shall in any Manner affect the first and fourth Clauses in the Ninth Section of the first Article; and that no State, without its Consent, shall be deprived of its equal Suffrage in the Senate.

Article. VI.

Clause 1: All Debts contracted and Engagements entered into, before the Adoption of this Constitution, shall be as valid against the United States under this Constitution, as under the Confederation.

Clause 2: This Constitution, and the Laws of the United States which shall be made in Pursuance thereof; and all Treaties made, or which shall be made, under the Authority of the United States, shall be the supreme Law of the Land; and the Judges in every State shall be bound thereby, any Thing in the Constitution or Laws of any State to the Contrary notwithstanding.

Clause 3: The Senators and Representatives before mentioned, and the Members of the several State Legislatures, and all executive and judicial Officers, both of the United States and of the several States, shall be bound by Oath or Affirmation, to support this Constitution; but no religious Test shall ever be required as a Qualification to any Office or public Trust under the United States.

Article. VII.

The Ratification of the Conventions of nine States, shall be sufficient for the Establishment of this Constitution between the States so ratifying the Same.

Done in convention by the unanimous consent of the states present the seventeenth day of September in the year of our Lord one thousand seven hundred and eighty seven and of the independence of the United States of America the twelfth.

In witness whereof We have hereunto subscribed our Names,

G. Washington-Presidt. and deputy from Virginia

New Hampshire: John Langdon, Nicholas Gilman

Massachusetts: Nathaniel Gorham, Rufus King

Connecticut: Wm: Saml. Johnson, Roger Sherman

New York: Alexander Hamilton

New Jersey: Wil: Livingston, David Brearly, Wm. Paterson, Jona: Dayton

Pennsylvania: B. Franklin, Thomas Mifflin, Robt. Morris, Geo. Clymer, Thos. FitzSimons, Jared Ingersoll, James Wilson, Gouv Morris

Delaware: Geo: Read, Gunning Bedford jun, John Dickinson, Richard Bassett, Jaco: Broom

Maryland: James McHenry, Dan of St Thos. Jenifer, Danl Carroll

Virginia: John Blair—, James Madison Jr.

North Carolina: Wm. Blount, Richd. Dobbs Spaight, Hu Williamson

South Carolina: J. Rutledge, Charles Cotesworth Pinckney, Charles Pinckney, Pierce Butler

Georgia: William Few, Abr Baldwin

Amendment I

Congress shall make no law respecting an establishment of religion, or prohibiting the free exercise thereof; or abridging the freedom of speech, or of the press; or the right of the people peaceably to assemble, and to petition the government for a redress of grievances.

Amendment II

A well regulated militia, being necessary to the security of a free state, the right of the people to keep and bear arms, shall not be infringed.

Amendment III

No soldier shall, in time of peace be quartered in any house, without the consent of the owner, nor in time of war, but in a manner to be prescribed by law.

Amendment IV

The right of the people to be secure in their persons, houses, papers, and effects, against unreasonable searches and seizures, shall not be violated, and no warrants shall issue, but upon probable cause, supported by oath or affirmation, and particularly describing the place to be searched, and the persons or things to be seized.

Amendment V

No person shall be held to answer for a capital, or otherwise infamous crime, unless on a presentment or indictment of a grand jury, except in cases arising in the land or naval forces, or in the militia, when in actual service in time of war or public danger; nor shall any person be subject for the same offense to be twice put in jeopardy of life or limb; nor shall be compelled in any criminal case to be a witness against himself, nor be deprived of life, liberty, or property, without due process of law; nor shall private property be taken for public use, without just compensation.

Amendment VI

In all criminal prosecutions, the accused shall enjoy the right to a speedy and public trial, by an impartial jury of the state and district wherein the crime shall have been committed, which district shall have been previously ascertained by law, and to be informed of the nature and cause of the accusation; to be confronted with the witnesses against him; to have compulsory process for obtaining witnesses in his favor, and to have the assistance of counsel for his defense.

Amendment VII

In suits at common law, where the value in controversy shall exceed twenty dollars, the right of trial by jury shall be preserved, and no fact tried by a jury, shall be otherwise reexamined in any court of the United States, than according to the rules of the common law.

Amendment VIII

Excessive bail shall not be required, nor excessive fines imposed, nor cruel and unusual punishments inflicted.

Amendment IX

The enumeration in the Constitution, of certain rights, shall not be construed to deny or disparage others retained by the people.

Amendment X

The powers not delegated to the United States by the Constitution, nor prohibited by it to the states, are reserved to the states respectively, or to the people.

Amendment XI

The judicial power of the United States shall not be construed to extend to any suit in law or equity, commenced or prosecuted against one of the United States by citizens of another state, or by citizens or subjects of any foreign state.

Amendment XII

The electors shall meet in their respective states and vote by ballot for President and Vice-President, one of whom, at least, shall not be an inhabitant of the same state with themselves; they shall name in their ballots the person voted for as President, and in distinct ballots the person voted for as Vice-President, and they shall make distinct lists of all persons voted for as President, and of all persons voted for as Vice-President, and of the number of votes for each, which lists they shall sign and certify, and transmit sealed to the seat of the government of the United States, directed to the President of the Senate;—The President of the Senate shall, in the presence of the Senate and House of Representatives, open all the certificates and the votes shall then be counted;—the person having the greatest number of votes for President, shall be the President, if such number be a majority of the whole number of electors appointed; and if no person have such majority, then from the persons having the highest numbers not exceeding three on the list of those voted for as President, the House of Representatives shall choose immediately, by ballot, the President. But in choosing the President, the votes shall be taken by states, the representation from each state having one vote; a quorum for this purpose shall consist of a member or members from two-thirds of the states, and a majority of all the states shall be necessary to a choice. And if the House of Representatives shall not choose a President whenever the right of choice shall devolve upon them, before the fourth day of March next following, then the Vice-President shall act as President, as in the case of the death or other constitutional disability of the President. The person having the greatest number of votes as Vice-President, shall be the Vice-President, if such number be a majority of the whole number of electors appointed, and if no person have a majority, then from the two highest numbers on the list, the Senate shall choose the Vice-President; a quorum for the purpose shall consist of two-thirds of the whole number of Senators, and a majority of the whole number shall be necessary to a choice. But no person constitutionally ineligible to the office of President shall be eligible to that of Vice-President of the United States.

Amendment XIII

Section 1.

Neither slavery nor involuntary servitude, except as a punishment for crime whereof the party shall have been duly convicted, shall exist within the United States, or any place subject to their jurisdiction.

Section 2.

Congress shall have power to enforce this article by appropriate legislation.

Amendment XIV

Section 1.

All persons born or naturalized in the United States, and subject to the jurisdiction thereof, are citizens of the United States and of the state wherein they reside. No state shall make or enforce any law which shall abridge the privileges or immunities of citizens of the United States; nor shall any state deprive any person of life, liberty, or property, without due process of law; nor deny to any person within its jurisdiction the equal protection of the laws.

Section 2.

Representatives shall be apportioned among the several states according to their respective numbers, counting the whole number of persons in each state, excluding

Indians not taxed. But when the right to vote at any election for the choice of electors for President and Vice President of the United States, Representatives in Congress, the executive and judicial officers of a state, or the members of the legislature thereof, is denied to any of the male inhabitants of such state, being twenty-one years of age, and citizens of the United States, or in any way abridged, except for participation in rebellion, or other crime, the basis of representation therein shall be reduced in the proportion which the number of such male citizens shall bear to the whole number of male citizens twenty-one years of age in such state.

Section 3.

No person shall be a Senator or Representative in Congress, or elector of President and Vice President, or hold any office, civil or military, under the United States, or under any state, who, having previously taken an oath, as a member of Congress, or as an officer of the United States, or as a member of any state legislature, or as an executive or judicial officer of any state, to support the Constitution of the United States, shall have engaged in insurrection or rebellion against the same, or given aid or comfort to the enemies thereof. But Congress may by a vote of two-thirds of each House, remove such disability.

Section 4.

The validity of the public debt of the United States, authorized by law, including debts incurred for payment of pensions and bounties for services in suppressing insurrection or rebellion, shall not be questioned. But neither the United States nor any state shall assume or pay any debt or obligation incurred in aid of insurrection or rebellion against the United States, or any claim for the loss or emancipation of any slave; but all such debts, obligations and claims shall be held illegal and void.

Section 5.

The Congress shall have power to enforce, by appropriate legislation, the provisions of this article.

Amendment XV

Section 1.

The right of citizens of the United States to vote shall not be denied or abridged by the United States or by any state on account of race, color, or previous condition of servitude.

Section 2.

The Congress shall have power to enforce this article by appropriate legislation.

Amendment XVI

The Congress shall have power to lay and collect taxes on incomes, from whatever source derived, without apportionment among the several states, and without regard to any census or enumeration.

Amendment XVII

The Senate of the United States shall be composed of two Senators from each state, elected by the people thereof, for six years; and each Senator shall have one vote. The electors in each state shall have the qualifications requisite for electors of the most numerous branch of the state legislatures.

When vacancies happen in the representation of any state in the Senate, the executive authority of such state shall issue writs of election to fill such vacancies: Provided, that the legislature of any state may empower the executive thereof to make temporary appointments until the people fill the vacancies by election as the legislature may direct.

This amendment shall not be so construed as to affect the election or term of any Senator chosen before it becomes valid as part of the Constitution.

Amendment XVIII

Section 1.

After one year from the ratification of this article the manufacture, sale, or transportation of intoxicating liquors within, the importation thereof into, or the exportation thereof from the United States and all territory subject to the jurisdiction thereof for beverage purposes is hereby prohibited.

Section 2.

The Congress and the several states shall have concurrent power to enforce this article by appropriate legislation.

Section 3.

This article shall be inoperative unless it shall have been ratified as an amendment to the Constitution by the legislatures of the several states, as provided in the Constitution, within seven years from the date of the submission hereof to the states by the Congress.

Amendment XIX

The right of citizens of the United States to vote shall not be denied or abridged by the United States or by any state on account of sex.

Congress shall have power to enforce this article by appropriate legislation.

Amendment XX

Section 1.

The terms of the President and Vice President shall end at noon on the 20th day of January, and the terms of Senators and Representatives at noon on the 3d day of January, of the years in which such terms would have ended if this article had not been ratified; and the terms of their successors shall then begin.

Section 2.

The Congress shall assemble at least once in every year, and such meeting shall begin at noon on the 3d day of January, unless they shall by law appoint a different day.

Section 3.

If, at the time fixed for the beginning of the term of the President, the President elect shall have died, the Vice President elect shall become President. If a President shall not have been chosen before the time fixed for the beginning of his term, or if the President elect shall have failed to qualify, then the Vice President elect shall act as President until a President shall have qualified; and the Congress may by law provide for the case wherein neither a President elect nor a Vice President elect shall have qualified, declaring who shall then act as President, or the manner in which one who is to act shall be selected, and such person shall act accordingly until a President or Vice President shall have qualified.

Section 4.

The Congress may by law provide for the case of the death of any of the persons from whom the House of Representatives may choose a President whenever the right of choice shall have devolved upon them, and for the case of the death of any of the persons from whom the Senate may choose a Vice President whenever the right of choice shall have devolved upon them.

Section 5.

Sections 1 and 2 shall take effect on the 15th day of October following the ratification of this article.

Section 6.

This article shall be inoperative unless it shall have been ratified as an amendment to the Constitution by the legislatures of three-fourths of the several states within seven years from the date of its submission.

Amendment XXI

Section 1.

The eighteenth article of amendment to the Constitution of the United States is hereby repealed.

Section 2.

The transportation or importation into any state, territory, or possession of the United States for delivery or use therein of intoxicating liquors, in violation of the laws thereof, is hereby prohibited.

Section 3.

This article shall be inoperative unless it shall have been ratified as an amendment to the Constitution by conventions in the several states, as provided in the Constitution, within seven years from the date of the submission hereof to the states by the Congress.

Amendment XXII

Section 1.

No person shall be elected to the office of the President more than twice, and no person who has held the office of President, or acted as President, for more than two years of a term to which some other person was elected President shall be elected to the office of the President more than once. But this article shall not apply to any person holding the office of President when this article was proposed by the Congress, and shall not prevent any person who may be holding the office of President, or acting as President, during the term within which this article becomes operative from holding the office of President or acting as President during the remainder of such term.

Section 2.

This article shall be inoperative unless it shall have been ratified as an amendment to the Constitution by the legislatures of three-fourths of the several states within seven years from the date of its submission to the states by the Congress.

Amendment XXIII

Section 1.

The District constituting the seat of government of the United States shall appoint in such manner as the Congress may direct:

A number of electors of President and Vice President equal to the whole number of Senators and Representatives in Congress to which the District would be entitled if it were a state, but in no event more than the least populous state; they shall be in addition to those appointed by the states, but they shall be considered, for the purposes of the election of President and Vice President, to be electors appointed by a state; and they shall meet in the District and perform such duties as provided by the twelfth article of amendment.

Section 2.

The Congress shall have power to enforce this article by appropriate legislation.

Amendment XXIV

Section 1.

The right of citizens of the United States to vote in any primary or other election for President or Vice President, for electors for President or Vice President, or for Senator or Representative in Congress, shall not be denied or abridged by the United States or any state by reason of failure to pay any poll tax or other tax.

Section 2.

The Congress shall have power to enforce this article by appropriate legislation.

Amendment XXV

Section 1.

In case of the removal of the President from office or of his death or resignation, the Vice President shall become President.

Section 2.

Whenever there is a vacancy in the office of the Vice President, the President shall nominate a Vice President who shall take office upon confirmation by a majority vote of both Houses of Congress.

Section 3.

Whenever the President transmits to the President pro tempore of the Senate and the Speaker of the House of Representatives his written declaration that he is unable to discharge the powers and duties of his office, and until he transmits to them a written declaration to the contrary, such powers and duties shall be discharged by the Vice President as Acting President.

Section 4.

Whenever the Vice President and a majority of either the principal officers of the executive departments or of such other body as Congress may by law provide, transmit to the President pro tempore of the Senate and the Speaker of the House of Representatives their written declaration that the President is unable to discharge the powers and duties of his office, the Vice President shall immediately assume the powers and duties of the office as Acting President.

Thereafter, when the President transmits to the President pro tempore of the Senate and the Speaker of the House of Representatives his written declaration that no inability exists, he shall resume the powers and duties of his office unless the Vice President and a majority of either the principal officers of the executive department or of such other body as Congress may by law provide, transmit within four days to the President pro tempore of the Senate and the Speaker of the House of Representatives their written declaration that the President is unable to discharge the powers and duties of his office. Thereupon Congress shall decide the issue, assembling within forty-eight hours for that purpose if not in session. If the Congress, within twenty-one days after receipt of the latter written declaration, or, if Congress is not in session, within twenty-one days after Congress is required to assemble, determines by two-thirds vote of both Houses that the President is unable to discharge the powers and duties of his office, the Vice President shall continue to discharge the same as Acting President; otherwise, the President shall resume the powers and duties of his office.

Amendment XXVI

Section 1.

The right of citizens of the United States, who are 18 years of age or older, to vote, shall not be denied or abridged by the United States or any state on account of age.

Section 2.

The Congress shall have the power to enforce this article by appropriate legislation.

Amendment XXVII

No law, varying the compensation for the services of the Senators and Representatives, shall take effect, until an election of Representatives shall have intervened.

Administrative Procedure Act

Title 5 U.S. Code, Chapter 5, Subchapter II (2013)

SHORT TITLE

The provisions of this subchapter and chapter 7 of this title were originally enacted by act June 11, 1946, ch. 324, 60 Stat. 237, popularly known as the "Administrative Procedure Act". That Act was repealed as part of the general revision of this title by Pub. L. 89-554 and its provisions incorporated into this subchapter and chapter 7 hereof.

§ 551. Definitions

For the purpose of this subchapter—

(1) "agency" means each authority of the Government of the United States, whether or not it is within or subject to review by another agency, but does not include—

(A) the Congress;

(B) the courts of the United States;

(C) the governments of the territories or possessions of the United States;

(D) the government of the District of Columbia;

or except as to the requirements of section 552 of this title—

(E) agencies composed of representatives of the parties or of representatives of organizations of the parties to the disputes determined by them;

(F) courts martial and military commissions;

(G) military authority exercised in the field in time of war or in occupied territory; or

(H) functions conferred by sections 1738, 1739, 1743, and 1744 of title 12; subchapter II of chapter 471 of title 49; or sections 1884, 1891–1902, and former section 1641(b)(2), of title 50, appendix;

(2) "person" includes an individual, partnership, corporation, association, or public or private organization other than an agency;

(3) "party" includes a person or agency named or admitted as a party, or properly seeking and entitled as of right to be admitted as a party, in an agency proceeding, and a person or agency admitted by an agency as a party for limited purposes;

(4) "rule" means the whole or a part of an agency statement of general or particular applicability and future effect designed to implement, interpret, or prescribe law or policy or describing the organization, procedure, or practice requirements of an agency and includes the approval or prescription for the future of rates, wages, corporate or financial structures or reorganizations thereof, prices, facilities, appliances, services or allowances therefor or of valuations, costs, or accounting, or practices bearing on any of the foregoing;

(5) "rule making" means agency process for formulating, amending, or repealing a rule;

(6) "order" means the whole or a part of a final disposition, whether affirmative, negative, injunctive, or declaratory in form, of an agency in a matter other than rule making but including licensing;

(7) "adjudication" means agency process for the formulation of an order;

(8) "license" includes the whole or a part of an agency permit, certificate, approval, registration, charter, membership, statutory exemption or other form of permission;

(9) "licensing" includes agency process respecting the grant, renewal, denial, revocation, suspension, annulment, withdrawal, limitation, amendment, modification, or conditioning of a license;

(10) "sanction" includes the whole or a part of an agency—

(A) prohibition, requirement, limitation, or other condition affecting the freedom of a person;

(B) withholding of relief;

(C) imposition of penalty or fine;

(D) destruction, taking, seizure, or withholding of property;

(E) assessment of damages, reimbursement, restitution, compensation, costs, charges, or fees;

(F) requirement, revocation, or suspension of a license; or

(G) taking other compulsory or restrictive action;

(11) "relief" includes the whole or a part of an agency—

(A) grant of money, assistance, license, authority, exemption, exception, privilege, or remedy;

(B) recognition of a claim, right, immunity, privilege, exemption, or exception; or

(C) taking of other action on the application or petition of, and beneficial to, a person;

(12) "agency proceeding" means an agency process as defined by paragraphs (5), (7), and (9) of this section;

(13) "agency action" includes the whole or a part of an agency rule, order, license, sanction, relief, or the equivalent or denial thereof, or failure to act; and

(14) "ex parte communication" means an oral or written communication not on the public record with respect to which reasonable prior notice to all parties is not given, but it shall not include requests for status reports on any matter or proceeding covered by this subchapter.

§ 552. Public information; agency rules, opinions, orders, records, and proceedings

(a) Each agency shall make available to the public information as follows:

(1) Each agency shall separately state and currently publish in the Federal Register for the guidance of the public —

(A) descriptions of its central and field organization and the established places at which, the employees (and in the case of a uniformed service, the members) from whom, and the methods whereby, the public may obtain information, make submittals or requests, or obtain decisions;

(B) statements of the general course and method by which its functions are channeled and determined, including the nature and requirements of all formal and informal procedures available;

(C) rules of procedure, descriptions of forms available or the places at which forms may be obtained, and instructions as to the scope and contents of all papers, reports, or examinations;

(D) substantive rules of general applicability adopted as authorized by law, and statements of general policy or interpretations of general applicability formulated and adopted by the agency; and

(E) each amendment, revision, or repeal of the foregoing.

Except to the extent that a person has actual and timely notice of the terms thereof, a person may not in any manner be required to resort to, or be adversely affected by, a matter required to be published in the Federal Register and not so published. For the purpose of this paragraph, matter reasonably available to the class of persons affected thereby is deemed published in the Federal Register when incorporated by reference therein with the approval of the Director of the Federal Register.

(2) Each agency, in accordance with published rules, shall make available for public inspection in an electronic format —

(A) final opinions, including concurring and dissenting opinions, as well as orders, made in the adjudication of cases;

(B) those statements of policy and interpretations which have been adopted by the agency and are not published in the Federal Register;

(C) administrative staff manuals and instructions to staff that affect a member of the public;

(D) copies of all records, regardless of form or format —

(i) that have been released to any person under paragraph (3); and

(ii)(I) that because of the nature of their subject matter, the agency determines have become or are likely to become the subject of subsequent requests for substantially the same records; or

(II) that have been requested 3 or more times; and

(E) a general index of the records referred to under subparagraph (D); unless the materials are promptly published and copies offered for sale. ***

(3)(A) Except with respect to the records made available under paragraphs (1) and (2) of this subsection, and except as provided in subparagraph (E), each agency, upon any request for records which (i) reasonably describes such records and (ii) is made in accordance with published rules stating the time, place, fees (if any), and procedures to be followed, shall make the records promptly available to any person.

(B) In making any record available to a person under this paragraph, an agency shall provide the record in any form or format requested by the person if the record is readily reproducible by the agency in that form or format. Each agency shall make reasonable efforts to maintain its records in forms or formats that are reproducible for purposes of this section.

(C) In responding under this paragraph to a request for records, an agency shall make reasonable efforts to search for the records in electronic form or format, except when such efforts would significantly interfere with the operation of the agency's automated information system.

(D) For purposes of this paragraph, the term "search" means to review, manually or by automated means, agency records for the purpose of locating those records which are responsive to a request.

(E) An agency, or part of an agency, that is an element of the intelligence community (as that term is defined in section 3(4) of the National Security Act of 1947 (50 U.S.C. 401a(4))) shall not make any record available under this paragraph to —

(i) any government entity, other than a State, territory, commonwealth, or district of the United States, or any subdivision thereof; or

(ii) a representative of a government entity described in clause (i).

(4)(A)(i) In order to carry out the provisions of this section, each agency shall promulgate regulations, pursuant to notice and receipt of public comment, specifying the schedule of fees applicable to the processing of requests under this section and establishing procedures and guidelines for determining when such fees should be waived or reduced. Such schedule shall conform to the guidelines which shall be promulgated, pursuant to notice and receipt of public comment, by the Director of the Office of Management and Budget and which shall provide for a uniform schedule of fees for all agencies. ***

(B) On complaint, the district court of the United States in the district in which the complainant resides, or has his principal place of business, or in which the agency records are situated, or in the District of Columbia, has jurisdiction to enjoin the agency from withholding agency records and to order the production of any agency records improperly withheld from the complainant. In such a case the court shall determine the matter de novo, and may examine the contents of such agency records in camera to determine whether such records or any part thereof shall be withheld under any of the exemptions set forth in subsection (b) of this section, and the burden is on the agency to sustain its action. ***

(E)(i) The court may assess against the United States reasonable attorney fees and other litigation costs reasonably incurred in any case under this section in which the complainant has substantially prevailed. ***

(6)

(A) Each agency, upon any request for records made under paragraph (1), (2), or (3) of this subsection, shall—

(i) determine within 20 days (excepting Saturdays, Sundays, and legal public holidays) after the receipt of any such request whether to comply with such request and shall immediately notify the person making such request of—

(I) such determination and the reasons therefor; ***

(C)(i) Any person making a request to any agency for records under paragraph (1), (2), or (3) of this subsection shall be deemed to have exhausted his administrative remedies with respect to such request if the agency fails to comply with the applicable time limit provisions of this paragraph. If the Government can show exceptional circumstances exist and that the agency is exercising due diligence in responding to the request, the court may retain jurisdiction and allow the agency additional time to complete its review of the records. ***

(7) Each agency shall—

(A) establish a system to assign an individualized tracking number for each request received that will take longer than ten days to process and provide to each person making a request the tracking number assigned to the request; and

(B) establish a telephone line or Internet service that provides information about the status of a request to the person making the request using the assigned tracking number, including—

(i) the date on which the agency originally received the request; and

(ii) an estimated date on which the agency will complete action on the request.

(8)(A) An agency shall—

(i) withhold information under this section only if—

(I) the agency reasonably foresees that disclosure would harm an interest protected by an exemption described in subsection (b); or

(II) disclosure is prohibited by law; and

(ii)(I) consider whether partial disclosure of information is possible whenever the agency determines that a full disclosure of a requested record is not possible; and

(II) take reasonable steps necessary to segregate and release nonexempt information; and

(B) Nothing in this paragraph requires disclosure of information that is otherwise prohibited from disclosure by law, or otherwise exempted from disclosure under subsection (b)(3).

(b) This section does not apply to matters that are—

(1)(A) specifically authorized under criteria established by an Executive order to be kept secret in the interest of national defense or foreign policy and (B) are in fact properly classified pursuant to such Executive order;

(2) related solely to the internal personnel rules and practices of an agency;

(3) specifically exempted from disclosure by statute (other than section 552b of this title [the Government in the Sunshine Act]), if that statute—

(A)(i) requires that the matters be withheld from the public in such a manner as to leave no discretion on the issue; or

(ii) establishes particular criteria for withholding or refers to particular types of matters to be withheld; and

(B) if enacted after the date of enactment of the OPEN FOIA Act of 2009 [section 564 of the Department of Homeland Security Appropriations Act, 2010, Pub. L. No. 111-83, 123 Stat. 2142, 2184], specifically cites to this paragraph.

(4) trade secrets and commercial or financial information obtained from a person and privileged or confidential;

(5) inter-agency or intra-agency memorandums or letters that would not be available by law to a party other than an agency in litigation with the agency, provided that the deliberative process privilege shall not apply to records created 25 years or more before the date on which the records were requested;

(6) personnel and medical files and similar files the disclosure of which would constitute a clearly unwarranted invasion of personal privacy;

(7) records or information compiled for law enforcement purposes, but only to the extent that the production of such law enforcement records or information (A) could reasonably be expected to interfere with enforcement proceedings, (B) would deprive a person of a right to a fair trial or an impartial adjudication, (C) could reasonably be expected to constitute an unwarranted invasion of personal privacy, (D) could reasonably be expected to disclose the identity of a confidential

source, including a State, local, or foreign agency or authority or any private institution which furnished information on a confidential basis, and, in the case of a record or information compiled by criminal law enforcement authority in the course of a criminal investigation or by an agency conducting a lawful national security intelligence investigation, information furnished by a confidential source, (E) would disclose techniques and procedures for law enforcement investigations or prosecutions, or would disclose guidelines for law enforcement investigations or prosecutions if such disclosure could reasonably be expected to risk circumvention of the law, or (F) could reasonably be expected to endanger the life or physical safety of any individual;

(8) contained in or related to examination, operating, or condition reports prepared by, on behalf of, or for the use of an agency responsible for the regulation or supervision of financial institutions; or

(9) geological and geophysical information and data, including maps, concerning wells.

Any reasonably segregable portion of a record shall be provided to any person requesting such record after deletion of the portions which are exempt under this subsection. The amount of information deleted, and the exemption under which the deletion is made, shall be indicated on the released portion of the record, unless including that indication would harm an interest protected by the exemption in this subsection under which the deletion is made. If technically feasible, the amount of the information deleted, and the exemption under which the deletion is made, shall be indicated at the place in the record where such deletion is made. ***

(d) This section does not authorize withholding of information or limit the availability of records to the public, except as specifically stated in this section. This section is not authority to withhold information from Congress. ***

(f) For purposes of this section, the term—

(1) "agency" as defined in section 551(1) of this title includes any executive department, military department, Government corporation, Government controlled corporation, or other establishment in the executive branch of the Government (including the Executive Office of the President), or any independent regulatory agency; and

(2) "record" and any other term used in this section in reference to information includes—

(A) any information that would be an agency record subject to the requirements of this section when maintained by an agency in any format, including an electronic format; and

(B) any information described under subparagraph (A) that is maintained for an agency by an entity under Government contract, for the purposes of records management. * * *

§ 553.   Rule making

(a) This section applies, according to the provisions thereof, except to the extent that there is involved—

(1) a military or foreign affairs function of the United States; or

(2) a matter relating to agency management or personnel or to public property, loans, grants, benefits, or contracts.

(b) General notice of proposed rule making shall be published in the Federal Register, unless persons subject thereto are named and either personally served or otherwise have actual notice thereof in accordance with law. The notice shall include—

(1) a statement of the time, place, and nature of public rule making proceedings;

(2) reference to the legal authority under which the rule is proposed; and

(3) either the terms or substance of the proposed rule or a description of the subjects and issues involved.

Except when notice or hearing is required by statute, this subsection does not apply—

(A) to interpretative rules, general statements of policy, or rules of agency organization, procedure, or practice; or

(B) when the agency for good cause finds (and incorporates the finding and a brief statement of reasons therefor in the rules issued) that notice and public procedure thereon are impracticable, unnecessary, or contrary to the public interest.

(c) After notice required by this section, the agency shall give interested persons an opportunity to participate in the rule making through submission of written data, views, or arguments with or without opportunity for oral presentation. After consideration of the relevant matter presented, the agency shall incorporate in the rules adopted a concise general statement of their basis and purpose. When rules are required by statute to be made on the record after opportunity for an agency hearing, sections 556 and 557 of this title apply instead of this subsection.

(d) The required publication or service of a substantive rule shall be made not less than 30 days before its effective date, except—

(1) a substantive rule which grants or recognizes an exemption or relieves a restriction;

(2) interpretative rules and statements of policy; or

(3) as otherwise provided by the agency for good cause found and published with the rule.

(e) Each agency shall give an interested person the right to petition for the issuance, amendment, or repeal of a rule.

§ 554. Adjudications

(a) This section applies, according to the provisions thereof, in every case of adjudication required by statute to be determined on the record after opportunity for an agency hearing, except to the extent that there is involved—

(1) a matter subject to a subsequent trial of the law and the facts de novo in a court;

(2) the selection or tenure of an employee, except an administrative law judge appointed under section 3105 of this title;

(3) proceedings in which decisions rest solely on inspections, tests, or elections;

(4) the conduct of military or foreign affairs functions;

(5) cases in which an agency is acting as an agent for a court; or

(6) the certification of worker representatives.

(b) Persons entitled to notice of an agency hearing shall be timely informed of—

(1) the time, place, and nature of the hearing;

(2) the legal authority and jurisdiction under which the hearing is to be held; and

(3) the matters of fact and law asserted.

When private persons are the moving parties, other parties to the proceeding shall give prompt notice of issues controverted in fact or law; and in other instances agencies may by rule require responsive pleading. In fixing the time and place for hearings, due regard shall be had for the convenience and necessity of the parties or their representatives.

(c) The agency shall give all interested parties opportunity for—

(1) the submission and consideration of facts, arguments, offers of settlement, or proposals of adjustment when time, the nature of the proceeding, and the public interest permit; and

(2) to the extent that the parties are unable so to determine a controversy by consent, hearing and decision on notice and in accordance with sections 556 and 557 of this title.

(d) The employee who presides at the reception of evidence pursuant to section 556 of this title shall make the recommended decision or initial decision required by section 557 of this title, unless he becomes unavailable to the agency. Except to the extent required for the disposition of ex parte matters as authorized by law, such an employee may not—

(1) consult a person or party on a fact in issue, unless on notice and opportunity for all parties to participate; or

(2) be responsible to or subject to the supervision or direction of an employee or agent engaged in the performance of investigative or prosecuting functions for an agency.

An employee or agent engaged in the performance of investigative or prosecuting functions for an agency in a case may not, in that or a factually related case, participate or advise in the decision, recommended decision, or agency review pursuant to section 557 of this title, except as witness or counsel in public proceedings. This subsection does not apply—

(A) in determining applications for initial licenses;

(B) to proceedings involving the validity or application of rates, facilities, or practices of public utilities or carriers; or

(C) to the agency or a member or members of the body comprising the agency.

(e) The agency, with like effect as in the case of other orders, and in its sound discretion, may issue a declaratory order to terminate a controversy or remove uncertainty.

§ 555. Ancillary matters

(a) This section applies, according to the provisions thereof, except as otherwise provided by this subchapter.

(b) A person compelled to appear in person before an agency or representative thereof is entitled to be accompanied, represented, and advised by counsel or, if permitted by the agency, by other qualified representative. A party is entitled to appear in person or by or with counsel or other duly qualified representative in an agency proceeding. So far as the orderly conduct of public business permits, an interested person may appear before an agency or its responsible employees for the presentation, adjustment, or determination of an issue, request, or controversy in a proceeding, whether interlocutory, summary, or otherwise, or in connection with an agency function. With due regard for the convenience and necessity of the parties or their representatives and within a reasonable time, each agency shall proceed to conclude a matter presented to it. This subsection does not grant or deny a person who is not a lawyer the right to appear for or represent others before an agency or in an agency proceeding.

(c) Process, requirement of a report, inspection, or other investigative act or demand may not be issued, made, or enforced except as authorized by law. A person compelled to submit data or evidence is entitled to retain or, on payment of lawfully prescribed costs, procure a copy or transcript thereof, except that in a nonpublic investigatory proceeding the witness may for good cause be limited to inspection of the official transcript of his testimony.

(d) Agency subpenas authorized by law shall be issued to a party on request and, when required by rules of procedure, on a statement or showing of general relevance and reasonable scope of the evidence sought. On contest, the court shall sustain the subpena or similar process or demand to the extent that it is found to be in accordance with law. In a proceeding for enforcement, the court shall issue an order requiring the appearance of the witness or the production of the evidence or data within a reasonable time under penalty of punishment for contempt in case of contumacious failure to comply.

(e) Prompt notice shall be given of the denial in whole or in part of a written application, petition, or other request of an interested person made in connection with any agency proceeding. Except in affirming a prior denial or when the denial is self-explanatory, the notice shall be accompanied by a brief statement of the grounds for denial.

§ 556. Hearings; presiding employees; powers and duties; burden of proof; evidence; record as basis of decision

(a) This section applies, according to the provisions thereof, to hearings required by section 553 or 554 of this title to be conducted in accordance with this section.

(b) There shall preside at the taking of evidence —

(1) the agency;

(2) one or more members of the body which comprises the agency; or

(3) one or more administrative law judges appointed under section 3105 of this title.

This subchapter does not supersede the conduct of specified classes of proceedings, in whole or in part, by or before boards or other employees specially provided for by or designated under statute. The functions of presiding employees and of employees participating in decisions in accordance with section 557 of this title shall be conducted in an impartial manner. A presiding or participating employee may at any time disqualify himself. On the filing in good faith of a timely and sufficient affidavit of personal bias or other disqualification of a presiding or participating employee, the agency shall determine the matter as a part of the record and decision in the case.

(c) Subject to published rules of the agency and within its powers, employees presiding at hearings may —

(1) administer oaths and affirmations;

(2) issue subpenas authorized by law;

(3) rule on offers of proof and receive relevant evidence;

(4) take depositions or have depositions taken when the ends of justice would be served;

(5) regulate the course of the hearing;

(6) hold conferences for the settlement or simplification of the issues by consent of the parties or by the use of alternative means of dispute resolution as provided in subchapter IV of this chapter;

(7) inform the parties as to the availability of one or more alternative means of dispute resolution, and encourage use of such methods;

(8) require the attendance at any conference held pursuant to paragraph (6) of at least one representative of each party who has authority to negotiate concerning resolution of issues in controversy;

(9) dispose of procedural requests or similar matters;

(10) make or recommend decisions in accordance with section 557 of this title; and

(11) take other action authorized by agency rule consistent with this subchapter.

(d) Except as otherwise provided by statute, the proponent of a rule or order has the burden of proof. Any oral or documentary evidence may be received, but the agency as a matter of policy shall provide for the exclusion of irrelevant, immaterial, or unduly repetitious evidence. A sanction may not be imposed or rule or order issued except on consideration of the whole record or those parts thereof cited by a party and supported by and in accordance with the reliable, probative, and substantial evidence. The agency may, to the extent consistent with the interests of justice and the policy of the underlying statutes administered by the agency, consider a violation of section 557(d) of this title sufficient grounds for a decision adverse to a party who has knowingly committed such violation or knowingly caused such violation to occur. A party is entitled to present his case or defense by oral or documentary evidence, to submit rebuttal evidence, and to conduct such cross-examination as may be required for a full and true disclosure of the facts. In rule making or determining claims for money or benefits or applications for initial licenses an agency may, when a party will not be prejudiced thereby, adopt procedures for the submission of all or part of the evidence in written form.

(e) The transcript of testimony and exhibits, together with all papers and requests filed in the proceeding, constitutes the exclusive record for decision in accordance with section 557 of this title and, on payment of lawfully prescribed costs, shall be made available to the parties. When an agency decision rests on official notice of a material fact not appearing in the evidence in the record, a party is entitled, on timely request, to an opportunity to show the contrary.

§ 557. Initial decisions; conclusiveness; review by agency; submissions by parties; contents of decisions; record

(a) This section applies, according to the provisions thereof, when a hearing is required to be conducted in accordance with section 556 of this title.

(b) When the agency did not preside at the reception of the evidence, the presiding employee or, in cases not subject to section 554(d) of this title, an employee qualified to preside at hearings pursuant to section 556 of this title, shall initially decide the case unless the agency requires, either in specific cases or by general rule, the entire record to be certified to it for decision. When the presiding employee makes an initial decision, that decision then becomes the decision of the agency without further proceedings unless there is an appeal to, or review on motion of, the agency within time provided by rule. On appeal from or review of the initial decision, the agency has all the powers which it would have in making the initial decision except as it may limit the issues on notice or by rule. When the agency makes the decision without having presided at the reception of the evidence, the presiding employee or an employee qualified to preside at hearings pursuant to section 556 of this title shall first recommend a decision, except that in rule making or determining applications for initial licenses—

(1) instead thereof the agency may issue a tentative decision or one of its responsible employees may recommend a decision; or

(2) this procedure may be omitted in a case in which the agency finds on the record that due and timely execution of its functions imperatively and unavoidably so requires.

(c) Before a recommended, initial, or tentative decision, or a decision on agency review of the decision of subordinate employees, the parties are entitled to a reasonable opportunity to submit for the consideration of the employees participating in the decisions—

(1) proposed findings and conclusions; or

(2) exceptions to the decisions or recommended decisions of subordinate employees or to tentative agency decisions; and

(3) supporting reasons for the exceptions or proposed findings or conclusions.

The record shall show the ruling on each finding, conclusion, or exception presented. All decisions, including initial, recommended, and tentative decisions, are a part of the record and shall include a statement of—

(A) findings and conclusions, and the reasons or basis therefor, on all the material issues of fact, law, or discretion presented on the record; and

(B) the appropriate rule, order, sanction, relief, or denial thereof.

(d)(1) In any agency proceeding which is subject to subsection (a) of this section, except to the extent required for the disposition of ex parte matters as authorized by law—

(A) no interested person outside the agency shall make or knowingly cause to be made to any member of the body comprising the agency, administrative law judge, or other employee who is or may reasonably be expected to be involved in the decisional process of the proceeding, an ex parte communication relevant to the merits of the proceeding;

(B) no member of the body comprising the agency, administrative law judge, or other employee who is or may reasonably be expected to be involved in the decisional process of the proceeding, shall make or knowingly cause to be made to any interested person outside the agency an ex parte communication relevant to the merits of the proceeding;

(C) a member of the body comprising the agency, administrative law judge, or other employee who is or may reasonably be expected to be involved in the decisional process of such proceeding who receives, or who makes or knowingly causes to be made, a communication prohibited by this subsection shall place on the public record of the proceeding:

(i) all such written communications;

(ii) memoranda stating the substance of all such oral communications; and

(iii) all written responses, and memoranda stating the substance of all oral responses, to the materials described in clauses (i) and (ii) of this subparagraph;

(D) upon receipt of a communication knowingly made or knowingly caused to be made by a party in violation of this subsection, the agency, administrative law judge, or other employee presiding at the hearing may, to the extent consistent with the interests of justice and the policy of the underlying statutes, require the party to show cause why his claim or interest in the proceeding should not be dismissed, denied, disregarded, or otherwise adversely affected on account of such violation; and

(E) the prohibitions of this subsection shall apply beginning at such time as the agency may designate, but in no case shall they begin to apply later than the time at which a proceeding is noticed for hearing unless the person responsible for the communication has knowledge that it will be noticed, in which case the prohibitions shall apply beginning at the time of his acquisition of such knowledge.

(2) This subsection does not constitute authority to withhold information from Congress.

§ 558. Imposition of sanctions; determination of applications for licenses; suspension, revocation, and expiration of licenses

(a) This section applies, according to the provisions thereof, to the exercise of a power or authority.

(b) A sanction may not be imposed or a substantive rule or order issued except within jurisdiction delegated to the agency and as authorized by law.

(c) When application is made for a license required by law, the agency, with due regard for the rights and privileges of all the interested parties or adversely affected persons and within a reasonable time, shall set and complete proceedings required to be conducted in accordance with sections 556 and 557 of this title or other proceedings required by law and shall make its decision. Except in cases of willfulness or those in which public health, interest, or safety requires otherwise, the withdrawal, suspension, revocation, or annulment of a license is lawful only if, before the institution of agency proceedings therefor, the licensee has been given—

(1) notice by the agency in writing of the facts or conduct which may warrant the action; and

(2) opportunity to demonstrate or achieve compliance with all lawful requirements.

When the licensee has made timely and sufficient application for a renewal or a new license in accordance with agency rules, a license with reference to an activity of a continuing nature does not expire until the application has been finally determined by the agency.

§ 559. Effect on other laws; effect of subsequent statute

This subchapter, chapter 7, and sections 1305, 3105, 3344, 4301(2)(E), 5372, and 7521 of this title, and the provisions of section 5335(a)(B) of this title that relate to administrative law judges, do not limit or repeal additional requirements imposed by statute or otherwise recognized by law. Except as otherwise required by law, requirements or privileges relating to evidence or procedure apply equally to agencies and persons. Each agency is granted the authority necessary to comply with the requirements of this subchapter through the issuance of rules or otherwise. Subsequent statute may not be held to supersede or modify this subchapter, chapter 7, sections 1305, 3105, 3344, 4301(2)(E), 5372, or 7521 of this title, or the provisions of section 5335(a)(B) of this title that relate to administrative law judges, except to the extent that it does so expressly.

Title 5 U.S. Code, Chapter 7

JUDICIAL REVIEW

SHORT TITLE

The provisions of sections 551 to 559 of this title and this chapter were originally enacted by act June 11, 1946, ch. 423, 60 Stat. 237, popularly known as the "Administrative Procedure Act". That Act was repealed as part of the general revision of this title by Pub. L. 89-554 and its provisions incorporated into sections 551 to 559 of this title and this chapter.

§ 701. Application; definitions

(a) This chapter applies, according to the provisions thereof, except to the extent that—

(1) statutes preclude judicial review; or

(2) agency action is committed to agency discretion by law.

(b) For the purpose of this chapter—

(1) "agency" means each authority of the Government of the United States, whether or not it is within or subject to review by another agency, but does not include—

(A) the Congress;

(B) the courts of the United States;

(C) the governments of the territories or possessions of the United States;

(D) the government of the District of Columbia;

(E) agencies composed of representatives of the parties or of representatives of organizations of the parties to the disputes determined by them;

(F) courts martial and military commissions;

(G) military authority exercised in the field in time of war or in occupied territory; ***

(2) "person", "rule", "order", "license", "sanction", "relief", and "agency action" have the meanings given them by section 551 of this title.

§ 702. Right of review

A person suffering legal wrong because of agency action, or adversely affected or aggrieved by agency action within the meaning of a relevant statute, is entitled to judicial review thereof. An action in a court of the United States seeking relief other than money damages and stating a claim that an agency or an officer or employee thereof acted or failed to act in an official capacity or under color of legal authority shall not be dismissed nor relief therein be denied on the ground that it is against the United States or that the United States is an indispensable party. The United States may be named as a defendant in any such action, and a judgment or decree may be entered against the United States: *Provided*, That any mandatory or injunctive decree shall specify the Federal officer or officers (by name or by title), and their successors in office, personally responsible for compliance. Nothing herein (1) affects other limitations on judicial review or the power or duty of the court to dismiss any action or deny relief on any other appropriate legal or equitable ground; or (2) confers authority to grant relief if any other statute that grants consent to suit expressly or impliedly forbids the relief which is sought.

§ 703. Form and venue of proceeding

The form of proceeding for judicial review is the special statutory review proceeding relevant to the subject matter in a court specified by statute or, in the absence or inadequacy thereof, any applicable form of legal action, including actions for declaratory judgments or writs of prohibitory or mandatory injunction or habeas corpus, in a court of competent jurisdiction. If no special statutory review proceeding is applicable, the action for judicial review may be brought against the United States, the agency by its official title, or the appropriate officer. Except to the extent that prior, adequate, and exclusive opportunity for judicial review is provided by law, agency action is subject to judicial review in civil or criminal proceedings for judicial enforcement.

§ 705. Relief pending review

When an agency finds that justice so requires, it may postpone the effective date of action taken by it, pending judicial review. On such conditions as may be required and to the extent necessary to prevent irreparable injury, the reviewing court, including the court to which a case may be taken on appeal from or on application for certiorari or other writ to a reviewing court, may issue all necessary and appropriate process to postpone the effective date of an agency action or to preserve status or rights pending conclusion of the review proceedings.

§ 706. Scope of review

To the extent necessary to decision and when presented, the reviewing court shall decide all relevant questions of law, interpret constitutional and statutory provisions, and determine the meaning or applicability of the terms of an agency action. The reviewing court shall—

(1) compel agency action unlawfully withheld or unreasonably delayed; and

(2) hold unlawful and set aside agency action, findings, and conclusions found to be—

(A) arbitrary, capricious, an abuse of discretion, or otherwise not in accordance with law;

(B) contrary to constitutional right, power, privilege, or immunity;

(C) in excess of statutory jurisdiction, authority, or limitations, or short of statutory right;

(D) without observance of procedure required by law;

(E) unsupported by substantial evidence in a case subject to sections 556 and 557 of this title or otherwise reviewed on the record of an agency hearing provided by statute; or

(F) unwarranted by the facts to the extent that the facts are subject to trial de novo by the reviewing court.

In making the foregoing determinations, the court shall review the whole record or those parts of it cited by a party, and due account shall be taken of the rule of prejudicial error.

Government in the Sunshine Act

5 U.S. Code § 552b (2013)

(a) For purposes of this section—

(1) the term "agency" means any agency, as defined in section 552(e) of this title, headed by a collegial body composed of two or more individual members, a majority of whom are appointed to such position by the President with the advice and consent of the Senate, and any subdivision thereof authorized to act on behalf of the agency;

(2) the term "meeting" means the deliberations of at least the number of individual agency members required to take action on behalf of the agency where such deliberations determine or result in the joint conduct or disposition of official agency business, but does not include deliberations required or permitted by subsection (d) or (e); and

(3) the term "member" means an individual who belongs to a collegial body heading an agency.

(b) Members shall not jointly conduct or dispose of agency business other than in accordance with this section. Except as provided in subsection (c), every portion of every meeting of an agency shall be open to public observation.

(c) Except in a case where the agency finds that the public interest requires otherwise, the second sentence of subsection (b) shall not apply to any portion of an agency meeting, and the requirements of subsections (d) and (e) shall not apply to any information pertaining to such meeting otherwise required by this section to be disclosed to the public, where the agency properly determines that such portion or portions of its meeting or the disclosure of such information is likely to—

(1) disclose matters that are (A) specifically authorized under criteria established by an Executive order to be kept secret in the interests of national defense or foreign policy and (B) in fact properly classified pursuant to such Executive order;

(2) relate solely to the internal personnel rules and practices of an agency;

(3) disclose matters specifically exempted from disclosure by statute (other than section 552 of this title), provided that such statute (A) requires that the matters be withheld from the public in such a manner as to leave no discretion on the issue, or (B) establishes particular criteria for withholding or refers to particular types of matters to be withheld;

(4) disclose trade secrets and commercial or financial information obtained from a person and privileged or confidential;

(5) involve accusing any person of a crime, or formally censuring any person;

(6) disclose information of a personal nature where disclosure would constitute a clearly unwarranted invasion of personal privacy;

(7) disclose investigatory records compiled for law enforcement purposes, or information which if written would be contained in such records, but only to the extent that the production of such records or information would (A) interfere with enforcement proceedings, (B) deprive a person of a right to a fair trial or an impartial adjudication, (C) constitute an unwarranted invasion of personal privacy, (D) disclose the identity of a confidential source and, in the case of a record compiled by a criminal law enforcement authority in the course of a criminal investigation, or by an agency conducting a lawful national security intelligence investigation, confidential information furnished only by the confidential source, (E) disclose investigative techniques and procedures, or (F) endanger the life or physical safety of law enforcement personnel;

(8) disclose information contained in or related to examination, operating, or condition reports prepared by, on behalf of, or for the use of an agency responsible for the regulation or supervision of financial institutions;

(9) disclose information the premature disclosure of which would—

(A) in the case of an agency which regulates currencies, securities, commodities, or financial institutions, be likely to (i) lead to significant financial speculation in currencies, securities, or commodities, or (ii) significantly endanger the stability of any financial institution; or

(B) in the case of any agency, be likely to significantly frustrate implementation of a proposed agency action, except that subparagraph (B) shall not apply in any instance where the agency has already disclosed to the public the content or nature of its proposed action, or where the agency is required by law to make such disclosure on its own initiative prior to taking final agency action on such proposal; or

(10) specifically concern the agency's issuance of a subpena, or the agency's participation in a civil action or proceeding, an action in a foreign court or international tribunal, or an arbitration, or the initiation, conduct, or disposition by the agency of a particular case of formal agency adjudication pursuant to the procedures in section 554 of this title or otherwise involving a determination on the record after opportunity for a hearing.

(d)(1) Action under subsection (c) shall be taken only when a majority of the entire membership of the agency (as defined in subsection (a)(1)) votes to take such action. A separate vote of the agency members shall be taken with respect to each agency meeting a portion or portions of which are proposed to be closed to the public pursuant to subsection (c), or with respect to any information which is proposed to be withheld under subsection (c). A single vote may be taken with respect to a series of meetings, a portion or portions of which are proposed to be closed to the public, or with respect to any information concerning such series of meetings, so long as each meeting in such series involves the same particular matters and is scheduled to be held no more than thirty days after the initial meeting in such series. The vote of each agency member participating in such vote shall be recorded and no proxies shall be allowed.

(2) Whenever any person whose interests may be directly affected by a portion of a meeting requests that the agency close such portion to the public for any of the reasons referred to in paragraph (5), (6), or (7) of subsection (c), the agency, upon request of any one of its members, shall vote by recorded vote whether to close such meeting.

(3) Within one day of any vote taken pursuant to paragraph (1) or (2), the agency shall make publicly available a written copy of such vote reflecting the vote of each member on the question. If a portion of a meeting is to be closed to the public, the agency shall, within one day of the vote taken pursuant to paragraph (1) or (2) of this subsection, make publicly available a full written explanation of its action closing the portion together with a list of all persons expected to attend the meeting and their affiliation.

(4) Any agency, a majority of whose meetings may properly be closed to the public pursuant to paragraph (4), (8), (9)(A), or (10) of subsection (c), or any combination thereof, may provide by regulation for the closing of such meetings or portions thereof in the event that a majority of the members of the agency votes by recorded vote at the beginning of such meeting, or portion thereof, to close the exempt portion or portions of the meeting, and a copy of such vote, reflecting the vote of each member on the question, is made available to the public. The provisions of paragraphs (1), (2), and (3) of this subsection and subsection (e) shall not apply to any portion of a meeting to which such regulations apply: *Provided*, That the agency shall, except to the extent that such information is exempt from disclosure under the provisions of subsection (c), provide the public with public announcement of the time, place, and subject matter of the meeting and of each portion thereof at the earliest practicable time.

(e)(1) In the case of each meeting, the agency shall make public announcement, at least one week before the meeting, of the time, place, and subject matter of the meeting, whether it is to be open or closed to the public, and the name and phone number of the official designated by the agency to respond to requests for information about the meeting. Such announcement shall be made unless a majority of the members of the agency determines by a recorded vote that agency business requires that such meeting be called at an earlier date, in which case the agency shall make public announcement of the time, place, and subject matter of such meeting, and whether open or closed to the public, at the earliest practicable time.

(2) The time or place of a meeting may be changed following the public announcement required by paragraph (1) only if the agency publicly announces such change at the earliest practicable time. The subject matter of a meeting, or the determination of the agency to open or close a meeting, or portion of a meeting, to the public, may be changed following the public announcement required by this subsection only if (A) a majority of the entire membership of the agency determines by a recorded vote that agency business so requires and that no earlier announcement of the change was possible, and (B) the agency publicly announces such change and the vote of each member upon such change at the earliest practicable time.

(3) Immediately following each public announcement required by this subsection, notice of the time, place, and subject matter of a meeting, whether the meeting is open or closed, any change in one of the preceding, and the name and phone number of the official designated by the agency to respond to requests for information about the meeting, shall also be submitted for publication in the Federal Register.

(f)(1) For every meeting closed pursuant to paragraphs (1) through (10) of subsection (c), the General Counsel or chief legal officer of the agency shall publicly certify that, in his or her opinion, the meeting may be closed to the public and shall state each relevant exemptive provision. A copy of such certification, together with a statement from the presiding officer of the meeting setting forth the time and place of the meeting, and the persons present, shall be retained by the agency. The agency shall maintain a complete transcript or electronic recording adequate to record fully the proceedings of each meeting, or portion of a meeting, closed to the public, except that in the case of a meeting, or portion of a meeting, closed to the public pursuant to paragraph (8), (9)(A), or (10) of subsection (c), the agency shall maintain either such a transcript or recording, or a set of minutes. Such minutes shall fully and clearly describe all matters discussed and shall provide a full and accurate summary of any actions taken, and the reasons therefor, including a description of each of the views expressed on any item and the record of any rollcall vote (reflecting the vote of each member on the question). All documents considered in connection with any action shall be identified in such minutes.

(2) The agency shall make promptly available to the public, in a place easily accessible to the public, the transcript, electronic recording, or minutes (as required by paragraph (1)) of the discussion of any item on the agenda, or of any item of the testimony of any witness received at the meeting, except for such item or items of such discussion or testimony as the agency determines to contain information which may be withheld under subsection (c). Copies of such transcript, or minutes, or a transcription of such recording disclosing the identity of each speaker, shall be furnished to any person at the actual cost of duplication or transcription. The agency shall maintain a complete verbatim copy of the transcript, a complete copy of the minutes, or a complete electronic recording of each meeting, or portion of a meeting, closed to the public, for a period of at least two years after such

meeting, or until one year after the conclusion of any agency proceeding with respect to which the meeting or portion was held, whichever occurs later.

(g) Each agency subject to the requirements of this section shall, within 180 days after the date of enactment of this section, following consultation with the Office of the Chairman of the Administrative Conference of the United States and published notice in the Federal Register of at least thirty days and opportunity for written comment by any person, promulgate regulations to implement the requirements of subsections (b) through (f) of this section. Any person may bring a proceeding in the United States District Court for the District of Columbia to require an agency to promulgate such regulations if such agency has not promulgated such regulations within the time period specified herein. Subject to any limitations of time provided by law, any person may bring a proceeding in the United States Court of Appeals for the District of Columbia to set aside agency regulations issued pursuant to this subsection that are not in accord with the requirements of subsections (b) through (f) of this section and to require the promulgation of regulations that are in accord with such subsections.

(h)(1) The district courts of the United States shall have jurisdiction to enforce the requirements of subsections (b) through (f) of this section by declaratory judgment, injunctive relief, or other relief as may be appropriate. Such actions may be brought by any person against an agency prior to, or within sixty days after, the meeting out of which the violation of this section arises, except that if public announcement of such meeting is not initially provided by the agency in accordance with the requirements of this section, such action may be instituted pursuant to this section at any time prior to sixty days after any public announcement of such meeting. Such actions may be brought in the district court of the United States for the district in which the agency meeting is held or in which the agency in question has its headquarters, or in the District Court for the District of Columbia. In such actions a defendant shall serve his answer within thirty days after the service of the complaint. The burden is on the defendant to sustain his action. In deciding such cases the court may examine in camera any portion of the transcript, electronic recording, or minutes of a meeting closed to the public, and may take such additional evidence as it deems necessary. The court, having due regard for orderly administration and the public interest, as well as the interests of the parties, may grant such equitable relief as it deems appropriate, including granting an injunction against future violations of this section or ordering the agency to make available to the public such portion of the transcript, recording, or minutes of a meeting as is not authorized to be withheld under subsection (c) of this section.

(2) Any Federal court otherwise authorized by law to review agency action may, at the application of any person properly participating in the proceeding pursuant to other applicable law, inquire into violations by the agency of the requirements of this section and afford such relief as it deems appropriate. Nothing in this section authorizes any Federal court having jurisdiction solely on the basis of paragraph (1) to set aside, enjoin, or invalidate any agency action (other than an action

to close a meeting or to withhold information under this section) taken or discussed at any agency meeting out of which the violation of this section arose.

(i) The court may assess against any party reasonable attorney fees and other litigation costs reasonably incurred by any other party who substantially prevails in any action brought in accordance with the provisions of subsection (g) or (h) of this section, except that costs may be assessed against the plaintiff only where the court finds that the suit was initiated by the plaintiff primarily for frivolous or dilatory purposes. In the case of assessment of costs against an agency, the costs may be assessed by the court against the United States.

(j) Each agency subject to the requirements of this section shall annually report to the Congress regarding the following:

(1) The changes in the policies and procedures of the agency under this section that have occurred during the preceding 1-year period.

(2) A tabulation of the number of meetings held, the exemptions applied to close meetings, and the days of public notice provided to close meetings.

(3) A brief description of litigation or formal complaints concerning the implementation of this section by the agency.

(4) A brief explanation of any changes in law that have affected the responsibilities of the agency under this section.

(k) Nothing herein expands or limits the present rights of any person under section 552 of this title, except that the exemptions set forth in subsection (c) of this section shall govern in the case of any request made pursuant to section 552 to copy or inspect the transcripts, recordings, or minutes described in subsection (f) of this section. The requirements of chapter 33 of title 44, United States Code, shall not apply to the transcripts, recordings, and minutes described in subsection (f) of this section.

(l) This section does not constitute authority to withhold any information from Congress, and does not authorize the closing of any agency meeting or portion thereof required by any other provision of law to be open.

(m) Nothing in this section authorizes any agency to withhold from any individual any record, including transcripts, recordings, or minutes required by this section, which is otherwise accessible to such individual under section 552a of this title.

Congressional Review Act

5 U.S.C. §§ 801–808 (2013)

§ 801.   Congressional review

(a)(1)(A) Before a rule can take effect, the Federal agency promulgating such rule shall submit to each House of the Congress and to the Comptroller General a report containing—

(i) a copy of the rule;

(ii) a concise general statement relating to the rule, including whether it is a major rule; and

(iii) the proposed effective date of the rule.

(B) On the date of the submission of the report under subparagraph (A), the Federal agency promulgating the rule shall submit to the Comptroller General and make available to each House of Congress—

(i) a complete copy of the cost-benefit analysis of the rule, if any;

(ii) the agency's actions relevant to sections 603, 604, 605, 607, and 609;

(iii) the agency's actions relevant to sections 202, 203, 204, and 205 of the Unfunded Mandates Reform Act of 1995; and

(iv) any other relevant information or requirements under any other Act and any relevant Executive orders.

(C) Upon receipt of a report submitted under subparagraph (A), each House shall provide copies of the report to the chairman and ranking member of each standing committee with jurisdiction under the rules of the House of Representatives or the Senate to report a bill to amend the provision of law under which the rule is issued.

(2)(A) The Comptroller General shall provide a report on each major rule to the committees of jurisdiction in each House of the Congress by the end of 15 calendar days after the submission or publication date as provided in section 802(b)(2). The report of the Comptroller General shall include an assessment of the agency's compliance with procedural steps required by paragraph (1)(B).

(B) Federal agencies shall cooperate with the Comptroller General by providing information relevant to the Comptroller General's report under subparagraph (A).

(3) A major rule relating to a report submitted under paragraph (1) shall take effect on the latest of—

(A) the later of the date occurring 60 days after the date on which—

(i) the Congress receives the report submitted under paragraph (1); or

(ii) the rule is published in the Federal Register, if so published;

(B) if the Congress passes a joint resolution of disapproval described in section 802 relating to the rule, and the President signs a veto of such resolution, the earlier date—

(i) on which either House of Congress votes and fails to override the veto of the President; or

(ii) occurring 30 session days after the date on which the Congress received the veto and objections of the President; or

(C) the date the rule would have otherwise taken effect, if not for this section (unless a joint resolution of disapproval under section 802 is enacted).

(4) Except for a major rule, a rule shall take effect as otherwise provided by law after submission to Congress under paragraph (1).

(5) Notwithstanding paragraph (3), the effective date of a rule shall not be delayed by operation of this chapter beyond the date on which either House of Congress votes to reject a joint resolution of disapproval under section 802.

(b)(1) A rule shall not take effect (or continue), if the Congress enacts a joint resolution of disapproval, described under section 802, of the rule.

(2) A rule that does not take effect (or does not continue) under paragraph (1) may not be reissued in substantially the same form, and a new rule that is substantially the same as such a rule may not be issued, unless the reissued or new rule is specifically authorized by a law enacted after the date of the joint resolution disapproving the original rule.

(c)(1) Notwithstanding any other provision of this section (except subject to paragraph (3)), a rule that would not take effect by reason of subsection (a)(3) may take effect, if the President makes a determination under paragraph (2) and submits written notice of such determination to the Congress.

(2) Paragraph (1) applies to a determination made by the President by Executive order that the rule should take effect because such rule is—

(A) necessary because of an imminent threat to health or safety or other emergency;

(B) necessary for the enforcement of criminal laws;

(C) necessary for national security; or

(D) issued pursuant to any statute implementing an international trade agreement.

(3) An exercise by the President of the authority under this subsection shall have no effect on the procedures under section 802 or the effect of a joint resolution of disapproval under this section.

(d)(1) In addition to the opportunity for review otherwise provided under this chapter, in the case of any rule for which a report was submitted in accordance with subsection (a)(1)(A) during the period beginning on the date occurring—

(A) in the case of the Senate, 60 session days, or

(B) in the case of the House of Representatives, 60 legislative days, before the date the Congress adjourns a session of Congress through the date on which the same or succeeding Congress first convenes its next session, section 802 shall apply to such rule in the succeeding session of Congress.

(2)(A) In applying section 802 for purposes of such additional review, a rule described under paragraph (1) shall be treated as though—

(i) such rule were published in the Federal Register (as a rule that shall take effect) on—

(I) in the case of the Senate, the 15th session day, or

(II) in the case of the House of Representatives, the 15th legislative day, after the succeeding session of Congress first convenes; and

(ii) a report on such rule were submitted to Congress under subsection (a)(1) on such date.

(B) Nothing in this paragraph shall be construed to affect the requirement under subsection (a)(1) that a report shall be submitted to Congress before a rule can take effect.

(3) A rule described under paragraph (1) shall take effect as otherwise provided by law (including other subsections of this section).

(e)(1) For purposes of this subsection, section 802 shall also apply to any major rule promulgated between March 1, 1996, and the date of the enactment of this chapter.

(2) In applying section 802 for purposes of Congressional review, a rule described under paragraph (1) shall be treated as though—

(A) such rule were published in the Federal Register on the date of enactment of this chapter; and

(B) a report on such rule were submitted to Congress under subsection (a) (1) on such date.

(3) The effectiveness of a rule described under paragraph (1) shall be as otherwise provided by law, unless the rule is made of no force or effect under section 802.

(f) Any rule that takes effect and later is made of no force or effect by enactment of a joint resolution under section 802 shall be treated as though such rule had never taken effect.

(g) If the Congress does not enact a joint resolution of disapproval under section 802 respecting a rule, no court or agency may infer any intent of the Congress from any action or inaction of the Congress with regard to such rule, related statute, or joint resolution of disapproval.

§ 802.   Congressional disapproval procedure

(a) For purposes of this section, the term "joint resolution" means only a joint resolution introduced in the period beginning on the date on which the report referred to in section 801(a)(1)(A) is received by Congress and ending 60 days thereafter (excluding days either House of Congress is adjourned for more than 3 days during a session of Congress), the matter after the resolving clause of which is as follows: "That Congress disapproves the rule submitted by the _____ relating to _____, and such rule shall have no force or effect." (The blank spaces being appropriately filled in).

(b)(1) A joint resolution described in subsection (a) shall be referred to the committees in each House of Congress with jurisdiction.

(2) For purposes of this section, the term "submission or publication date" means the later of the date on which—

(A) the Congress receives the report submitted under section 801(a)(1); or

(B) the rule is published in the Federal Register, if so published.

(c) In the Senate, if the committee to which is referred a joint resolution described in subsection (a) has not reported such joint resolution (or an identical joint resolution) at the end of 20 calendar days after the submission or publication date defined under subsection (b)(2), such committee may be discharged from further consideration of such joint resolution upon a petition supported in writing by 30 Members of the Senate, and such joint resolution shall be placed on the calendar.

(d)(1) In the Senate, when the committee to which a joint resolution is referred has reported, or when a committee is discharged (under subsection (c)) from further consideration of a joint resolution described in subsection (a), it is at any time thereafter in order (even though a previous motion to the same effect has been disagreed to) for a motion to proceed to the consideration of the joint resolution, and all points of order against the joint resolution (and against consideration of the joint resolution) are waived. The motion is not subject to amendment, or to a motion to postpone, or to a motion to proceed to the consideration of other business. A motion to reconsider the vote by which the motion is agreed to or disagreed to shall not be in order. If a motion to proceed to the consideration of the joint resolution is agreed to, the joint resolution shall remain the unfinished business of the Senate until disposed of.

(2) In the Senate, debate on the joint resolution, and on all debatable motions and appeals in connection therewith, shall be limited to not more than 10 hours, which shall be divided equally between those favoring and those opposing the

joint resolution. A motion further to limit debate is in order and not debatable. An amendment to, or a motion to postpone, or a motion to proceed to the consideration of other business, or a motion to recommit the joint resolution is not in order.

(3) In the Senate, immediately following the conclusion of the debate on a joint resolution described in subsection (a), and a single quorum call at the conclusion of the debate if requested in accordance with the rules of the Senate, the vote on final passage of the joint resolution shall occur.

(4) Appeals from the decisions of the Chair relating to the application of the rules of the Senate to the procedure relating to a joint resolution described in subsection (a) shall be decided without debate.

(e) In the Senate the procedure specified in subsection (c) or (d) shall not apply to the consideration of a joint resolution respecting a rule—

(1) after the expiration of the 60 session days beginning with the applicable submission or publication date, or

(2) if the report under section 801(a)(1)(A) was submitted during the period referred to in section 801(d)(1), after the expiration of the 60 session days beginning on the 15th session day after the succeeding session of Congress first convenes.

(f) If, before the passage by one House of a joint resolution of that House described in subsection (a), that House receives from the other House a joint resolution described in subsection (a), then the following procedures shall apply:

(1) The joint resolution of the other House shall not be referred to a committee.

(2) With respect to a joint resolution described in subsection (a) of the House receiving the joint resolution—

(A) the procedure in that House shall be the same as if no joint resolution had been received from the other House; but

(B) the vote on final passage shall be on the joint resolution of the other House.

(g) This section is enacted by Congress—

(1) as an exercise of the rulemaking power of the Senate and House of Representatives, respectively, and as such it is deemed a part of the rules of each House, respectively, but applicable only with respect to the procedure to be followed in that House in the case of a joint resolution described in subsection (a), and it supersedes other rules only to the extent that it is inconsistent with such rules; and

(2) with full recognition of the constitutional right of either House to change the rules (so far as relating to the procedure of that House) at any time, in the same manner, and to the same extent as in the case of any other rule of that House.

§ 803.   Special rule on statutory, regulatory, and judicial deadlines

(a) In the case of any deadline for, relating to, or involving any rule which does not take effect (or the effectiveness of which is terminated) because of enactment of a joint resolution under section 802, that deadline is extended until the date 1 year after the date of enactment of the joint resolution. Nothing in this subsection shall be construed to affect a deadline merely by reason of the postponement of a rule's effective date under section 801(a).

(b) The term "deadline" means any date certain for fulfilling any obligation or exercising any authority established by or under any Federal statute or regulation, or by or under any court order implementing any Federal statute or regulation.

§ 804.   Definitions

For purposes of this chapter—

(1) The term "Federal agency" means any agency as that term is defined in section 551(1).

(2) The term "major rule" means any rule that the Administrator of the Office of Information and Regulatory Affairs of the Office of Management and Budget finds has resulted in or is likely to result in—

(A) an annual effect on the economy of $100,000,000 or more;

(B) a major increase in costs or prices for consumers, individual industries, Federal, State, or local government agencies, or geographic regions; or

(C) significant adverse effects on competition, employment, investment, productivity, innovation, or on the ability of United States-based enterprises to compete with foreign-based enterprises in domestic and export markets.

The term does not include any rule promulgated under the Telecommunications Act of 1996 and the amendments made by that Act.

(3) The term "rule" has the meaning given such term in section 551, except that such term does not include—

(A) any rule of particular applicability, including a rule that approves or prescribes for the future rates, wages, prices, services, or allowances therefor, corporate or financial structures, reorganizations, mergers, or acquisitions thereof, or accounting practices or disclosures bearing on any of the foregoing;

(B) any rule relating to agency management or personnel; or

(C) any rule of agency organization, procedure, or practice that does not substantially affect the rights or obligations of non-agency parties.

§ 805.   Judicial review

No determination, finding, action, or omission under this chapter shall be subject to judicial review.

§ 806.   Applicability; severability

(a) This chapter shall apply notwithstanding any other provision of law.

(b) If any provision of this chapter or the application of any provision of this chapter to any person or circumstance, is held invalid, the application of such provision to other persons or circumstances, and the remainder of this chapter, shall not be affected thereby.

§ 807.   Exemption for monetary policy

Nothing in this chapter shall apply to rules that concern monetary policy proposed or implemented by the Board of Governors of the Federal Reserve System or the Federal Open Market Committee.

§ 808.   Effective date of certain rules

Notwithstanding section 801 —

(1) any rule that establishes, modifies, opens, closes, or conducts a regulatory program for a commercial, recreational, or subsistence activity related to hunting, fishing, or camping, or

(2) any rule which an agency for good cause finds (and incorporates the finding and a brief statement of reasons therefor in the rule issued) that notice and public procedure thereon are impracticable, unnecessary, or contrary to the public interest, shall take effect at such time as the Federal agency promulgating the rule determines.

Federal Advisory Committee Act

Pub. L. 92-463, Oct. 6, 1972, 86 Stat. 770, as amended by Pub. L. 94-409, §5(c), Sept. 13, 1976, 90 Stat. 1247; Pub. L. 96-523, §2, Dec. 12, 1980, 94 Stat. 3040; Pub. L. 97-375, title II, §201(c), Dec. 21, 1982, 96 Stat. 1822; Pub. L. 105-153, §2(a), (b), Dec. 17, 1997, 111 Stat. 2689; Pub. L. 111-259, title IV, §410(a), Oct. 7, 2010, 124 Stat. 2724

§ 1.   Short title

This Act may be cited as the "Federal Advisory Committee Act".

§ 2.   Findings and purpose

(a) The Congress finds that there are numerous committees, boards, commissions, councils, and similar groups which have been established to advise officers and agencies in the executive branch of the Federal Government and that they are frequently a useful and beneficial means of furnishing expert advice, ideas, and diverse opinions to the Federal Government.

(b) The Congress further finds and declares that—

(1) the need for many existing advisory committees has not been adequately reviewed:

(2) new advisory committees should be established only when they are determined to be essential and their number should be kept to the minimum necessary;

(3) advisory committees should be terminated when they are no longer carrying out the purposes for which they were established;

(4) standards and uniform procedures should govern the establishment, operation, administration, and duration of advisory committees;

(5) the Congress and the public should be kept informed with respect to the number, purpose, membership, activities, and cost of advisory committees; and

(6) the function of advisory committees should be advisory only, and that all matters under their consideration should be determined, in accordance with law, by the official, agency, or officer involved.

§ 3.   Definitions

For the purpose of this Act —

(1) The term "Administrator" means the Administrator of General Services.

(2) The term "advisory committee" means any committee, board, commission, council, conference, panel, task force, or other similar group, or any subcommittee or other subgroup thereof (hereafter in this paragraph referred to as "committee"), which is —

(A) established by statute or reorganization plan, or

(B) established or utilized by the President, or

(C) established or utilized by one or more agencies,

in the interest of obtaining advice or recommendations for the President or one or more agencies or officers of the Federal Government, except that such term excludes (i) any committee that is composed wholly of full-time, or permanent part-time, officers or employees of the Federal Government, and (ii) any committee that is created by the National Academy of Sciences or the National Academy of Public Administration.

(3) The term "agency" has the same meaning as in section 551(1) of title 5, United States Code.

(4) The term "Presidential advisory committee" means an advisory committee which advises the President.

4.   Applicability; restrictions

(a) The provisions of this Act or of any rule, order, or regulation promulgated under this Act shall apply to each advisory committee except to the extent that any Act of Congress establishing any such advisory committee specifically provides otherwise.

(b) Nothing in this Act shall be construed to apply to any advisory committee established or utilized by —

(1) the Central Intelligence Agency;

(2) the Federal Reserve System; or

(3) the Office of the Director of National Intelligence, if the Director of National Intelligence determines that for reasons of national security such advisory committee cannot comply with the requirements of this Act.

(c) Nothing in this Act shall be construed to apply to any local civic group whose primary function is that of rendering a public service with respect to a Federal program, or any State or local committee, council, board, commission, or similar group established to advise or make recommendations to State or local officials or agencies.

§ 5. Responsibilities of Congressional committees; review; guidelines

(a) In the exercise of its legislative review function, each standing committee of the Senate and the House of Representatives shall make a continuing review of the activities of each advisory committee under its jurisdiction to determine whether such advisory committee should be abolished or merged with any other advisory committee, whether the responsibilities of such advisory committee should be revised, and whether such advisory committee performs a necessary function not already being performed. Each such standing committee shall take appropriate action to obtain the enactment of legislation necessary to carry out the purpose of this subsection.

(b) In considering legislation establishing, or authorizing the establishment of any advisory committee, each standing committee of the Senate and of the House of Representatives shall determine, and report such determination to the Senate or to the House of Representatives, as the case may be, whether the functions of the proposed advisory committee are being or could be performed by one or more agencies or by an advisory committee already in existence, or by enlarging the mandate of an existing advisory committee. Any such legislation shall—

(1) contain a clearly defined purpose for the advisory committee;

(2) require the membership of the advisory committee to be fairly balanced in terms of the points of view represented and the functions to be performed by the advisory committee;

(3) contain appropriate provisions to assure that the advice and recommendations of the advisory committee will not be inappropriately influenced by the appointing authority or by any special interest, but will instead be the result of the advisory committee's independent judgment;

(4) contain provisions dealing with authorization of appropriations, the date for submission of reports (if any), the duration of the advisory committee, and the publication of reports and other materials, to the extent that the standing committee determines the provisions of section 10 of this Act to be inadequate; and

(5) contain provisions which will assure that the advisory committee will have adequate staff (either supplied by an agency or employed by it), will be provided adequate quarters, and will have funds available to meet its other necessary expenses.

(c) To the extent they are applicable, the guidelines set out in subsection (b) of this section shall be followed by the President, agency heads, or other Federal officials in creating an advisory committee.

§ 6. Responsibilities of the President; report to Congress; annual report to Congress; exclusion

(a) The President may delegate responsibility for evaluating and taking action, where appropriate, with respect to all public recommendations made to him by Presidential advisory committees.

(b) Within one year after a Presidential advisory committee has submitted a public report to the President, the President or his delegate shall make a report to the Congress stating either his proposals for action or his reasons for inaction, with respect to the recommendations contained in the public report.

(c) The President shall, not later than December 31 of each year, make an annual report to the Congress on the activities, status, and changes in the composition of advisory committees in existence during the preceding fiscal year. The report shall contain the name of every advisory committee, the date of and authority for its creation, its termination date or the date it is to make a report, its functions, a reference to the reports it has submitted, a statement of whether it is an ad hoc or continuing body, the dates of its meetings, the names and occupations of its current members, and the total estimated annual cost to the United States to fund, service, supply, and maintain such committee. Such report shall include a list of those advisory committees abolished by the President, and in the case of advisory committees established by statute, a list of those advisory committees which the President recommends be abolished together with his reasons therefor. The President shall exclude from this report any information which, in his judgment, should be withheld for reasons of national security, and he shall include in such report a statement that such information is excluded.

§ 7. Responsibilities of the Administrator of General Services; Committee Management Secretariat, establishment; review; recommendations to President and Congress; agency cooperation; performance guidelines; uniform pay guidelines; travel expenses; expense recommendations

(a) The Administrator shall establish and maintain within the General Services Administration a Committee Management Secretariat, which shall be responsible for all matters relating to advisory committees.

(b) The Administrator shall, immediately after October 6, 1972, institute a comprehensive review of the activities and responsibilities of each advisory committee to determine—

(1) whether such committee is carrying out its purpose;

(2) whether, consistent with the provisions of applicable statutes, the responsibilities assigned to it should be revised;

(3) whether it should be merged with other advisory committees; or

(4) whether it should be abolished.

The Administrator may from time to time request such information as he deems necessary to carry out his functions under this subsection. Upon the completion of the Administrator's review he shall make recommendations to the President and to either the agency head or the Congress with respect to action he believes should be taken. Thereafter, the Administrator shall carry out a similar review annually. Agency heads shall cooperate with the Administrator in making the reviews required by this subsection.

(c) The Administrator shall prescribe administrative guidelines and management controls applicable to advisory committees, and, to the maximum extent feasible, provide advice, assistance, and guidance to advisory committees to improve their performance. In carrying out his functions under this subsection, the Administrator shall consider the recommendations of each agency head with respect to means of improving the performance of advisory committees whose duties are related to such agency.

(d)(1) The Administrator, after study and consultation with the Director of the Office of Personnel Management, shall establish guidelines with respect to uniform fair rates of pay for comparable services of members, staffs, and consultants of advisory committees in a manner which gives appropriate recognition to the responsibilities and qualifications required and other relevant factors. Such regulations shall provide that—

(A) no member of any advisory committee or of the staff of any advisory committee shall receive compensation at a rate in excess of the rate specified for GS-18 of the General Schedule under section 5332 of title 5, United States Code;

(B) such members, while engaged in the performance of their duties away from their homes or regular places of business, may be allowed travel expenses, including per diem in lieu of subsistence, as authorized by section 5703 of title 5, United States Code, for persons employed intermittently in the Government service; and

(C) such members—

(i) who are blind or deaf or who otherwise qualify as handicapped individuals (within the meaning of section 501 of the Rehabilitation Act of 1973 (29 U.S.C. 794)), and

(ii) who do not otherwise qualify for assistance under section 3102 of title 5, United States Code, by reason of being an employee of an agency (within the meaning of section 3102(a)(1) of such title 5),

may be provided services pursuant to section 3102 of such title 5 while in performance of their advisory committee duties.

(2) Nothing in this subsection shall prevent—

(A) an individual who (without regard to his service with an advisory committee) is a full-time employee of the United States, or

(B) an individual who immediately before his service with an advisory committee was such an employee, from receiving compensation at the rate at which he otherwise would be compensated (or was compensated) as a full-time employee of the United States.

(e) The Administrator shall include in budget recommendations a summary of the amounts he deems necessary for the expenses of advisory committees, including the expenses for publication of reports where appropriate.

§ 8. Responsibilities of agency heads; Advisory Committee Management Officer, designation

(a) Each agency head shall establish uniform administrative guidelines and management controls for advisory committees established by that agency, which shall be consistent with directives of the Administrator under section 7 and section 10. Each agency shall maintain systematic information on the nature, functions, and operations of each advisory committee within its jurisdiction.

(b) The head of each agency which has an advisory committee shall designate an Advisory Committee Management Officer who shall—

(1) exercise control and supervision over the establishment, procedures, and accomplishments of advisory committees established by that agency;

(2) assemble and maintain the reports, records, and other papers of any such committee during its existence; and

(3) carry out, on behalf of that agency, the provisions of section 552 of title 5, United States Code, with respect to such reports, records, and other papers.

§ 9. Establishment and purpose of advisory committees; publication in Federal Register; charter: filing, contents, copy

(a) No advisory committee shall be established unless such establishment is—

(1) specifically authorized by statute or by the President; or

(2) determined as a matter of formal record, by the head of the agency involved after consultation with the Administrator, with timely notice published in the Federal Register, to be in the public interest in connection with the performance of duties imposed on that agency by law.

(b) Unless otherwise specifically provided by statute or Presidential directive, advisory committees shall be utilized solely for advisory functions. Determinations of action to be taken and policy to be expressed with respect to matters upon which an advisory committee reports or makes recommendations shall be made solely by the President or an officer of the Federal Government.

(c) No advisory committee shall meet or take any action until an advisory committee charter has been filed with (1) the Administrator, in the case of Presidential advisory committees, or (2) with the head of the agency to whom any advisory committee reports and with the standing committees of the Senate and of the House of Representatives having legislative jurisdiction of such agency. Such charter shall contain the following information:

(A) the committee's official designation;

(B) the committee's objectives and the scope of its activity;

(C) the period of time necessary for the committee to carry out its purposes;

(D) the agency or official to whom the committee reports;

(E) the agency responsible for providing the necessary support for the committee;

(F) a description of the duties for which the committee is responsible, and, if such duties are not solely advisory, a specification of the authority for such functions;

(G) the estimated annual operating costs in dollars and man-years for such committee;

(H) the estimated number and frequency of committee meetings;

(I) the committee's termination date, if less than two years from the date of the committee's establishment; and

(J) the date the charter is filed.

A copy of any such charter shall also be furnished to the Library of Congress.

§ 10. Advisory committee procedures; meetings; notice, publication in Federal Register; regulations; minutes; certification; annual report; Federal officer or employee, attendance

(a)(1) Each advisory committee meeting shall be open to the public.

(2) Except when the President determines otherwise for reasons of national security, timely notice of each such meeting shall be published in the Federal Register, and the Administrator shall prescribe regulations to provide for other types of public notice to insure that all interested persons are notified of such meeting prior thereto.

(3) Interested persons shall be permitted to attend, appear before, or file statements with any advisory committee, subject to such reasonable rules or regulations as the Administrator may prescribe.

(b) Subject to section 552 of title 5, United States Code, the records, reports, transcripts, minutes, appendixes, working papers, drafts, studies, agenda, or other documents which were made available to or prepared for or by each advisory committee shall be available for public inspection and copying at a single location in the offices of the advisory committee or the agency to which the advisory committee reports until the advisory committee ceases to exist.

(c) Detailed minutes of each meeting of each advisory committee shall be kept and shall contain a record of the persons present, a complete and accurate description of matters discussed and conclusions reached, and copies of all reports received, issued, or approved by the advisory committee. The accuracy of all minutes shall be certified to by the chairman of the advisory committee.

(d) Subsections (a)(1) and (a)(3) of this section shall not apply to any portion of an advisory committee meeting where the President, or the head of the agency to which the advisory committee reports, determines that such portion of such meeting may be closed to the public in accordance with subsection (c) of section 552b of title 5, United States Code. Any such determination shall be in writing and shall contain the reasons for such determination. If such a determination is made, the advisory committee shall issue a report at least annually setting forth a summary of its activities and such related matters as would be informative to the public consistent with the policy of section 552(b) of title 5, United States Code.

(e) There shall be designated an officer or employee of the Federal Government to chair or attend each meeting of each advisory committee. The officer or employee so designated is authorized, whenever he determines it to be in the public interest, to adjourn any such meeting. No advisory committee shall conduct any meeting in the absence of that officer or employee.

(f) Advisory committees shall not hold any meetings except at the call of, or with the advance approval of, a designated officer or employee of the Federal Government, and in the case of advisory committees (other than Presidential advisory committees), with an agenda approved by such officer or employee.

§ 11.　Availability of transcripts; "agency proceeding"

(a) Except where prohibited by contractual agreements entered into prior to the effective date of this Act, agencies and advisory committees shall make available to any person, at actual cost of duplication, copies of transcripts of agency proceedings or advisory committee meetings.

(b) As used in this section "agency proceeding" means any proceeding as defined in section 551(12) of title 5, United States Code.

§ 12.　Fiscal and administrative provisions; record-keeping; audit; agency support services

(a) Each agency shall keep records as will fully disclose the disposition of any funds which may be at the disposal of its advisory committees and the nature and extent of their activities. The General Services Administration, or such other agency as the President may designate, shall maintain financial records with respect to Presidential advisory committees. The Comptroller General of the United States, or any of his authorized representatives, shall have access, for the purpose of audit and examination, to any such records.

(b) Each agency shall be responsible for providing support services for each advisory committee established by or reporting to it unless the establishing authority provides otherwise. Where any such advisory committee reports to more than one agency, only one agency shall be responsible for support services at any one time. In the case of Presidential advisory committees, such services may be provided by the General Services Administration.

§ 13. Responsibilities of Library of Congress; reports and background papers; depository

Subject to section 552 of title 5, United States Code, the Administrator shall provide for the filing with the Library of Congress of at least eight copies of each report made by every advisory committee and, where appropriate, background papers prepared by consultants. The Librarian of Congress shall establish a depository for such reports and papers where they shall be available to public inspection and use.

§ 14. Termination of advisory committees; renewal; continuation

(a)(1) Each advisory committee which is in existence on the effective date of this Act shall terminate not later than the expiration of the two-year period following such effective date unless —

(A) in the case of an advisory committee established by the President or an officer of the Federal Government, such advisory committee is renewed by the President or that officer by appropriate action prior to the expiration of such two-year period; or

(B) in the case of an advisory committee established by an Act of Congress, its duration is otherwise provided for by law.

(2) Each advisory committee established after such effective date shall terminate not later than the expiration of the two-year period beginning on the date of its establishment unless —

(A) in the case of an advisory committee established by the President or an officer of the Federal Government such advisory committee is renewed by the President or such officer by appropriate action prior to the end of such period; or

(B) in the case of an advisory committee established by an Act of Congress, its duration is otherwise provided for by law.

(b)(1) Upon the renewal of any advisory committee, such advisory committee shall file a charter in accordance with section 9(c).

(2) Any advisory committee established by an Act of Congress shall file a charter in accordance with such section upon the expiration of each successive two-year period following the date of enactment of the Act establishing such advisory committee.

(3) No advisory committee required under this subsection to file a charter shall take any action (other than preparation and filing of such charter) prior to the date on which such charter is filed.

(c) Any advisory committee which is renewed by the President or any officer of the Federal Government may be continued only for successive two-year periods by appropriate action taken by the President or such officer prior to the date on which such advisory committee would otherwise terminate.

§ 15.   Requirements relating to the National Academy of Sciences and the National Academy of Public Administration

(a) In General. — An agency may not use any advice or recommendation provided by the National Academy of Sciences or National Academy of Public Administration that was developed by use of a committee created by that academy under an agreement with an agency, unless —

(1) the committee was not subject to any actual management or control by an agency or an officer of the Federal Government;

(2) in the case of a committee created after the date of the enactment of the Federal Advisory Committee Act Amendments of 1997, the membership of the committee was appointed in accordance with the requirements described in subsection (b)(1); and

(3) in developing the advice or recommendation, the academy complied with —

(A) subsection (b)(2) through (6), in the case of any advice or recommendation provided by the National Academy of Sciences; or

(B) subsection (b)(2) and (5), in the case of any advice or recommendation provided by the National Academy of Public Administration.

(b) Requirements. — The requirements referred to in subsection (a) are as follows:

(1) The Academy shall determine and provide public notice of the names and brief biographies of individuals that the Academy appoints or intends to appoint to serve on the committee. The Academy shall determine and provide a reasonable opportunity for the public to comment on such appointments before they are made or, if the Academy determines such prior comment is not practicable, in the period immediately following the appointments. The Academy shall make its best efforts to ensure that (A) no individual appointed to serve on the committee has a conflict of interest that is relevant to the functions to be performed, unless such conflict is promptly and publicly disclosed and the Academy determines that the conflict is unavoidable, (B) the committee membership is fairly balanced as determined by the Academy to be appropriate for the functions to be performed, and (C) the final report of the Academy will be the result of the Academy's independent judgment. The Academy shall require that individuals that the Academy appoints or intends to appoint to serve on the committee inform the Academy of

the individual's conflicts of interest that are relevant to the functions to be performed.

(2) The Academy shall determine and provide public notice of committee meetings that will be open to the public.

(3) The Academy shall ensure that meetings of the committee to gather data from individuals who are not officials, agents, or employees of the Academy are open to the public, unless the Academy determines that a meeting would disclose matters described in section 552(b) of title 5, United States Code. The Academy shall make available to the public, at reasonable charge if appropriate, written materials presented to the committee by individuals who are not officials, agents, or employees of the Academy, unless the Academy determines that making material available would disclose matters described in that section.

(4) The Academy shall make available to the public as soon as practicable, at reasonable charge if appropriate, a brief summary of any committee meeting that is not a data gathering meeting, unless the Academy determines that the summary would disclose matters described in section 552(b) of title 5, United States Code. The summary shall identify the committee members present, the topics discussed, materials made available to the committee, and such other matters that the Academy determines should be included.

(5) The Academy shall make available to the public its final report, at reasonable charge if appropriate, unless the Academy determines that the report would disclose matters described in section 552(b) of title 5, United States Code. If the Academy determines that the report would disclose matters described in that section, the Academy shall make public an abbreviated version of the report that does not disclose those matters.

(6) After publication of the final report, the Academy shall make publicly available the names of the principal reviewers who reviewed the report in draft form and who are not officials, agents, or employees of the Academy.

(c) Regulations.—The Administrator of General Services may issue regulations implementing this section.

§ 16.   Effective date

Except as provided in section 7(b), this Act shall become effective upon the expiration of ninety days following October 6, 1972.

Paperwork Reduction Act

44 U.S.C. §§ 3501–3521 (2013)

§ 3501. Purposes

The purposes of this subchapter are to —

(1) minimize the paperwork burden for individuals, small businesses, educational and nonprofit institutions, Federal contractors, State, local and tribal governments, and other persons resulting from the collection of information by or for the Federal Government;

(2) ensure the greatest possible public benefit from and maximize the utility of information created, collected, maintained, used, shared and disseminated by or for the Federal Government;

(3) coordinate, integrate, and to the extent practicable and appropriate, make uniform Federal information resources management policies and practices as a means to improve the productivity, efficiency, and effectiveness of Government programs, including the reduction of information collection burdens on the public and the improvement of service delivery to the public;

(4) improve the quality and use of Federal information to strengthen decision-making, accountability, and openness in Government and society;

(5) minimize the cost to the Federal Government of the creation, collection, maintenance, use, dissemination, and disposition of information;

(6) strengthen the partnership between the Federal Government and State, local, and tribal governments by minimizing the burden and maximizing the utility of information created, collected, maintained, used, disseminated, and retained by or for the Federal Government;

(7) provide for the dissemination of public information on a timely basis, on equitable terms, and in a manner that promotes the utility of the information to the public and makes effective use of information technology;

(8) ensure that the creation, collection, maintenance, use, dissemination, and disposition of information by or for the Federal Government is consistent with applicable laws, including laws relating to —

(A) privacy and confidentiality, including section 552a of title 5;

(B) security of information, including section 11332 of title 40; and

(C) access to information, including section 552 of title 5;

(9) ensure the integrity, quality, and utility of the Federal statistical system;

(10) ensure that information technology is acquired, used, and managed to improve performance of agency missions, including the reduction of information collection burdens on the public; and

(11) improve the responsibility and accountability of the Office of Management and Budget and all other Federal agencies to Congress and to the public for implementing the information collection review process, information resources management, and related policies and guidelines established under this subchapter.

§ 3502.   Definitions

As used in this subchapter —

(1) the term "agency" means any executive department, military department, Government corporation, Government controlled corporation, or other establishment in the executive branch of the Government (including the Executive Office of the President), or any independent regulatory agency, but does not include —

(A) the Government Accountability Office;

(B) Federal Election Commission;

(C) the governments of the District of Columbia and of the territories and possessions of the United States, and their various subdivisions; or

(D) Government-owned contractor-operated facilities, including laboratories engaged in national defense research and production activities;

(2) the term "burden" means time, effort, or financial resources expended by persons to generate, maintain, or provide information to or for a Federal agency, including the resources expended for —

(A) reviewing instructions;

(B) acquiring, installing, and utilizing technology and systems;

(C) adjusting the existing ways to comply with any previously applicable instructions and requirements;

(D) searching data sources;

(E) completing and reviewing the collection of information; and

(F) transmitting, or otherwise disclosing the information;

(3) the term "collection of information" —

(A) means the obtaining, causing to be obtained, soliciting, or requiring the disclosure to third parties or the public, of facts or opinions by or for an agency, regardless of form or format, calling for either —

(i) answers to identical questions posed to, or identical reporting or record-keeping requirements imposed on, ten or more persons, other than agencies, instrumentalities, or employees of the United States; or

(ii) answers to questions posed to agencies, instrumentalities, or employees of the United States which are to be used for general statistical purposes; and

(B) shall not include a collection of information described under section 3518(c)(1);

(4) the term "Director" means the Director of the Office of Management and Budget;

(5) the term "independent regulatory agency" means the Board of Governors of the Federal Reserve System, the Commodity Futures Trading Commission, the Consumer Product Safety Commission, the Federal Communications Commission, the Federal Deposit Insurance Corporation, the Federal Energy Regulatory Commission, the Federal Housing Finance Agency, the Federal Maritime Commission, the Federal Trade Commission, the Interstate Commerce Commission, the Mine Enforcement Safety and Health Review Commission, the National Labor Relations Board, the Nuclear Regulatory Commission, the Occupational Safety and Health Review Commission, the Postal Regulatory Commission, the Securities and Exchange Commission, the Bureau of Consumer Financial Protection, the Office of Financial Research, Office of the Comptroller of the Currency, and any other similar agency designated by statute as a Federal independent regulatory agency or commission;

(6) the term "information resources" means information and related resources, such as personnel, equipment, funds, and information technology;

(7) the term "information resources management" means the process of managing information resources to accomplish agency missions and to improve agency performance, including through the reduction of information collection burdens on the public;

(8) the term "information system" means a discrete set of information resources organized for the collection, processing, maintenance, use, sharing, dissemination, or disposition of information;

(9) the term "information technology" has the meaning given that term in section 11101 of title 40 but does not include national security systems as defined in section 11103 of title 40;

(10) the term "person" means an individual, partnership, association, corporation, business trust, or legal representative, an organized group of individuals, a State, territorial, tribal, or local government or branch thereof, or a political subdivision of a State, territory, tribal, or local government or a branch of a political subdivision;

(11) the term "practical utility" means the ability of an agency to use information, particularly the capability to process such information in a timely and useful fashion;

(12) the term "public information" means any information, regardless of form or format, that an agency discloses, disseminates, or makes available to the public;

(13) the term "recordkeeping requirement" means a requirement imposed by or for an agency on persons to maintain specified records, including a requirement to—

(A) retain such records;

(B) notify third parties, the Federal Government, or the public of the existence of such records;

(C) disclose such records to third parties, the Federal Government, or the public; or

(D) report to third parties, the Federal Government, or the public regarding such records; and

(14) the term "penalty" includes the imposition by an agency or court of a fine or other punishment; a judgment for monetary damages or equitable relief; or the revocation, suspension, reduction, or denial of a license, privilege, right, grant, or benefit.

§ 3503.   Office of Information and Regulatory Affairs

(a) There is established in the Office of Management and Budget an office to be known as the Office of Information and Regulatory Affairs.

(b) There shall be at the head of the Office an Administrator who shall be appointed by the President, by and with the advice and consent of the Senate. The Director shall delegate to the Administrator the authority to administer all functions under this subchapter, except that any such delegation shall not relieve the Director of responsibility for the administration of such functions. The Administrator shall serve as principal adviser to the Director on Federal information resources management policy.

§ 3504.   Authority and functions of Director

(a)(1) The Director shall oversee the use of information resources to improve the efficiency and effectiveness of governmental operations to serve agency missions, including burden reduction and service delivery to the public. In performing such oversight, the Director shall—

(A) develop, coordinate and oversee the implementation of Federal information resources management policies, principles, standards, and guidelines; and

(B) provide direction and oversee—

(i) the review and approval of the collection of information and the reduction of the information collection burden;

(ii) agency dissemination of and public access to information;

(iii) statistical activities;

(iv) records management activities;

(v) privacy, confidentiality, security, disclosure, and sharing of information; and

(vi) the acquisition and use of information technology, including alternative information technologies that provide for electronic submission, maintenance, or disclosure of information as a substitute for paper and for the use and acceptance of electronic signatures.

(2) The authority of the Director under this subchapter shall be exercised consistent with applicable law.

(b) With respect to general information resources management policy, the Director shall—

(1) develop and oversee the implementation of uniform information resources management policies, principles, standards, and guidelines;

(2) foster greater sharing, dissemination, and access to public information, including through—

(A) the use of the Government Information Locator Service; and

(B) the development and utilization of common standards for information collection, storage, processing and communication, including standards for security, interconnectivity and interoperability;

(3) initiate and review proposals for changes in legislation, regulations, and agency procedures to improve information resources management practices;

(4) oversee the development and implementation of best practices in information resources management, including training; and

(5) oversee agency integration of program and management functions with information resources management functions.

(c) With respect to the collection of information and the control of paperwork, the Director shall—

(1) review and approve proposed agency collections of information;

(2) coordinate the review of the collection of information associated with Federal procurement and acquisition by the Office of Information and Regulatory Affairs with the Office of Federal Procurement Policy, with particular emphasis on applying information technology to improve the efficiency and effectiveness of Federal procurement, acquisition and payment, and to reduce information collection burdens on the public;

(3) minimize the Federal information collection burden, with particular emphasis on those individuals and entities most adversely affected;

(4) maximize the practical utility of and public benefit from information collected by or for the Federal Government;

(5) establish and oversee standards and guidelines by which agencies are to estimate the burden to comply with a proposed collection of information;

(6) publish in the Federal Register and make available on the Internet (in consultation with the Small Business Administration) on an annual basis a list of the compliance assistance resources available to small businesses, with the first such publication occurring not later than 1 year after the date of enactment of the Small Business Paperwork Relief Act of 2002.

(d) With respect to information dissemination, the Director shall develop and oversee the implementation of policies, principles, standards, and guidelines to—

(1) apply to Federal agency dissemination of public information, regardless of the form or format in which such information is disseminated; and

(2) promote public access to public information and fulfill the purposes of this subchapter, including through the effective use of information technology.

(e) With respect to statistical policy and coordination, the Director shall—

(1) coordinate the activities of the Federal statistical system to ensure—

(A) the efficiency and effectiveness of the system; and

(B) the integrity, objectivity, impartiality, utility, and confidentiality of information collected for statistical purposes;

(2) ensure that budget proposals of agencies are consistent with system-wide priorities for maintaining and improving the quality of Federal statistics and prepare an annual report on statistical program funding;

(3) develop and oversee the implementation of Governmentwide policies, principles, standards, and guidelines concerning—

(A) statistical collection procedures and methods;

(B) statistical data classification;

(C) statistical information presentation and dissemination;

(D) timely release of statistical data; and

(E) such statistical data sources as may be required for the administration of Federal programs;

(4) evaluate statistical program performance and agency compliance with Governmentwide policies, principles, standards and guidelines;

(5) promote the sharing of information collected for statistical purposes consistent with privacy rights and confidentiality pledges;

(6) coordinate the participation of the United States in international statistical activities, including the development of comparable statistics;

(7) appoint a chief statistician who is a trained and experienced professional statistician to carry out the functions described under this subsection;

(8) establish an Interagency Council on Statistical Policy to advise and assist the Director in carrying out the functions under this subsection that shall—

(A) be headed by the chief statistician; and

(B) consist of—

(i) the heads of the major statistical programs; and

(ii) representatives of other statistical agencies under rotating membership; and

(9) provide opportunities for training in statistical policy functions to employees of the Federal Government under which—

(A) each trainee shall be selected at the discretion of the Director based on agency requests and shall serve under the chief statistician for at least 6 months and not more than 1 year; and

(B) all costs of the training shall be paid by the agency requesting training.

(f) With respect to records management, the Director shall—

(1) provide advice and assistance to the Archivist of the United States and the Administrator of General Services to promote coordination in the administration of chapters 29, 31, and 33 of this title with the information resources management policies, principles, standards, and guidelines established under this subchapter;

(2) review compliance by agencies with—

(A) the requirements of chapters 29, 31, and 33 of this title; and

(B) regulations promulgated by the Archivist of the United States and the Administrator of General Services; and

(3) oversee the application of records management policies, principles, standards, and guidelines, including requirements for archiving information maintained in electronic format, in the planning and design of information systems.

(g) With respect to privacy and security, the Director shall—

(1) develop and oversee the implementation of policies, principles, standards, and guidelines on privacy, confidentiality, security, disclosure and sharing of information collected or maintained by or for agencies; and

(2) oversee and coordinate compliance with sections 552 and 552a of title 5, sections 20 and 21 of the National Institute of Standards and Technology Act (15 U.S.C. 278g-3 and 278g-4), section 11331 of title 40 and subchapter II of this chapter, and related information management laws.

(h) With respect to Federal information technology, the Director shall—

(1) in consultation with the Director of the National Institute of Standards and Technology and the Administrator of General Services —

(A) develop and oversee the implementation of policies, principles, standards, and guidelines for information technology functions and activities of the Federal Government, including periodic evaluations of major information systems; and

(B) oversee the development and implementation of standards under section 11331 of title 40;

(2) monitor the effectiveness of, and compliance with, directives issued under subtitle III of title 40 and directives issued under section 322 of title 40;

(3) coordinate the development and review by the Office of Information and Regulatory Affairs of policy associated with Federal procurement and acquisition of information technology with the Office of Federal Procurement Policy;

(4) ensure, through the review of agency budget proposals, information resources management plans and other means —

(A) agency integration of information resources management plans, program plans and budgets for acquisition and use of information technology; and

(B) the efficiency and effectiveness of inter-agency information technology initiatives to improve agency performance and the accomplishment of agency missions; and

(5) promote the use of information technology by the Federal Government to improve the productivity, efficiency, and effectiveness of Federal programs, including through dissemination of public information and the reduction of information collection burdens on the public.

§ 3505.   Assignment of tasks and deadlines

(a) In carrying out the functions under this subchapter, the Director shall—

(1) in consultation with agency heads, set an annual Governmentwide goal for the reduction of information collection burdens by at least 10 percent during each of fiscal years 1996 and 1997 and 5 percent during each of fiscal years 1998, 1999, 2000, and 2001, and set annual agency goals to—

(A) reduce information collection burdens imposed on the public that—

(i) represent the maximum practicable opportunity in each agency; and

(ii) are consistent with improving agency management of the process for the review of collections of information established under section 3506(c); and

(B) improve information resources management in ways that increase the productivity, efficiency and effectiveness of Federal programs, including service delivery to the public;

(2) with selected agencies and non-Federal entities on a voluntary basis, conduct pilot projects to test alternative policies, practices, regulations, and procedures to fulfill the purposes of this subchapter, particularly with regard to minimizing the Federal information collection burden; and

(3) in consultation with the Administrator of General Services, the Director of the National Institute of Standards and Technology, the Archivist of the United States, and the Director of the Office of Personnel Management, develop and maintain a Governmentwide strategic plan for information resources management, that shall include—

(A) a description of the objectives and the means by which the Federal Government shall apply information resources to improve agency and program performance;

(B) plans for—

(i) reducing information burdens on the public, including reducing such burdens through the elimination of duplication and meeting shared data needs with shared resources;

(ii) enhancing public access to and dissemination of, information, using electronic and other formats; and

(iii) meeting the information technology needs of the Federal Government in accordance with the purposes of this subchapter; and

(C) a description of progress in applying information resources management to improve agency performance and the accomplishment of missions.

(b) For purposes of any pilot project conducted under subsection (a)(2), the Director may, after consultation with the agency head, waive the application of any administrative directive issued by an agency with which the project is conducted, including any directive requiring a collection of information, after giving timely notice to the public and the Congress regarding the need for such waiver.

(c)[1] Inventory of Major Information Systems.—

(1) The head of each agency shall develop and maintain an inventory of major information systems (including major national security systems) operated by or under the control of such agency.

(2) The identification of information systems in an inventory under this subsection shall include an identification of the interfaces between each such system and all other systems or networks, including those not operated by or under the control of the agency.

(3) Such inventory shall be—

(A) updated at least annually;

(B) made available to the Comptroller General; and

---

1. So in original. Two subsecs. (c) have been enacted.

(C) used to support information resources management, including—

(i) preparation and maintenance of the inventory of information resources under section 3506(b)(4);

(ii) information technology planning, budgeting, acquisition, and management under section 3506(h), subtitle III of title 40, and related laws and guidance;

(iii) monitoring, testing, and evaluation of information security controls under subchapter II;

(iv) preparation of the index of major information systems required under section 552(g) of title 5, United States Code; and

(v) preparation of information system inventories required for records management under chapters 21, 29, 31, and 33.

(4) The Director shall issue guidance for and oversee the implementation of the requirements of this subsection.

(c) Inventory of Information Systems.—

(1) The head of each agency shall develop and maintain an inventory of the information systems (including national security systems) operated by or under the control of such agency;

(2) The identification of information systems in an inventory under this subsection shall include an identification of the interfaces between each such system and all other systems or networks, including those not operated by or under the control of the agency;

(3) Such inventory shall be—

(A) updated at least annually;

(B) made available to the Comptroller General; and

(C) used to support information resources management, including—

(i) preparation and maintenance of the inventory of information resources under section 3506(b)(4);

(ii) information technology planning, budgeting, acquisition, and management under section 3506(h), subtitle III of title 40, and related laws and guidance;

(iii) monitoring, testing, and evaluation of information security controls under subchapter II;

(iv) preparation of the index of major information systems required under section 552(g) of title 5, United States Code; and

(v) preparation of information system inventories required for records management under chapters 21, 29, 31, and 33.

(4) The Director shall issue guidance for and oversee the implementation of the requirements of this subsection.

§ 3506. Federal agency responsibilities

(a)(1) The head of each agency shall be responsible for—

(A) carrying out the agency's information resources management activities to improve agency productivity, efficiency, and effectiveness; and

(B) complying with the requirements of this subchapter and related policies established by the Director.

(2)(A) Except as provided under subparagraph (B), the head of each agency shall designate a Chief Information Officer who shall report directly to such agency head to carry out the responsibilities of the agency under this subchapter.

(B) The Secretary of the Department of Defense and the Secretary of each military department may each designate Chief Information Officers who shall report directly to such Secretary to carry out the responsibilities of the department under this subchapter. If more than one Chief Information Officer is designated, the respective duties of the Chief Information Officers shall be clearly delineated.

(3) The Chief Information Officer designated under paragraph (2) shall head an office responsible for ensuring agency compliance with and prompt, efficient, and effective implementation of the information policies and information resources management responsibilities established under this subchapter, including the reduction of information collection burdens on the public. The Chief Information Officer and employees of such office shall be selected with special attention to the professional qualifications required to administer the functions described under this subchapter.

(4) Each agency program official shall be responsible and accountable for information resources assigned to and supporting the programs under such official. In consultation with the Chief Information Officer designated under paragraph (2) and the agency Chief Financial Officer (or comparable official), each agency program official shall define program information needs and develop strategies, systems, and capabilities to meet those needs.

(b) With respect to general information resources management, each agency shall—

(1) manage information resources to—

(A) reduce information collection burdens on the public;

(B) increase program efficiency and effectiveness; and

(C) improve the integrity, quality, and utility of information to all users within and outside the agency, including capabilities for ensuring dissemination of public information, public access to government information, and protections for privacy and security;

(2) in accordance with guidance by the Director, develop and maintain a strategic information resources management plan that shall describe how information resources management activities help accomplish agency missions;

(3) develop and maintain an ongoing process to—

(A) ensure that information resources management operations and decisions are integrated with organizational planning, budget, financial management, human resources management, and program decisions;

(B) in cooperation with the agency Chief Financial Officer (or comparable official), develop a full and accurate accounting of information technology expenditures, related expenses, and results; and

(C) establish goals for improving information resources management's contribution to program productivity, efficiency, and effectiveness, methods for measuring progress towards those goals, and clear roles and responsibilities for achieving those goals;

(4) in consultation with the Director, the Administrator of General Services, and the Archivist of the United States, maintain a current and complete inventory of the agency's information resources, including directories necessary to fulfill the requirements of section 3511 of this subchapter; and

(5) in consultation with the Director and the Director of the Office of Personnel Management, conduct formal training programs to educate agency program and management officials about information resources management.

(c) With respect to the collection of information and the control of paperwork, each agency shall—

(1) establish a process within the office headed by the Chief Information Officer designated under subsection (a), that is sufficiently independent of program responsibility to evaluate fairly whether proposed collections of information should be approved under this subchapter, to—

(A) review each collection of information before submission to the Director for review under this subchapter, including—

(i) an evaluation of the need for the collection of information;

(ii) a functional description of the information to be collected;

(iii) a plan for the collection of the information;

(iv) a specific, objectively supported estimate of burden;

(v) a test of the collection of information through a pilot program, if appropriate; and

(vi) a plan for the efficient and effective management and use of the information to be collected, including necessary resources;

(B) ensure that each information collection—

(i) is inventoried, displays a control number and, if appropriate, an expiration date;

(ii) indicates the collection is in accordance with the clearance requirements of section 3507; and

(iii) informs the person receiving the collection of information of—

(I) the reasons the information is being collected;

(II) the way such information is to be used;

(III) an estimate, to the extent practicable, of the burden of the collection;

(IV) whether responses to the collection of information are voluntary, required to obtain a benefit, or mandatory; and

(V) the fact that an agency may not conduct or sponsor, and a person is not required to respond to, a collection of information unless it displays a valid control number; and

(C) assess the information collection burden of proposed legislation affecting the agency;

(2)(A) except as provided under subparagraph (B) or section 3507(j), provide 60-day notice in the Federal Register, and otherwise consult with members of the public and affected agencies concerning each proposed collection of information, to solicit comment to—

(i) evaluate whether the proposed collection of information is necessary for the proper performance of the functions of the agency, including whether the information shall have practical utility;

(ii) evaluate the accuracy of the agency's estimate of the burden of the proposed collection of information;

(iii) enhance the quality, utility, and clarity of the information to be collected; and

(iv) minimize the burden of the collection of information on those who are to respond, including through the use of automated collection techniques or other forms of information technology; and

(B) for any proposed collection of information contained in a proposed rule (to be reviewed by the Director under section 3507(d)), provide notice and comment through the notice of proposed rulemaking for the proposed rule and such notice shall have the same purposes specified under subparagraph (A)(i) through (iv);

(3) certify (and provide a record supporting such certification, including public comments received by the agency) that each collection of information submitted to the Director for review under section 3507—

(A) is necessary for the proper performance of the functions of the agency, including that the information has practical utility;

(B) is not unnecessarily duplicative of information otherwise reasonably accessible to the agency;

(C) reduces to the extent practicable and appropriate the burden on persons who shall provide information to or for the agency, including with respect to small entities, as defined under section 601(6) of title 5, the use of such techniques as —

(i) establishing differing compliance or reporting requirements or timetables that take into account the resources available to those who are to respond;

(ii) the clarification, consolidation, or simplification of compliance and reporting requirements; or

(iii) an exemption from coverage of the collection of information, or any part thereof;

(D) is written using plain, coherent, and unambiguous terminology and is understandable to those who are to respond;

(E) is to be implemented in ways consistent and compatible, to the maximum extent practicable, with the existing reporting and recordkeeping practices of those who are to respond;

(F) indicates for each recordkeeping requirement the length of time persons are required to maintain the records specified;

(G) contains the statement required under paragraph (1)(B)(iii);

(H) has been developed by an office that has planned and allocated resources for the efficient and effective management and use of the information to be collected, including the processing of the information in a manner which shall enhance, where appropriate, the utility of the information to agencies and the public;

(I) uses effective and efficient statistical survey methodology appropriate to the purpose for which the information is to be collected; and

(J) to the maximum extent practicable, uses information technology to reduce burden and improve data quality, agency efficiency and responsiveness to the public; and

(4) in addition to the requirements of this chapter regarding the reduction of information collection burdens for small business concerns (as defined in section 3 of the Small Business Act (15 U.S.C. 632)), make efforts to further reduce the information collection burden for small business concerns with fewer than 25 employees.

(d) With respect to information dissemination, each agency shall —

(1) ensure that the public has timely and equitable access to the agency's public information, including ensuring such access through —

(A) encouraging a diversity of public and private sources for information based on government public information;

(B) in cases in which the agency provides public information maintained in electronic format, providing timely and equitable access to the underlying data (in whole or in part); and

(C) agency dissemination of public information in an efficient, effective, and economical manner;

(2) regularly solicit and consider public input on the agency's information dissemination activities;

(3) provide adequate notice when initiating, substantially modifying, or terminating significant information dissemination products; and

(4) not, except where specifically authorized by statute—

(A) establish an exclusive, restricted, or other distribution arrangement that interferes with timely and equitable availability of public information to the public;

(B) restrict or regulate the use, resale, or redissemination of public information by the public;

(C) charge fees or royalties for resale or redissemination of public information; or

(D) establish user fees for public information that exceed the cost of dissemination.

(e) With respect to statistical policy and coordination, each agency shall—

(1) ensure the relevance, accuracy, timeliness, integrity, and objectivity of information collected or created for statistical purposes;

(2) inform respondents fully and accurately about the sponsors, purposes, and uses of statistical surveys and studies;

(3) protect respondents' privacy and ensure that disclosure policies fully honor pledges of confidentiality;

(4) observe Federal standards and practices for data collection, analysis, documentation, sharing, and dissemination of information;

(5) ensure the timely publication of the results of statistical surveys and studies, including information about the quality and limitations of the surveys and studies; and

(6) make data available to statistical agencies and readily accessible to the public.

(f) With respect to records management, each agency shall implement and enforce applicable policies and procedures, including requirements for archiving information maintained in electronic format, particularly in the planning, design and operation of information systems.

(g) With respect to privacy and security, each agency shall—

(1) implement and enforce applicable policies, procedures, standards, and guidelines on privacy, confidentiality, security, disclosure and sharing of information collected or maintained by or for the agency; and

(2) assume responsibility and accountability for compliance with and coordinated management of sections 552 and 552a of title 5, subchapter II of this chapter, and related information management laws.

(h) With respect to Federal information technology, each agency shall—

(1) implement and enforce applicable Governmentwide and agency information technology management policies, principles, standards, and guidelines;

(2) assume responsibility and accountability for information technology investments;

(3) promote the use of information technology by the agency to improve the productivity, efficiency, and effectiveness of agency programs, including the reduction of information collection burdens on the public and improved dissemination of public information;

(4) propose changes in legislation, regulations, and agency procedures to improve information technology practices, including changes that improve the ability of the agency to use technology to reduce burden; and

(5) assume responsibility for maximizing the value and assessing and managing the risks of major information systems initiatives through a process that is—

(A) integrated with budget, financial, and program management decisions; and

(B) used to select, control, and evaluate the results of major information systems initiatives.

(i)(1) In addition to the requirements described in subsection (c), each agency shall, with respect to the collection of information and the control of paperwork, establish 1 point of contact in the agency to act as a liaison between the agency and small business concerns (as defined in section 3 of the Small Business Act (15 U.S.C. 632)).

(2) Each point of contact described under paragraph (1) shall be established not later than 1 year after the date of enactment of the Small Business Paperwork Relief Act of 2002.

§ 3507. Public information collection activities; submission to Director; approval and delegation

(a) An agency shall not conduct or sponsor the collection of information unless in advance of the adoption or revision of the collection of information—

(1) the agency has—

(A) conducted the review established under section 3506(c)(1);

(B) evaluated the public comments received under section 3506(c)(2);

(C) submitted to the Director the certification required under section 3506(c) (3), the proposed collection of information, copies of pertinent statutory authority, regulations, and other related materials as the Director may specify; and

(D) published a notice in the Federal Register—

(i) stating that the agency has made such submission; and

(ii) setting forth—

(I) a title for the collection of information;

(II) a summary of the collection of information;

(III) a brief description of the need for the information and the proposed use of the information;

(IV) a description of the likely respondents and proposed frequency of response to the collection of information;

(V) an estimate of the burden that shall result from the collection of information; and

(VI) notice that comments may be submitted to the agency and Director;

(2) the Director has approved the proposed collection of information or approval has been inferred, under the provisions of this section; and

(3) the agency has obtained from the Director a control number to be displayed upon the collection of information.

(b) The Director shall provide at least 30 days for public comment prior to making a decision under subsection (c), (d), or (h), except as provided under subsection (j).

(c)(1) For any proposed collection of information not contained in a proposed rule, the Director shall notify the agency involved of the decision to approve or disapprove the proposed collection of information.

(2) The Director shall provide the notification under paragraph (1), within 60 days after receipt or publication of the notice under subsection (a)(1)(D), whichever is later.

(3) If the Director does not notify the agency of a denial or approval within the 60-day period described under paragraph (2)—

(A) the approval may be inferred;

(B) a control number shall be assigned without further delay; and

(C) the agency may collect the information for not more than 1 year.

(d)(1) For any proposed collection of information contained in a proposed rule—

(A) as soon as practicable, but no later than the date of publication of a notice of proposed rulemaking in the Federal Register, each agency shall forward to the Director a copy of any proposed rule which contains a collection of information and any information requested by the Director necessary to make the determination required under this subsection; and

(B) within 60 days after the notice of proposed rulemaking is published in the Federal Register, the Director may file public comments pursuant to the standards set forth in section 3508 on the collection of information contained in the proposed rule;

(2) When a final rule is published in the Federal Register, the agency shall explain —

(A) how any collection of information contained in the final rule responds to the comments, if any, filed by the Director or the public; or

(B) the reasons such comments were rejected.

(3) If the Director has received notice and failed to comment on an agency rule within 60 days after the notice of proposed rulemaking, the Director may not disapprove any collection of information specifically contained in an agency rule.

(4) No provision in this section shall be construed to prevent the Director, in the Director's discretion —

(A) from disapproving any collection of information which was not specifically required by an agency rule;

(B) from disapproving any collection of information contained in an agency rule, if the agency failed to comply with the requirements of paragraph (1) of this subsection;

(C) from disapproving any collection of information contained in a final agency rule, if the Director finds within 60 days after the publication of the final rule that the agency's response to the Director's comments filed under paragraph (2) of this subsection was unreasonable; or

(D) from disapproving any collection of information contained in a final rule, if—

(i) the Director determines that the agency has substantially modified in the final rule the collection of information contained in the proposed rule; and

(ii) the agency has not given the Director the information required under paragraph (1) with respect to the modified collection of information, at least 60 days before the issuance of the final rule.

(5) This subsection shall apply only when an agency publishes a notice of proposed rulemaking and requests public comments.

(6) The decision by the Director to approve or not act upon a collection of information contained in an agency rule shall not be subject to judicial review.

(e)(1) Any decision by the Director under subsection (c), (d), (h), or (j) to disapprove a collection of information, or to instruct the agency to make substantive or material change to a collection of information, shall be publicly available and include an explanation of the reasons for such decision.

(2) Any written communication between the Administrator of the Office of Information and Regulatory Affairs, or any employee of the Office of Information

and Regulatory Affairs, and an agency or person not employed by the Federal Government concerning a proposed collection of information shall be made available to the public.

(3) This subsection shall not require the disclosure of—

(A) any information which is protected at all times by procedures established for information which has been specifically authorized under criteria established by an Executive order or an Act of Congress to be kept secret in the interest of national defense or foreign policy; or

(B) any communication relating to a collection of information which is not approved under this subchapter, the disclosure of which could lead to retaliation or discrimination against the communicator.

(f)(1) An independent regulatory agency which is administered by 2 or more members of a commission, board, or similar body, may by majority vote void—

(A) any disapproval by the Director, in whole or in part, of a proposed collection of information of that agency; or

(B) an exercise of authority under subsection (d) of section 3507 concerning that agency.

(2) The agency shall certify each vote to void such disapproval or exercise to the Director, and explain the reasons for such vote. The Director shall without further delay assign a control number to such collection of information, and such vote to void the disapproval or exercise shall be valid for a period of 3 years.

(g) The Director may not approve a collection of information for a period in excess of 3 years.

(h)(1) If an agency decides to seek extension of the Director's approval granted for a currently approved collection of information, the agency shall—

(A) conduct the review established under section 3506(c), including the seeking of comment from the public on the continued need for, and burden imposed by the collection of information; and

(B) after having made a reasonable effort to seek public comment, but no later than 60 days before the expiration date of the control number assigned by the Director for the currently approved collection of information, submit the collection of information for review and approval under this section, which shall include an explanation of how the agency has used the information that it has collected.

(2) If under the provisions of this section, the Director disapproves a collection of information contained in an existing rule, or recommends or instructs the agency to make a substantive or material change to a collection of information contained in an existing rule, the Director shall—

(A) publish an explanation thereof in the Federal Register; and

(B) instruct the agency to undertake a rulemaking within a reasonable time limited to consideration of changes to the collection of information contained in the rule and thereafter to submit the collection of information for approval or disapproval under this subchapter.

(3) An agency may not make a substantive or material modification to a collection of information after such collection has been approved by the Director, unless the modification has been submitted to the Director for review and approval under this subchapter.

(i)(1) If the Director finds that a senior official of an agency designated under section 3506(a) is sufficiently independent of program responsibility to evaluate fairly whether proposed collections of information should be approved and has sufficient resources to carry out this responsibility effectively, the Director may, by rule in accordance with the notice and comment provisions of chapter 5 of title 5, United States Code, delegate to such official the authority to approve proposed collections of information in specific program areas, for specific purposes, or for all agency purposes.

(2) A delegation by the Director under this section shall not preclude the Director from reviewing individual collections of information if the Director determines that circumstances warrant such a review. The Director shall retain authority to revoke such delegations, both in general and with regard to any specific matter. In acting for the Director, any official to whom approval authority has been delegated under this section shall comply fully with the rules and regulations promulgated by the Director.

(j)(1) The agency head may request the Director to authorize a collection of information, if an agency head determines that —

(A) a collection of information —

(i) is needed prior to the expiration of time periods established under this subchapter; and

(ii) is essential to the mission of the agency; and

(B) the agency cannot reasonably comply with the provisions of this subchapter because —

(i) public harm is reasonably likely to result if normal clearance procedures are followed;

(ii) an unanticipated event has occurred; or

(iii) the use of normal clearance procedures is reasonably likely to prevent or disrupt the collection of information or is reasonably likely to cause a statutory or court ordered deadline to be missed.

(2) The Director shall approve or disapprove any such authorization request within the time requested by the agency head and, if approved, shall assign the collection of information a control number. Any collection of information conducted under this subsection may be conducted without compliance with the provisions of this subchapter for a maximum of 180 days after the date on which the Director received the request to authorize such collection.

§ 3512. Public protection

(a) Notwithstanding any other provision of law, no person shall be subject to any penalty for failing to comply with a collection of information that is subject to this subchapter if—

(1) the collection of information does not display a valid control number assigned by the Director in accordance with this subchapter; or

(2) the agency fails to inform the person who is to respond to the collection of information that such person is not required to respond to the collection of information unless it displays a valid control number.

(b) The protection provided by this section may be raised in the form of a complete defense, bar, or otherwise at any time during the agency administrative process or judicial action applicable thereto.

§ 3513. Director review of agency activities; reporting; agency response

(a) In consultation with the Administrator of General Services, the Archivist of the United States, the Director of the National Institute of Standards and Technology, and the Director of the Office of Personnel Management, the Director shall periodically review selected agency information resources management activities to ascertain the efficiency and effectiveness of such activities to improve agency performance and the accomplishment of agency missions.

(b) Each agency having an activity reviewed under subsection (a) shall, within 60 days after receipt of a report on the review, provide a written plan to the Director describing steps (including milestones) to—

(1) be taken to address information resources management problems identified in the report; and

(2) improve agency performance and the accomplishment of agency missions.

(c) Comparable Treatment.—Notwithstanding any other provision of law, the Director shall treat or review a rule or order prescribed or proposed by the Director of the Bureau of Consumer Financial Protection on the same terms and conditions as apply to any rule or order prescribed or proposed by the Board of Governors of the Federal Reserve System.

§ 3514. Responsiveness to Congress

(a)(1) The Director shall—

(A) keep the Congress and congressional committees fully and currently informed of the major activities under this subchapter; and

(B) submit a report on such activities to the President of the Senate and the Speaker of the House of Representatives annually and at such other times as the Director determines necessary.

(2) The Director shall include in any such report a description of the extent to which agencies have—

(A) reduced information collection burdens on the public, including—

(i) a summary of accomplishments and planned initiatives to reduce collection of information burdens;

(ii) a list of all violations of this subchapter and of any rules, guidelines, policies, and procedures issued pursuant to this subchapter;

(iii) a list of any increase in the collection of information burden, including the authority for each such collection; and

(iv) a list of agencies that in the preceding year did not reduce information collection burdens in accordance with section 3505(a)(1), a list of the programs and statutory responsibilities of those agencies that precluded that reduction, and recommendations to assist those agencies to reduce information collection burdens in accordance with that section;

(B) improved the quality and utility of statistical information;

(C) improved public access to Government information; and

(D) improved program performance and the accomplishment of agency missions through information resources management.

(b) The preparation of any report required by this section shall be based on performance results reported by the agencies and shall not increase the collection of information burden on persons outside the Federal Government.

§ 3515. Administrative powers

Upon the request of the Director, each agency (other than an independent regulatory agency) shall, to the extent practicable, make its services, personnel, and facilities available to the Director for the performance of functions under this subchapter.

§ 3516. Rules and regulations

The Director shall promulgate rules, regulations, or procedures necessary to exercise the authority provided by this subchapter.

§ 3517. Consultation with other agencies and the public

(a) In developing information resources management policies, plans, rules, regulations, procedures, and guidelines and in reviewing collections of information, the Director shall provide interested agencies and persons early and meaningful opportunity to comment.

(b) Any person may request the Director to review any collection of information conducted by or for an agency to determine, if, under this subchapter, a person shall maintain, provide, or disclose the information to or for the agency. Unless the request is frivolous, the Director shall, in coordination with the agency responsible for the collection of information—

(1) respond to the request within 60 days after receiving the request, unless such period is extended by the Director to a specified date and the person making the request is given notice of such extension; and

(2) take appropriate remedial action, if necessary.

§ 3518.   Effect on existing laws and regulations

(a) Except as otherwise provided in this subchapter, the authority of an agency under any other law to prescribe policies, rules, regulations, and procedures for Federal information resources management activities is subject to the authority of the Director under this subchapter.

(b) Nothing in this subchapter shall be deemed to affect or reduce the authority of the Secretary of Commerce or the Director of the Office of Management and Budget pursuant to Reorganization Plan No. 1 of 1977 (as amended) and Executive order, relating to telecommunications and information policy, procurement and management of telecommunications and information systems, spectrum use, and related matters.

(c)(1) Except as provided in paragraph (2), this subchapter shall not apply to the collection of information—

(A) during the conduct of a Federal criminal investigation or prosecution, or during the disposition of a particular criminal matter;

(B) during the conduct of—

(i) a civil action to which the United States or any official or agency thereof is a party; or

(ii) an administrative action or investigation involving an agency against specific individuals or entities;

(C) by compulsory process pursuant to the Antitrust Civil Process Act and section 13 of the Federal Trade Commission Improvements Act of 1980; or

(D) during the conduct of intelligence activities as defined in section 3.4(e) of Executive Order No. 12333, issued December 4, 1981, or successor orders, or during the conduct of cryptologic activities that are communications security activities.

(2) This subchapter applies to the collection of information during the conduct of general investigations (other than information collected in an antitrust investigation to the extent provided in subparagraph (C) of paragraph (1)) undertaken with reference to a category of individuals or entities such as a class of licensees or an entire industry.

(d) Nothing in this subchapter shall be interpreted as increasing or decreasing the authority conferred by sections 11331 and 11332 of title 40 on the Secretary of Commerce or the Director of the Office of Management and Budget.

(e) Nothing in this subchapter shall be interpreted as increasing or decreasing the authority of the President, the Office of Management and Budget or the Director thereof, under the laws of the United States, with respect to the substantive policies and programs of departments, agencies and offices, including the substantive authority of any Federal agency to enforce the civil rights laws.

§ 3519.   Access to information

Under the conditions and procedures prescribed in section 716 of title 31, the Director and personnel in the Office of Information and Regulatory Affairs shall furnish such information as the Comptroller General may require for the discharge of the responsibilities of the Comptroller General. For the purpose of obtaining such information, the Comptroller General or representatives thereof shall have access to all books, documents, papers and records, regardless of form or format, of the Office.

§ 3520.   Establishment of task force on information collection and dissemination

(a) There is established a task force to study the feasibility of streamlining requirements with respect to small business concerns regarding collection of information and strengthening dissemination of information (in this section referred to as the "task force").

(b)(1) The Director shall determine—

(A) subject to the minimum requirements under paragraph (2), the number of representatives to be designated under each subparagraph of that paragraph; and

(B) the agencies to be represented under paragraph (2)(K).

(2) After all determinations are made under paragraph (1), the members of the task force shall be designated by the head of each applicable department or agency, and include—

(A) 1 representative of the Director, who shall convene and chair the task force;

(B) not less than 2 representatives of the Department of Labor, including 1 representative of the Bureau of Labor Statistics and 1 representative of the Occupational Safety and Health Administration;

(C) not less than 1 representative of the Environmental Protection Agency;

(D) not less than 1 representative of the Department of Transportation;

(E) not less than 1 representative of the Office of Advocacy of the Small Business Administration;

(F) not less than 1 representative of the Internal Revenue Service;

(G) not less than 2 representatives of the Department of Health and Human Services, including 1 representative of the Centers for Medicare and Medicaid Services;

(H) not less than 1 representative of the Department of Agriculture;

(I) not less than 1 representative of the Department of the Interior;

(J) not less than 1 representative of the General Services Administration; and

(K) not less than 1 representative of each of 2 agencies not represented by representatives described under subparagraphs (A) through (J).

(c) The task force shall—

(1) identify ways to integrate the collection of information across Federal agencies and programs and examine the feasibility and desirability of requiring each agency to consolidate requirements regarding collections of information with respect to small business concerns within and across agencies, without negatively impacting the effectiveness of underlying laws and regulations regarding such collections of information, in order that each small business concern may submit all information required by the agency—

(A) to 1 point of contact in the agency;

(B) in a single format, such as a single electronic reporting system, with respect to the agency; and

(C) with synchronized reporting for information submissions having the same frequency, such as synchronized quarterly, semiannual, and annual reporting dates;

(2) examine the feasibility and benefits to small businesses of publishing a list by the Director of the collections of information applicable to small business concerns (as defined in section 3 of the Small Business Act (15 U.S.C. 632)), organized—

(A) by North American Industry Classification System code;

(B) by industrial sector description; or

(C) in another manner by which small business concerns can more easily identify requirements with which those small business concerns are expected to comply;

(3) examine the savings, including cost savings, and develop recommendations for implementing—

(A) systems for electronic submissions of information to the Federal Government; and

(B) interactive reporting systems, including components that provide immediate feedback to assure that data being submitted—

(i) meet requirements of format; and

(ii) are within the range of acceptable options for each data field;

(4) make recommendations to improve the electronic dissemination of information collected under Federal requirements;

(5) recommend a plan for the development of an interactive Governmentwide system, available through the Internet, to allow each small business to—

(A) better understand which Federal requirements regarding collection of information (and, when possible, which other Federal regulatory requirements) apply to that particular business; and

(B) more easily comply with those Federal requirements; and

(6) in carrying out this section, consider opportunities for the coordination—

(A) of Federal and State reporting requirements; and

(B) among the points of contact described under section 3506(i), such as to enable agencies to provide small business concerns with contacts for information collection requirements for other agencies.

(d) The task force shall—

(1) by publication in the Federal Register, provide notice and an opportunity for public comment on each report in draft form; and

(2) make provision in each report for the inclusion of—

(A) any additional or dissenting views of task force members; and

(B) a summary of significant public comments.

(e) Not later than 1 year after the date of enactment of the Small Business Paperwork Relief Act of 2002, the task force shall submit a report of its findings under subsection (c) (1), (2), and (3) to—

(1) the Director;

(2) the chairpersons and ranking minority members of—

(A) the Committee on Governmental Affairs and the Committee on Small Business and Entrepreneurship of the Senate; and

(B) the Committee on Government Reform and the Committee on Small Business of the House of Representatives; and

(3) the Small Business and Agriculture Regulatory Enforcement Ombudsman designated under section 30(b) of the Small Business Act (15 U.S.C. 657(b)).

(f) Not later than 2 years after the date of enactment of the Small Business Paperwork Relief Act of 2002, the task force shall submit a report of its findings under subsection (c) (4) and (5) to—

(1) the Director;

(2) the chairpersons and ranking minority members of—

(A) the Committee on Governmental Affairs and the Committee on Small Business and Entrepreneurship of the Senate; and

(B) the Committee on Government Reform and the Committee on Small Business of the House of Representatives; and

(3) the Small Business and Agriculture Regulatory Enforcement Ombudsman designated under section 30(b) of the Small Business Act (15 U.S.C. 657(b)).

(g) The task force shall terminate after completion of its work.

(h) In this section, the term "small business concern" has the meaning given under section 3 of the Small Business Act (15 U.S.C. 632).

§ 3521.   Authorization of appropriations

There are authorized to be appropriated to the Office of Information and Regulatory Affairs to carry out the provisions of this subchapter, and for no other purpose, $8,000,000 for each of the fiscal years 1996, 1997, 1998, 1999, 2000, and 2001.

Selected Rules of the U.S. House of Representatives (Jan. 6, 2015)

RULE I

THE SPEAKER

Questions of order

5. The Speaker shall decide all questions of order, subject to appeal by a Member, Delegate, or Resident Commissioner. On such an appeal a Member, Delegate, or Resident Commissioner may not speak more than once without permission of the House.

Form of a question

6. The Speaker shall rise to put a question but may state it sitting. The Speaker shall put a question in this form: "Those in favor (of the question), say 'Aye.'"; and after the affirmative voice is expressed, "Those opposed, say 'No.'". After a vote by voice under this clause, the Speaker may use such voting procedures as may be invoked under rule XX.

Discretion to vote

7. The Speaker is not required to vote in ordinary legislative proceedings, except when such vote would be decisive or when the House is engaged in voting by ballot.

Committee appointment

11. The Speaker shall appoint all select, joint, and conference committees ordered by the House. At any time after an original appointment, the Speaker may remove Members, Delegates, or the Resident Commissioner from, or appoint additional Members, Delegates, or the Resident Commissioner to, a select or conference committee. In appointing Members, Delegates, or the Resident Commissioner to conference committees, the Speaker shall appoint no less than a majority who generally supported the House position as determined by the Speaker, shall name those who are primarily responsible for the legislation, and shall, to the fullest extent feasible,

include the principal proponents of the major provisions of the bill or resolution passed or adopted by the House.

Recess and convening authorities

12. (a) To suspend the business of the House for a short time when no question is pending before the House, the Speaker may declare a recess subject to the call of the Chair.

(b)(1) To suspend the business of the House when notified of an imminent threat to its safety, the Speaker may declare an emergency recess subject to the call of the Chair. (2) To suspend the business of the Committee of the Whole House on the state of the Union when notified of an imminent threat to its safety, the chair of the Committee of the Whole may declare an emergency recess subject to the call of the Chair.

(c) During any recess or adjournment of not more than three days, if the Speaker is notified by the Sergeant-at-Arms of an imminent impairment of the place of reconvening at the time previously appointed, then the Speaker may, in consultation with the Minority Leader—

(1) postpone the time for reconvening within the limits of clause 4, section 5, article I of the Constitution and notify Members accordingly; or

(2) reconvene the House before the time previously appointed solely to declare the House in recess within the limits of clause 4, section 5, article I of the Constitution and notify Members accordingly.

(d) The Speaker may convene the House in a place at the seat of government other than the Hall of the House whenever, in the opinion of the Speaker, the public interest shall warrant it.

(e) During any recess or adjournment of not more than three days, if in the opinion of the Speaker the public interest so warrants, then the Speaker, after consultation with the Minority Leader, may reconvene the House at a time other than that previously appointed, within the limits of clause 4, section 5, article I of the Constitution, and notify Members accordingly.

(f) The Speaker may name a designee for purposes of paragraphs (c), (d), and (e).

RULE II

OTHER OFFICERS AND OFFICIALS

Clerk

2. (a) At the commencement of the first session of each Congress, the Clerk shall call the Members, Delegates, and Resident Commissioner to order and proceed to record their presence by States in alphabetical order, either by call of

the roll or by use of the electronic voting system. Pending the election of a Speaker or Speaker pro tempore, the Clerk shall preserve order and decorum and decide all questions of order, subject to appeal by a Member, Delegate, or Resident Commissioner.

(b) At the commencement of every regular session of Congress, the Clerk shall make and cause to be delivered to each Member, Delegate, and the Resident Commissioner a list of the reports that any officer or Department is required to make to Congress, citing the law or resolution in which the requirement may be contained and placing under the name of each officer the list of reports required to be made by such officer.

(c) The Clerk shall—

(1) note all questions of order, with the decisions thereon, the record of which shall be appended to the Journal of each session;

(2) enter on the Journal the hour at which the House adjourns;

(3) complete the distribution of the Journal to Members, Delegates, and the Resident Commissioner, together with an accurate and complete index, as soon as possible after the close of a session; and (4) send a copy of the Journal to the executive of and to each branch of the legislature of every State as may be requested by such State officials.

(d)(1) The Clerk shall attest and affix the seal of the House to all writs, warrants, and subpoenas issued by order of the House and certify the passage of all bills and joint resolutions.

(2) The Clerk shall examine all bills, amendments, and joint resolutions after passage by the House and, in cooperation with the Senate, examine all bills and joint resolutions that have passed both Houses to see that they are correctly enrolled and forthwith present those bills and joint resolutions that originated in the House to the President in person after their signature by the Speaker and the President of the Senate, and report to the House the fact and date of their presentment.

(e) The Clerk shall cause the calendars of the House to be distributed each legislative day.

(f) The Clerk shall—(1) retain in the library at the Office of the Clerk for the use of the Members, Delegates, Resident Commissioner, and officers of the House, and not to be withdrawn therefrom, two copies of all the books and printed documents deposited there; and (2) deliver to any Member, Delegate, or the Resident Commissioner an extra copy of each document requested by that Member, Delegate, or Resident Commissioner that has been printed by order of either House of Congress in any Congress in which the Member, Delegate, or Resident Commissioner served.

(g) The Clerk shall provide for the temporary absence or disability of the Clerk by designating an official in the Office of the Clerk to sign all papers that may require the official signature of the Clerk and to perform all other official acts that the Clerk may be required to perform under the rules and practices of the House, except such official acts as are provided for by statute. Official acts performed by the designated official shall be under the name of the Clerk. The designation shall be in writing and shall be laid before the House and entered on the Journal.

(h) The Clerk may receive messages from the President and from the Senate at any time when the House is in recess or adjournment.

(i)(1) The Clerk shall supervise the staff and manage the office of a Member, Delegate, or Resident Commissioner who has died, resigned, or been expelled until a successor is elected. The Clerk shall perform similar duties in the event that a vacancy is declared by the House in any congressional district because of the incapacity of the person representing such district or other reason. When acting as a supervisory authority over such staff, the Clerk shall have authority to terminate employees and, with the approval of the Committee on House Administration, may appoint such staff as is required to operate the office until a successor is elected.

(2) For 60 days following the death of a former Speaker, the Clerk shall maintain on the House payroll, and shall supervise in the same manner, staff appointed under House Resolution 1238, Ninety-first Congress (as enacted into permanent law by chapter VIII of the Supplemental Appropriations Act, 1971) (2 U.S.C. 5128).

(j) In addition to any other reports required by the Speaker or the Committee on House Administration, the Clerk shall report to the Committee on House Administration not later than 45 days following the close of each semiannual period ending on June 30 or on December 31 on the financial and operational status of each function under the jurisdiction of the Clerk. Each report shall include financial statements and a description or explanation of current operations, the implementation of new policies and procedures, and future plans for each function.

(k) The Clerk shall fully cooperate with the appropriate offices and persons in the performance of reviews and audits of financial records and administrative operations.

Office of Inspector General

6. (a) There is established an Office of Inspector General.

(b) The Inspector General shall be appointed for a Congress by the Speaker, the Majority Leader, and the Minority Leader, acting jointly.

(c) Subject to the policy direction and oversight of the Committee on House Administration, the Inspector General shall only—

(1) provide audit, investigative, and advisory services to the House and joint entities in a manner consistent with government-wide standards;

(2) inform the officers or other officials who are the subject of an audit of the results of that audit and suggesting appropriate curative actions;

(3) simultaneously notify the Speaker, the Majority Leader, the Minority Leader, and the chair and ranking minority member of the Committee on House Administration in the case of any financial irregularity discovered in the course of carrying out responsibilities under this clause;

(4) simultaneously submit to the Speaker, the Majority Leader, the Minority Leader, and the chair and ranking minority member of the Committee on Appropriations and the Committee on House Administration a report of each audit conducted under this clause; and

(5) report to the Committee on Ethics information involving possible violations by a Member, Delegate, Resident Commissioner, officer, or employee of the House of any rule of the House or of any law applicable to the performance of official duties or the discharge of official responsibilities that may require referral to the appropriate Federal or State authorities under clause 3(a)(3) of rule XI.

Office of General Counsel

8. (a) There is established an Office of General Counsel for the purpose of providing legal assistance and representation to the House. Legal assistance and representation shall be provided without regard to political affiliation. The Speaker shall appoint and set the annual rate of pay for employees of the Office of General Counsel. The Office of General Counsel shall function pursuant to the direction of the Speaker, who shall consult with the Bipartisan Legal Advisory Group. (b) There is established a Bipartisan Legal Advisory Group composed of the Speaker and the majority and minority leaderships. Unless otherwise provided by the House, the Bipartisan Legal Advisory Group speaks for, and articulates the institutional position of, the House in all litigation matters.

RULE III

THE MEMBERS, DELEGATES, AND RESIDENT COMMISSIONER OF PUERTO RICO

Voting

1. Every Member shall be present within the Hall of the House during its sittings, unless excused or necessarily prevented, and shall vote on each question put, unless having a direct personal or pecuniary interest in the event of such question.

2. (a) A Member may not authorize any other person to cast the vote of such Member or record the presence of such Member in the House or the Committee of the Whole House on the state of the Union.

(b) No other person may cast a Member's vote or record a Member's presence in the House or the Committee of the Whole House on the state of the Union.

RULE X

ORGANIZATION OF COMMITTEES

Committees and their legislative jurisdictions

1. There shall be in the House the following standing committees, each of which shall have the jurisdiction and related functions assigned by this clause and clauses 2, 3, and 4. All bills, resolutions, and other matters relating to subjects within the jurisdiction of the standing committees listed in this clause shall be referred to those committees, in accordance with clause 2 of rule XII, as follows:

(a) **Committee on Agriculture**.

(1) Adulteration of seeds, insect pests, and protection of birds and animals in forest reserves.

(2) Agriculture generally.

(3) Agricultural and industrial chemistry.

(4) Agricultural colleges and experiment stations.

(5) Agricultural economics and research.

(6) Agricultural education extension services.

(7) Agricultural production and marketing and stabilization of prices of agricultural products, and commodities (not including distribution outside of the United States).

(8) Animal industry and diseases of animals.

(9) Commodity exchanges.

(10) Crop insurance and soil conservation.

(11) Dairy industry.

(12) Entomology and plant quarantine.

(13) Extension of farm credit and farm security.

(14) Inspection of livestock, poultry, meat products, and seafood and seafood products.

(15) Forestry in general and forest reserves other than those created from the public domain.

(16) Human nutrition and home economics.

(17) Plant industry, soils, and agricultural engineering.

(18) Rural electrification.

(19) Rural development.

(20) Water conservation related to activities of the Department of Agriculture.

(b) **Committee on Appropriations.**

(1) Appropriation of the revenue for the support of the Government.

(2) Rescissions of appropriations contained in appropriation Acts.

(3) Transfers of unexpended balances.

(4) Bills and joint resolutions reported by other committees that provide new entitlement authority as defined in section 3(9) of the Congressional Budget Act of 1974 and referred to the committee under clause 4(a)(2).

(5) Bills and joint resolutions that provide new budget authority, limitation on the use of funds, or other authority relating to new direct loan obligations and new loan guarantee commitments referencing section 504(b) of the Congressional Budget Act of 1974.

(c) **Committee on Armed Services.**

(1) Ammunition depots; forts; arsenals; and Army, Navy, and Air Force reservations and establishments.

(2) Common defense generally.

(3) Conservation, development, and use of naval petroleum and oil shale reserves.

(4) The Department of Defense generally, including the Departments of the Army, Navy, and Air Force, generally.

(5) Interoceanic canals generally, including measures relating to the maintenance, operation, and administration of interoceanic canals.

(6) Merchant Marine Academy and State Maritime Academies.

(7) Military applications of nuclear energy.

(8) Tactical intelligence and intelligence-related activities of the Department of Defense.

(9) National security aspects of merchant marine, including financial assistance for the construction and operation of vessels, maintenance of the U.S. shipbuilding and ship repair industrial base, cabotage, cargo preference, and merchant marine officers and seamen as these matters relate to the national security.

(10) Pay, promotion, retirement, and other benefits and privileges of members of the armed forces.

(11) Scientific research and development in support of the armed services.

(12) Selective service.

(13) Size and composition of the Army, Navy, Marine Corps, and Air Force.

(14) Soldiers' and sailors' homes.

(15) Strategic and critical materials necessary for the common defense.

(16) Cemeteries administered by the Department of Defense.

(d) **Committee on the Budget.**

(1) Concurrent resolutions on the budget (as defined in section 3(4) of the Congressional Budget Act of 1974), other matters required to be referred to the committee under titles III and IV of that Act, and other measures setting forth appropriate levels of budget totals for the United States Government.

(2) Budget process generally.

(3) Establishment, extension, and enforcement of special controls over the Federal budget, including the budgetary treatment of off-budget Federal agencies and measures providing exemption from reduction under any order issued under part C of the Balanced Budget and Emergency Deficit Control Act of 1985.

(e) **Committee on Education and the Workforce.**

(1) Child labor.

(2) Gallaudet University and Howard University and Hospital.

(3) Convict labor and the entry of goods made by convicts into interstate commerce.

(4) Food programs for children in schools.

(5) Labor standards and statistics.

(6) Education or labor generally.

(7) Mediation and arbitration of labor disputes.

(8) Regulation or prevention of importation of foreign laborers under contract.

(9) Workers' compensation.

(10) Vocational rehabilitation.

(11) Wages and hours of labor.

(12) Welfare of miners.

(13) Work incentive programs.

(f) **Committee on Energy and Commerce.**

(1) Biomedical research and development.

(2) Consumer affairs and consumer protection.

(3) Health and health facilities (except health care supported by payroll deductions).

(4) Interstate energy compacts.

(5) Interstate and foreign commerce generally.

(6) Exploration, production, storage, supply, marketing, pricing, and regulation of energy resources, including all fossil fuels, solar energy, and other unconventional or renewable energy resources.

(7) Conservation of energy resources.

(8) Energy information generally.

(9) The generation and marketing of power (except by federally chartered or Federal regional power marketing authorities); reliability and interstate transmission of, and ratemaking for, all power; and siting of generation facilities (except the installation of interconnections between Government waterpower projects).

(10) General management of the Department of Energy and management and all functions of the Federal Energy Regulatory Commission.

(11) National energy policy generally.

(12) Public health and quarantine.

(13) Regulation of the domestic nuclear energy industry, including regulation of research and development reactors and nuclear regulatory research.

(14) Regulation of interstate and foreign communications.

(15) Travel and tourism.

The committee shall have the same jurisdiction with respect to regulation of nuclear facilities and of use of nuclear energy as it has with respect to regulation of nonnuclear facilities and of use of nonnuclear energy.

(g) **Committee on Ethics.**

The Code of Official Conduct.

(h) **Committee on Financial Services.**

(1) Banks and banking, including deposit insurance and Federal monetary policy.

(2) Economic stabilization, defense production, renegotiation, and control of the price of commodities, rents, and services.

(3) Financial aid to commerce and industry (other than transportation).

(4) Insurance generally.

(5) International finance.

(6) International financial and monetary organizations.

(7) Money and credit, including currency and the issuance of notes and redemption thereof; gold and silver, including the coinage thereof; valuation and revaluation of the dollar.

(8) Public and private housing.

(9) Securities and exchanges.

(10) Urban development.

(i) **Committee on Foreign Affairs.**

(1) Relations of the United States with foreign nations generally.

(2) Acquisition of land and buildings for embassies and legations in foreign countries.

(3) Establishment of boundary lines between the United States and foreign nations.

(4) Export controls, including nonproliferation of nuclear technology and nuclear hardware.

(5) Foreign loans.

(6) International commodity agreements (other than those involving sugar), including all agreements for cooperation in the export of nuclear technology and nuclear hardware.

(7) International conferences and congresses.

(8) International education.

(9) Intervention abroad and declarations of war.

(10) Diplomatic service.

(11) Measures to foster commercial intercourse with foreign nations and to safeguard American business interests abroad.

(12) International economic policy.

(13) Neutrality.

(14) Protection of American citizens abroad and expatriation.

(15) The American National Red Cross.

(16) Trading with the enemy.

(17) United Nations organizations.

(j) **Committee on Homeland Security.**

(1) Overall homeland security policy.

(2) Organization, administration, and general management of the Department of Homeland Security.

(3) Functions of the Department of Homeland Security relating to the following:

(A) Border and port security (except immigration policy and non-border enforcement).

(B) Customs (except customs revenue).

(C) Integration, analysis, and dissemination of homeland security information.

(D) Domestic preparedness for and collective response to terrorism.

(E) Research and development.

(F) Transportation security.

(k) **Committee on House Administration**.

(1) Appropriations from accounts for committee salaries and expenses (except for the Committee on Appropriations); House Information Resources; and allowance and expenses of Members, Delegates, the Resident Commissioner, officers, and administrative offices of the House.

(2) Auditing and settling of all accounts described in subparagraph (1).

(3) Employment of persons by the House, including staff for Members, Delegates, the Resident Commissioner, and committees; and reporters of debates, subject to rule VI.

(4) Except as provided in paragraph (r)(11), the Library of Congress, including management thereof; the House Library; statuary and pictures; acceptance or purchase of works of art for the Capitol; the Botanic Garden; and purchase of books and manuscripts.

(5) The Smithsonian Institution and the incorporation of similar institutions (except as provided in paragraph (r)(11)).

(6) Expenditure of accounts described in subparagraph (1).

(7) Franking Commission.

(8) Printing and correction of the Congressional Record.

(9) Accounts of the House generally.

(10) Assignment of office space for Members, Delegates, the Resident Commissioner, and committees.

(11) Disposition of useless executive papers.

(12) Election of the President, Vice President, Members, Senators, Delegates, or the Resident Commissioner; corrupt practices; contested elections; credentials and qualifications; and Federal elections generally.

(13) Services to the House, including the House Restaurant, parking facilities, and administration of the House Office Buildings and of the House wing of the Capitol.

(14) Travel of Members, Delegates, and the Resident Commissioner.

(15) Raising, reporting, and use of campaign contributions for candidates for office of Representative, of Delegate, and of Resident Commissioner.

(16) Compensation, retirement, and other benefits of the Members, Delegates, the Resident Commissioner, officers, and employees of Congress.

(l) **Committee on the Judiciary**.

(1) The judiciary and judicial proceedings, civil and criminal.

(2) Administrative practice and procedure.

(3) Apportionment of Representatives.

(4) Bankruptcy, mutiny, espionage, and counterfeiting.

(5) Civil liberties.

(6) Constitutional amendments.

(7) Criminal law enforcement and criminalization.

(8) Federal courts and judges, and local courts in the Territories and possessions.

(9) Immigration policy and nonborder enforcement.

(10) Interstate compacts generally.

(11) Claims against the United States.

(12) Meetings of Congress; attendance of Members, Delegates, and the Resident Commissioner; and their acceptance of incompatible offices.

(13) National penitentiaries.

(14) Patents, the Patent and Trademark Office, copyrights, and trademarks.

(15) Presidential succession.

(16) Protection of trade and commerce against unlawful restraints and monopolies.

(17) Revision and codification of the Statutes of the United States.

(18) State and territorial boundary lines.

(19) Subversive activities affecting the internal security of the United States.

(m) **Committee on Natural Resources**.

(1) Fisheries and wildlife, including research, restoration, refuges, and conservation.

(2) Forest reserves and national parks created from the public domain.

(3) Forfeiture of land grants and alien ownership, including alien ownership of mineral lands.

(4) Geological Survey.

(5) International fishing agreements.

(6) Interstate compacts relating to apportionment of waters for irrigation purposes.

(7) Irrigation and reclamation, including water supply for reclamation projects and easements of public lands for irrigation projects; and acquisition of private lands when necessary to complete irrigation projects.

(8) Native Americans generally, including the care and allotment of Native American lands and general and special measures relating to claims that are paid out of Native American funds.

(9) Insular areas of the United States generally (except those affecting the revenue and appropriations).

(10) Military parks and battlefields, national cemeteries administered by the Secretary of the Interior, parks within the District of Columbia, and the erection of monuments to the memory of individuals.

(11) Mineral land laws and claims and entries thereunder.

(12) Mineral resources of public lands.

(13) Mining interests generally.

(14) Mining schools and experimental stations.

(15) Marine affairs, including coastal zone management (except for measures relating to oil and other pollution of navigable waters).

(16) Oceanography.

(17) Petroleum conservation on public lands and conservation of the radium supply in the United States.

(18) Preservation of prehistoric ruins and objects of interest on the public domain.

(19) Public lands generally, including entry, easements, and grazing thereon.

(20) Relations of the United States with Native Americans and Native American tribes.

(21) Trans-Alaska Oil Pipeline (except ratemaking).

(n) **Committee on Oversight and Government Reform.**

(1) Federal civil service, including intergovernmental personnel; and the status of officers and employees of the United States, including their compensation, classification, and retirement.

(2) Municipal affairs of the District of Columbia in general (other than appropriations).

(3) Federal paperwork reduction.

(4) Government management and accounting measures generally.

(5) Holidays and celebrations.

(6) Overall economy, efficiency, and management of government operations and activities, including Federal procurement.

(7) National archives.

(8) Population and demography generally, including the Census.

(9) Postal service generally, including transportation of the mails.

(10) Public information and records.

(11) Relationship of the Federal Government to the States and municipalities generally.

(12) Reorganizations in the executive branch of the Government.

(o) **Committee on Rules.**

(1) Rules and joint rules (other than those relating to the Code of Official Conduct) and the order of business of the House.

(2) Recesses and final adjournments of Congress.

(p) **Committee on Science, Space, and Technology.**

(1) All energy research, development, and demonstration, and projects therefor, and all federally owned or operated nonmilitary energy laboratories.

(2) Astronautical research and development, including resources, personnel, equipment, and facilities.

(3) Civil aviation research and development.

(4) Environmental research and development.

(5) Marine research.

(6) Commercial application of energy technology.

(7) National Institute of Standards and Technology, standardization of weights and measures, and the metric system.

(8) National Aeronautics and Space Administration.

(9) National Space Council.

(10) National Science Foundation.

(11) National Weather Service.

(12) Outer space, including exploration and control thereof.

(13) Science scholarships.

(14) Scientific research, development, and demonstration, and projects therefor.

(q) **Committee on Small Business.**

(1) Assistance to and protection of small business, including financial aid, regulatory flexibility, and paperwork reduction.

(2) Participation of small-business enterprises in Federal procurement and Government contracts.

(r) **Committee on Transportation and Infrastructure.**

(1) Coast Guard, including lifesaving service, lighthouses, lightships, ocean derelicts, and the Coast Guard Academy.

(2) Federal management of emergencies and natural disasters.

(3) Flood control and improvement of rivers and harbors.

(4) Inland waterways.

(5) Inspection of merchant marine vessels, lights and signals, lifesaving equipment, and fire protection on such vessels.

(6) Navigation and laws relating thereto, including pilotage.

(7) Registering and licensing of vessels and small boats.

(8) Rules and international arrangements to prevent collisions at sea.

(9) The Capitol Building and the Senate and House Office Buildings.

(10) Construction or maintenance of roads and post roads (other than appropriations therefor).

(11) Construction or reconstruction, maintenance, and care of buildings and grounds of the Botanic Garden, the Library of Congress, and the Smithsonian Institution.

(12) Merchant marine (except for national security aspects thereof).

(13) Purchase of sites and construction of post offices, customhouses, Federal courthouses, and Government buildings within the District of Columbia.

(14) Oil and other pollution of navigable waters, including inland, coastal, and ocean waters.

(15) Marine affairs, including coastal zone management, as they relate to oil and other pollution of navigable waters.

(16) Public buildings and occupied or improved grounds of the United States generally.

(17) Public works for the benefit of navigation, including bridges and dams (other than international bridges and dams).

(18) Related transportation regulatory agencies (except the Transportation Security Administration).

(19) Roads and the safety thereof.

(20) Transportation, including civil aviation, railroads, water transportation, transportation safety (except automobile safety and transportation security functions of the Department of Homeland Security), transportation infrastructure, transportation labor, and railroad retirement and unemployment (except revenue measures related thereto).

(21) Water power.

(s) **Committee on Veterans' Affairs.**

(1) Veterans' measures generally.

(2) Cemeteries of the United States in which veterans of any war or conflict are or may be buried, whether in the United States or abroad (except cemeteries administered by the Secretary of the Interior).

(3) Compensation, vocational rehabilitation, and education of veterans.

(4) Life insurance issued by the Government on account of service in the Armed Forces.

(5) Pensions of all the wars of the United States, general and special.

(6) Readjustment of servicemembers to civil life.

(7) Servicemembers' civil relief.

(8) Veterans' hospitals, medical care, and treatment of veterans.

(t) **Committee on Ways and Means.**

(1) Customs revenue, collection districts, and ports of entry and delivery.

(2) Reciprocal trade agreements.

(3) Revenue measures generally.

(4) Revenue measures relating to insular possessions.

(5) Bonded debt of the United States, subject to the last sentence of clause 4(f).

(6) Deposit of public monies.

(7) Transportation of dutiable goods.

(8) Tax exempt foundations and charitable trusts.

(9) National social security (except health care and facilities programs that are supported from general revenues as opposed to payroll deductions and except work incentive programs).

General oversight responsibilities

2. (a) The various standing committees shall have general oversight responsibilities as provided in paragraph (b) in order to assist the House in—

(1) its analysis, appraisal, and evaluation of—

(A) the application, administration, execution, and effectiveness of Federal laws; and

(B) conditions and circumstances that may indicate the necessity or desirability of enacting new or additional legislation; and

(2) its formulation, consideration, and enactment of changes in Federal laws, and of such additional legislation as may be necessary or appropriate.

(b)(1) In order to determine whether laws and programs addressing subjects within the jurisdiction of a committee are being implemented and carried out in accordance with the intent of Congress and whether they should be continued, curtailed, or eliminated, each standing committee (other than the Committee on Appropriations) shall review and study on a continuing basis —

(A) the application, administration, execution, and effectiveness of laws and programs addressing subjects within its jurisdiction;

(B) the organization and operation of Federal agencies and entities having responsibilities for the administration and execution of laws and programs addressing subjects within its jurisdiction;

(C) any conditions or circumstances that may indicate the necessity or desirability of enacting new or additional legislation addressing subjects within its jurisdiction (whether or not a bill or resolution has been introduced with respect thereto); and

(D) future research and forecasting on subjects within its jurisdiction.

(2) Each committee to which subparagraph (1) applies having more than 20 members shall establish an oversight subcommittee, or require its subcommittees to conduct oversight in their respective jurisdictions, to assist in carrying out its responsibilities under this clause. The establishment of an oversight subcommittee does not limit the responsibility of a subcommittee with legislative jurisdiction in carrying out its oversight responsibilities.

(c) Each standing committee shall review and study on a continuing basis the impact or probable impact of tax policies affecting subjects within its jurisdiction as described in clauses 1 and 3. * * *

(e) The Speaker, with the approval of the House, may appoint special ad hoc oversight committees for the purpose of reviewing specific matters within the jurisdiction of two or more standing committees.

Budget Act responsibilities

(f)(1) Each standing committee shall submit to the Committee on the Budget not later than six weeks after the submission of the budget by the President, or at such time as the Committee on the Budget may request —

(A) its views and estimates with respect to all matters to be set forth in the concurrent resolution on the budget for the ensuing fiscal year that are within its jurisdiction or functions; and

(B) an estimate of the total amounts of new budget authority, and budget outlays resulting therefrom, to be provided or authorized in all bills and resolutions within its jurisdiction that it intends to be effective during that fiscal year.

(2) The views and estimates submitted by the Committee on Ways and Means under subparagraph (1) shall include a specific recommendation, made after holding public hearings, as to the appropriate level of the public debt that should be set forth in the concurrent resolution on the budget.

Committee staffs

9. (a) (1) Subject to subparagraph (2) and paragraph (f), each standing committee may appoint, by majority vote, not more than 30 professional staff members to be compensated from the funds provided for the appointment of committee staff by primary and additional expense resolutions. Each professional staff member appointed under this subparagraph shall be assigned to the chair and the ranking minority member of the committee, as the committee considers advisable. * * *

RULE XI

PROCEDURES OF COMMITTEES AND UNFINISHED BUSINESS

In general

1. (a)(1)(A) The Rules of the House are the rules of its committees and subcommittees so far as applicable.

(B) Each subcommittee is a part of its committee and is subject to the authority and direction of that committee and to its rules, so far as applicable.

(2)(A) In a committee or subcommittee—

(i) a motion to recess from day to day, or to recess subject to the call of the Chair (within 24 hours), shall be privileged; and

(ii) a motion to dispense with the first reading (in full) of a bill or resolution shall be privileged if printed copies are available.

(B) A motion accorded privilege under this subparagraph shall be decided without debate.

(b)(1) Each committee may conduct at any time such investigations and studies as it considers necessary or appropriate in the exercise of its responsibilities under rule X. Subject to the adoption of expense resolutions as required by clause 6 of rule X, each committee may incur expenses, including travel expenses, in connection with such investigations and studies.

(2) A proposed investigative or oversight report shall be considered as read in committee if it has been available to the members for at least 24 hours (excluding Saturdays, Sundays, or legal holidays except when the House is in session on such a day).

(3) A report of an investigation or study conducted jointly by more than one committee may be filed jointly, provided that each of the committees complies independently with all requirements for approval and filing of the report.

(4) After an adjournment sine die of the last regular session of a Congress, an investigative or oversight report may be filed with the Clerk at any time, provided that a member who gives timely notice of intention to file supplemental, minority, additional, or dissenting views shall be entitled to not less than seven calendar days in which to submit such views for inclusion in the report.

(c) Each committee may have printed and bound such testimony and other data as may be presented at hearings held by the committee or its subcommittees. All costs of stenographic services and transcripts in connection with a meeting or hearing of a committee shall be paid from the applicable accounts of the House described in clause 1(k)(1) of rule X. * * *

Adoption of written rules

2. (a)(1) Each standing committee shall adopt written rules governing its procedure. Such rules—

(A) shall be adopted in a meeting that is open to the public unless the committee, in open session and with a quorum present, determines by record vote that all or part of the meeting on that day shall be closed to the public;

(B) may not be inconsistent with the Rules of the House or with those provisions of law having the force and effect of Rules of the House;

(C) shall in any event incorporate all of the succeeding provisions of this clause to the extent applicable; and

(D) shall include provisions to govern the implementation of clause 4 as provided in paragraph (f) of such clause.

(2) Each committee shall make its rules publicly available in electronic form and submit such rules for publication in the Congressional Record not later than 30 days after the chair of the committee is elected in each odd-numbered year.

(3) A committee may adopt a rule providing that the chair be directed to offer a motion under clause 1 of rule XXII whenever the chair considers it appropriate.

Regular meeting days

(b) Each standing committee shall establish regular meeting days for the conduct of its business, which shall be not less frequent than monthly. Each such committee shall meet for the consideration of a bill or resolution pending before the committee or the transaction of other committee business on all regular meeting days fixed by the committee if notice is given pursuant to paragraph (g)(3).

Additional and special meetings

(c) (1) The chair of each standing committee may call and convene, as the chair considers necessary, additional and special meetings of the committee for the consideration of a bill or resolution pending before the committee or for the conduct of other committee business, subject to such rules as the committee may adopt. The committee shall meet for such purpose under that call of the chair.

(2) Three or more members of a standing committee may file in the offices of the committee a written request that the chair call a special meeting of the committee. Such request shall specify the measure or matter to be considered. Immediately upon the filing of the request, the clerk of the committee shall notify the chair of the filing of the request. If the chair does not call the requested special meeting within three calendar days after the filing of the request (to be held within seven calendar days after the filing of the request) a majority of the members of the committee may file in the offices of the committee their written notice that a special meeting of the committee will be held. The written notice shall specify the date and hour of the special meeting and the measure or matter to be considered. The committee shall meet on that date and hour. Immediately upon the filing of the notice, the clerk of the committee shall notify all members of the committee that such special meeting will be held and inform them of its date and hour and the measure or matter to be considered. Such notice shall also be made publicly available in electronic form and shall be deemed to satisfy paragraph (g)(3)(A)(ii). Only the measure or matter specified in that notice may be considered at that special meeting. ***

Prohibition against proxy voting

(f) A vote by a member of a committee or subcommittee with respect to any measure or matter may not be cast by proxy.

Hearing procedures

(k)(1) The chair at a hearing shall announce in an opening statement the subject of the hearing.

(2) A copy of the committee rules and of this clause shall be made available to each witness on request.

(3) Witnesses at hearings may be accompanied by their own counsel for the purpose of advising them concerning their constitutional rights.

(4) The chair may punish breaches of order and decorum, and of professional ethics on the part of counsel, by censure and exclusion from the hearings; and the committee may cite the offender to the House for contempt.

(5) Whenever it is asserted by a member of the committee that the evidence or testimony at a hearing may tend to defame, degrade, or incriminate any person, or

it is asserted by a witness that the evidence or testimony that the witness would give at a hearing may tend to defame, degrade, or incriminate the witness—

(A) notwithstanding paragraph (g)(2), such testimony or evidence shall be presented in executive session if, in the presence of the number of members required under the rules of the committee for the purpose of taking testimony, the committee determines by vote of a majority of those present that such evidence or testimony may tend to defame, degrade, or incriminate any person; and

(B) the committee shall proceed to receive such testimony in open session only if the committee, a majority being present, determines that such evidence or testimony will not tend to defame, degrade, or incriminate any person. In either case the committee shall afford such person an opportunity voluntarily to appear as a witness, and receive and dispose of requests from such person to subpoena additional witnesses.

(6) Except as provided in subparagraph (5), the chair shall receive and the committee shall dispose of requests to subpoena additional witnesses.

(7) Evidence or testimony taken in executive session, and proceedings conducted in executive session, may be released or used in public sessions only when authorized by the committee, a majority being present.

(8) In the discretion of the committee, witnesses may submit brief and pertinent sworn statements in writing for inclusion in the record. The committee is the sole judge of the pertinence of testimony and evidence adduced at its hearing.

(9) A witness may obtain a transcript copy of the testimony of such witness given at a public session or, if given at an executive session, when authorized by the committee.

Supplemental, minority, additional, or dissenting views

(l) If at the time of approval of a measure or matter by a committee (other than the Committee on Rules) a member of the committee gives notice of intention to file supplemental, minority, additional, or dissenting views for inclusion in the report to the House thereon, all members shall be entitled to not less than two additional calendar days after the day of such notice (excluding Saturdays, Sundays, and legal holidays except when the House is in session on such a day) to file such written and signed views with the clerk of the committee.

Power to sit and act; subpoena power

(m)(1) For the purpose of carrying out any of its functions and duties under this rule and rule X (including any matters referred to it under clause 2 of rule XII), a committee or subcommittee is authorized (subject to subparagraph (3)(A))—

(A) to sit and act at such times and places within the United States, whether the House is in session, has recessed, or has adjourned, and to hold such hearings as it considers necessary; and

(B) to require, by subpoena or otherwise, the attendance and testimony of such witnesses and the production of such books, records, correspondence, memoranda, papers, and documents as it considers necessary.

(2) The chair of the committee, or a member designated by the chair, may administer oaths to witnesses.

(3)(A) (i) Except as provided in subdivision (A)(ii), a subpoena may be authorized and issued by a committee or subcommittee under subparagraph (1) (B) in the conduct of an investigation or series of investigations or activities only when authorized by the committee or subcommittee, a majority being present. The power to authorize and issue subpoenas under subparagraph (1)(B) may be delegated to the chair of the committee under such rules and under such limitations as the committee may prescribe. Authorized subpoenas shall be signed by the chair of the committee or by a member designated by the committee.

(ii) In the case of a subcommittee of the Committee on Ethics, a subpoena may be authorized and issued only by an affirmative vote of a majority of its members.

(B) A subpoena duces tecum may specify terms of return other than at a meeting or hearing of the committee or subcommittee authorizing the subpoena.

(C) Compliance with a subpoena issued by a committee or subcommittee under subparagraph (1)(B) may be enforced only as authorized or directed by the House.

(n)(1) Each standing committee, or a subcommittee thereof, shall hold at least one hearing during each 120-day period following the establishment of the committee on the topic of waste, fraud, abuse, or mismanagement in Government programs which that committee may authorize.

(2) A hearing described in subparagraph (1) shall include a focus on the most egregious instances of waste, fraud, abuse, or mismanagement as documented by any report the committee has received from a Federal Office of the Inspector General or the Comptroller General of the United States.

(o) Each committee, or a subcommittee thereof, shall hold at least one hearing in any session in which the committee has received disclaimers of agency financial statements from auditors of any Federal agency that the committee may authorize to hear testimony on such disclaimers from representatives of any such agency.

(p) Each standing committee, or a subcommittee thereof, shall hold at least one hearing on issues raised by reports issued by the Comptroller General of the United States indicating that Federal programs or operations that the committee may authorize are at high risk for waste, fraud, and mismanagement, known as the "high-risk list" or the "high-risk series."

RULE XIII

CALENDARS AND COMMITTEE REPORTS

Calendars

1. (a) All business reported by committees shall be referred to one of the following three calendars:

(1) A Calendar of the Committee of the Whole House on the state of the Union, to which shall be referred public bills and public resolutions raising revenue, involving a tax or charge on the people, directly or indirectly making appropriations of money or property or requiring such appropriations to be made, authorizing payments out of appropriations already made, releasing any liability to the United States for money or property, or referring a claim to the Court of Claims.

(2) A House Calendar, to which shall be referred all public bills and public resolutions not requiring referral to the Calendar of the Committee of the Whole House on the state of the Union.

(3) A Private Calendar as provided in clause 5 of rule XV, to which shall be referred all private bills and private resolutions. * * *

RULE XIV

ORDER AND PRIORITY OF BUSINESS

1. The daily order of business (unless varied by the application of other rules and except for the disposition of matters of higher precedence) shall be as follows:

First. Prayer by the Chaplain.

Second. Reading and approval of the Journal, unless postponed under clause 8 of rule XX.

Third. The Pledge of Allegiance to the Flag.

Fourth. Correction of reference of public bills.

Fifth. Disposal of business on the Speaker's table as provided in clause 2.

Sixth. Unfinished business as provided in clause 3.

Seventh. The morning hour for the consideration of bills called up by committees as provided in clause 4.

Eighth. Motions that the House resolve into the Committee of the Whole House on the state of the Union subject to clause 5.

Ninth. Orders of the day.

2. Business on the Speaker's table shall be disposed of as follows:

(a) Messages from the President shall be referred to the appropriate committees without debate.

(b) Communications addressed to the House, including reports and communications from heads of departments and bills, resolutions, and messages from the Senate, may be referred to the appropriate committees in the same manner and with the same right of correction as public bills and public resolutions presented by Members, Delegates, or the Resident Commissioner.

(c) Motions to dispose of Senate amendments on the Speaker's table may be entertained as provided in clauses 1, 2, and 4 of rule XXII.

(d) Senate bills and resolutions substantially the same as House measures already favorably reported and not required to be considered in the Committee of the Whole House on the state of the Union may be disposed of by motion. Such a motion shall be privileged if offered by direction of all reporting committees having initial jurisdiction of the House measure.

3. Consideration of unfinished business in which the House may have been engaged at an adjournment, except business in the morning hour and proceedings postponed under clause 8 of rule XX, shall be resumed as soon as the business on the Speaker's table is finished, and at the same time each day thereafter until disposed of. The consideration of all other unfinished business shall be resumed whenever the class of business to which it belongs shall be in order under the rules.

4. After the unfinished business has been disposed of, the Speaker shall call each standing committee in regular order and then select committees. Each committee when named may call up for consideration a bill or resolution reported by it on a previous day and on the House Calendar. If the Speaker does not complete the call of the committees before the House passes to other business, the next call shall resume at the point it left off, giving preference to the last bill or resolution under consideration. A committee that has occupied the call for two days may not call up another bill or resolution until the other committees have been called in their turn.

5. After consideration of bills or resolutions under clause 4 for one hour, it shall be in order, pending consideration thereof, to entertain a motion that the House resolve into the Committee of the Whole House on the state of the Union or, when authorized by a committee, that the House resolve into the Committee of the Whole House on the state of the Union to consider a particular bill. Such a motion shall be subject to only one amendment designating another bill. If such a motion is decided in the negative, another such motion may not be considered until the matter that was pending when such motion was offered is disposed of.

6. All questions relating to the priority of business shall be decided by a majority without debate.

RULE XVIII

THE COMMITTEE OF THE WHOLE HOUSE ON THE STATE OF THE UNION

Resolving into the Committee of the Whole

1. Whenever the House resolves into the Committee of the Whole House on the state of the Union, the Speaker shall leave the chair after appointing a Member as Chair to preside. In case of disturbance or disorderly conduct in the galleries or lobby, the Chair may cause the same to be cleared.

2. (a) Except as provided in paragraph (b) and in clause 6 of rule XV, the House resolves into the Committee of the Whole House on the state of the Union by motion. When such a motion is entertained, the Speaker shall put the question without debate: "Shall the House resolve itself into the Committee of the Whole House on the state of the Union for consideration of this matter?", naming it.

(b) After the House has adopted a resolution reported by the Committee on Rules providing a special order of business for the consideration of a measure in the Committee of the Whole House on the state of the Union, the Speaker may at any time, when no question is pending before the House, declare the House resolved into the Committee of the Whole for the consideration of that measure without intervening motion, unless the special order of business provides otherwise.

Measures requiring initial consideration in the Committee of the Whole

3. All public bills, resolutions, or Senate amendments (as provided in clause 3 of rule XXII) involving a tax or charge on the people, raising revenue, directly or indirectly making appropriations of money or property or requiring such appropriations to be made, authorizing payments out of appropriations already made, releasing any liability to the United States for money or property, or referring a claim to the Court of Claims, shall be first considered in the Committee of the Whole House on the state of the Union. A bill, resolution, or Senate amendment that fails to comply with this clause is subject to a point of order against its consideration.

Order of business

4. (a) Subject to subparagraph (b) business on the calendar of the Committee of the Whole House on the state of the Union may be taken up in regular order, or in such order as the Committee may determine, unless the measure to be considered was determined by the House at the time of resolving into the Committee of the Whole.

(b) Motions to resolve into the Committee of the Whole for consideration of bills and joint resolutions making general appropriations have precedence under this clause.

Reading for amendment

5. (a) Before general debate commences on a measure in the Committee of the Whole House on the state of the Union, it shall be read in full. When general debate is concluded or closed by order of the House, the measure under consideration shall be read for amendment. A Member, Delegate, or Resident Commissioner who offers an amendment shall be allowed five minutes to explain it, after which the Member, Delegate, or Resident Commissioner who shall first obtain the floor shall be allowed five minutes to speak in opposition to it. There shall be no further debate thereon, but the same privilege of debate shall be allowed in favor of and against any amendment that may be offered to an amendment. An amendment, or an amendment to an amendment, may be withdrawn by its proponent only by the unanimous consent of the Committee of the Whole.

(b) When a Member, Delegate, or Resident Commissioner offers an amendment in the Committee of the Whole House on the state of the Union, the Clerk shall promptly transmit five copies of the amendment to the majority committee table and five copies to the minority committee table. The Clerk also shall deliver at least one copy of the amendment to the majority cloakroom and at least one copy to the minority cloakroom.

Quorum and voting

6. (a) A quorum of a Committee of the Whole House on the state of the Union is 100 Members. The first time that a Committee of the Whole finds itself without a quorum during a day, the Chair shall invoke the procedure for a quorum call set forth in clause 2 of rule XX, unless the Chair elects to invoke an alternate procedure set forth in clause 3 or clause 4(a) of rule XX. If a quorum appears, the Committee of the Whole shall continue its business. If a quorum does not appear, the Committee of the Whole shall rise, and the Chair shall report the names of absentees to the House.

(b)(1) The Chair may refuse to entertain a point of order that a quorum is not present during general debate. (2) After a quorum has once been established on a day, the Chair may entertain a point of order that a quorum is not present only when the Committee of the Whole House on the state of the Union is operating under the five-minute rule and the Chair has put the pending proposition to a vote. (3) Upon sustaining a point of order that a quorum is not present, the Chair may announce that, following a regular quorum call under paragraph (a), the minimum time for electronic voting on the pending question shall be not less than two minutes.

(c) When ordering a quorum call in the Committee of the Whole House on the state of the Union, the Chair may announce an intention to declare that a quorum is constituted at any time during the quorum call when the Chair determines that a quorum has appeared. If the Chair interrupts the quorum call by declaring that a quorum is constituted, proceedings under the quorum call shall be considered as vacated, and the Committee of the Whole shall continue its sitting and resume its business.

(d) A quorum is not required in the Committee of the Whole House on the state of the Union for adoption of a motion that the Committee rise.

(e) In the Committee of the Whole House on the state of the Union, the Chair shall order a recorded vote on a request supported by at least 25 Members.

(f) In the Committee of the Whole House on the state of the Union, the Chair may reduce to not less than two minutes the minimum time for electronic voting without any intervening business or debate on any or all pending amendments after a record vote has been taken on the first pending amendment.

(g) The Chair may postpone a request for a recorded vote on any amendment. The Chair may resume proceedings on a postponed request at any time. The Chair may reduce to not less than two minutes the minimum time for electronic voting—

(1) on any postponed question that follows another electronic vote without intervening business, provided that the minimum time for electronic voting on the first in any series of questions shall be 15 minutes; or

(2) on any postponed question taken without intervening debate or motion after the Committee of the Whole resumes its sitting if in the discretion of the Chair Members would be afforded an adequate opportunity to vote.

Dispensing with the reading of an amendment

7. It shall be in order in the Committee of the Whole House on the state of the Union to move that the Committee of the Whole dispense with the reading of an amendment that has been printed in the bill or resolution as reported by a committee, or an amendment that a Member, Delegate, or Resident Commissioner has caused to be printed in the Congressional Record. Such a motion shall be decided without debate.

Closing debate

8. (a) Subject to paragraph (b) at any time after the Committee of the Whole House on the state of the Union has begun five-minute debate on amendments to any portion of a bill or resolution, it shall be in order to move that the Committee of the Whole close all debate on that portion of the bill or resolution or on the pending amendments only. Such a motion shall be decided without debate. The adoption of such a motion does not preclude further amendment, to be decided without debate.

(b) If the Committee of the Whole House on the state of the Union closes debate on any portion of a bill or resolution before there has been debate on an amendment that a Member, Delegate, or Resident Commissioner has caused to be printed in the Congressional Record at least one day before its consideration, the Member, Delegate, or Resident Commissioner who caused the amendment to be printed in the Record shall be allowed five minutes to explain it, after which the Member, Delegate, or Resident Commissioner who shall first obtain the floor shall be allowed five minutes to speak in opposition to it. There shall be no further debate thereon.

(c) Material submitted for printing in the Congressional Record under this clause shall indicate the full text of the proposed amendment, the name of the Member, Delegate, or Resident Commissioner proposing it, the number of the bill or resolution to which it will be offered, and the point in the bill or resolution or amendment thereto where the amendment is intended to be offered. The amendment shall appear in a portion of the Record designated for that purpose. Amendments to a specified measure submitted for printing in that portion of the Record shall be numbered in the order printed.

Concurrent resolution on the budget

10. (a) At the conclusion of general debate in the Committee of the Whole House on the state of the Union on a concurrent resolution on the budget under section 305(a) of the Congressional Budget Act of 1974, the concurrent resolution shall be considered as read for amendment.

(b) It shall not be in order in the House or in the Committee of the Whole House on the state of the Union to consider an amendment to a concurrent resolution on the budget, or an amendment thereto, unless the concurrent resolution, as amended by such amendment or amendments—

(1) would be mathematically consistent except as limited by paragraph (c); and

(2) would contain all the matter set forth in paragraphs (1) through (5) of section 301(a) of the Congressional Budget Act of 1974.

(c)(1) Except as specified in subparagraph (2), it shall not be in order in the House or in the Committee of the Whole House on the state of the Union to consider an amendment to a concurrent resolution on the budget, or an amendment thereto, that proposes to change the amount of the appropriate level of the public debt set forth in the concurrent resolution, as reported.

(2) Amendments to achieve mathematical consistency under section 305(a)(5) of the Congressional Budget Act of 1974, if offered by direction of the Committee on the Budget, may propose to adjust the amount of the appropriate level of the public debt set forth in the concurrent resolution, as reported, to reflect changes made in other figures contained in the concurrent resolution.

Applicability of Rules of the House

11. The Rules of the House are the rules of the Committee of the Whole House on the state of the Union so far as applicable.

RULE XIX

MOTIONS FOLLOWING THE AMENDMENT STAGE

Previous question

1. (a) There shall be a motion for the previous question, which, being ordered, shall have the effect of cutting off all debate and bringing the House to a direct vote on the immediate question or questions on which it has been ordered. Whenever the previous question has been ordered on an otherwise debatable question on which there has been no debate, it shall be in order to debate that question for 40 minutes, equally divided and controlled by a proponent of the question and an opponent. The previous question may be moved and ordered on a single question, on a series of questions allowable under the rules, or on an amendment or amendments, or may embrace all authorized motions or amendments and include the bill or resolution to its passage, adoption, or rejection.

(b) Incidental questions of order arising during the pendency of a motion for the previous question shall be decided, whether on appeal or otherwise, without debate.

(c) Notwithstanding paragraph (a), when the previous question is operating to adoption or passage of a measure pursuant to a special order of business, the Chair may postpone further consideration of such measure in the House to such time as may be designated by the Speaker.

Recommit

2. (a) After the previous question has been ordered on passage or adoption of a measure, or pending a motion to that end, it shall be in order to move that the House recommit (or commit, as the case may be) the measure, with or without instructions, to a standing or select committee. For such a motion to recommit, the Speaker shall give preference in recognition to a Member, Delegate, or Resident Commissioner who is opposed to the measure.

(b)(1) Except as provided in paragraph (c), a motion that the House recommit a bill or joint resolution on which the previous question has been ordered to passage shall be debatable for 10 minutes equally divided between the proponent and an opponent.

(2) A motion to recommit a bill or joint resolution may include instructions only in the form of a direction to report an amendment or amendments back to the House forthwith.

(c) On demand of the floor manager for the majority, it shall be in order to debate the motion for one hour equally divided and controlled by the proponent and an opponent.

Reconsideration

3. When a motion has been carried or lost, it shall be in order on the same or succeeding day for a Member on the prevailing side of the question to enter a motion for the reconsideration thereof. The entry of such a motion shall take precedence over all other questions except the consideration of a conference report or a motion to adjourn, and may not be withdrawn after such succeeding day without the consent of the House. Once entered, a motion may be called up for consideration by any Member. During the last six days of a session of Congress, such a motion shall be disposed of when entered.

4. A bill, petition, memorial, or resolution referred to a committee, or reported therefrom for printing and recommitment, may not be brought back to the House on a motion to reconsider.

RULE XXII

HOUSE AND SENATE RELATIONS

Senate amendments

1. A motion to disagree to Senate amendments to a House proposition and to request or agree to a conference with the Senate, or a motion to insist on House amendments to a Senate proposition and to request or agree to a conference with the Senate, shall be privileged in the discretion of the Speaker if offered by direction of the primary committee and of all reporting committees that had initial referral of the proposition.

2. A motion to dispose of House bills with Senate amendments not requiring consideration in the Committee of the Whole House on the state of the Union shall be privileged.

3. Except as permitted by clause 1, before the stage of disagreement, a Senate amendment to a House bill or resolution shall be subject to the point of order that it must first be considered in the Committee of the Whole House on the state of the Union if, originating in the House, it would be subject to such a point under clause 3 of rule XVIII.

4. When the stage of disagreement has been reached on a bill or resolution with House or Senate amendments, a motion to dispose of any amendment shall be privileged.

5. (a) Managers on the part of the House may not agree to a Senate amendment described in paragraph (b) unless specific authority to agree to the amendment first is given by the House by a separate vote with respect thereto. If specific

authority is not granted, the Senate amendment shall be reported in disagreement by the conference committee back to the two Houses for disposition by separate motion.

(b) The managers on the part of the House may not agree to a Senate amendment described in paragraph (a) that—

(1) would violate clause 2(a)(1) or (c) of rule XXI if originating in the House; or

(2) proposes an appropriation on a bill other than a general appropriation bill.

6. A Senate amendment carrying a tax or tariff measure in violation of clause 5(a) of rule XXI may not be agreed to.

Conference reports; amendments reported in disagreement

7. (a) The presentation of a conference report shall be in order at any time except during a reading of the Journal or the conduct of a record vote, a vote by division, or a quorum call.

(b)(1) Subject to subparagraph (2) the time allotted for debate on a motion to instruct managers on the part of the House shall be equally divided between the majority and minority parties.

(2) If the proponent of a motion to instruct managers on the part of the House and the Member, Delegate, or Resident Commissioner of the other party identified under subparagraph (1) both support the motion, one-third of the time for debate thereon shall be allotted to a Member, Delegate, or Resident Commissioner who opposes the motion on demand of that Member, Delegate, or Resident Commissioner.

(c)(1) A motion to instruct managers on the part of the House, or a motion to discharge all managers on the part of the House and to appoint new conferees, shall be privileged after a conference committee has been appointed for 45 calendar days and 25 legislative days without making a report, but only on the day after the calendar day on which the Member, Delegate, or Resident Commissioner offering the motion announces to the House intention to do so and the form of the motion.

(2) The Speaker may designate a time in the legislative schedule on that legislative day for consideration of a motion described in subparagraph (1).

(3) During the last six days of a session of Congress, a motion under subparagraph (1) shall be privileged after a conference committee has been appointed for 36 hours without making a report and the proponent meets the notice requirement in subparagraph (1).

(d) Instructions to conferees in a motion to instruct or in a motion to recommit to conference may not include argument.

(e) Each conference report to the House shall be printed as a report of the House. Each such report shall be accompanied by a joint explanatory statement prepared jointly by the managers on the part of the House and the managers on the part of the Senate. The joint explanatory statement shall be sufficiently detailed and explicit to inform the House of the effects of the report on the matters committed to conference. ***

RULE XXIX

GENERAL PROVISIONS

1. The provisions of law that constituted the Rules of the House at the end of the previous Congress shall govern the House in all cases to which they are applicable, and the rules of parliamentary practice comprised by Jefferson's Manual shall govern the House in all cases to which they are applicable and in which they are not inconsistent with the Rules and orders of the House.

2. In these rules words importing one gender include the other as well.

3. If a measure or matter is publicly available in electronic form at a location designated by the Committee on House Administration, it shall be considered as having been available to Members, Delegates, and the Resident Commissioner for purposes of these rules.

4. Authoritative guidance from the Committee on the Budget concerning the impact of a legislative proposition on the levels of new budget authority, outlays, direct spending, new entitlement authority and revenues may be provided by the chair of the committee.

Selected Standing Rules
of the U.S. Senate

RULE VI

QUORUM — ABSENT SENATORS
MAY BE SENT FOR

1. A quorum shall consist of a majority of the Senators duly chosen and sworn.

2. No Senator shall absent himself from the service of the Senate without leave.

3. If, at any time during the daily sessions of the Senate, a question shall be raised by any Senator as to the presence of a quorum, the Presiding Officer shall forthwith direct the Secretary to call the roll and shall announce the result, and these proceedings shall be without debate.

4. Whenever upon such roll call it shall be ascertained that a quorum is not present, a majority of the Senators present may direct the Sergeant at Arms to request, and, when necessary, to compel the attendance of the absent Senators, which order shall be determined without debate; and pending its execution, and until a quorum shall be present, no debate nor motion, except to adjourn, or to recess pursuant to a previous order entered by unanimous consent, shall be in order.

RULE XII

VOTING PROCEDURE

1. When the yeas and nays are ordered, the names of Senators shall be called alphabetically; and each Senator shall, without debate, declare his assent or dissent to the question, unless excused by the Senate; and no Senator shall be permitted to vote after the decision shall have been announced by the Presiding Officer, but may for sufficient reasons, with unanimous consent, change or withdraw his vote. No motion to suspend this rule shall be in order, nor shall the Presiding Officer entertain any request to suspend it by unanimous consent.

2. When a Senator declines to vote on call of his name, he shall be required to assign his reasons therefor, and having assigned them, the Presiding Officer shall submit the question to the Senate: "Shall the Senator for the reasons assigned by him, be excused

from voting?" which shall be decided without debate; and these proceedings shall be had after the rollcall and before the result is announced; and any further proceedings in reference thereto shall be after such announcement.

3. A Member, notwithstanding any other provisions of this rule, may decline to vote, in committee or on the floor, on any matter when he believes that his voting on such a matter would be a conflict of interest.

4. No request by a Senator for unanimous consent for the taking of a final vote on a specified date upon the passage of a bill or joint resolution shall be submitted to the Senate for agreement thereto until after a quorum call ordered for the purpose by the Presiding Officer, it shall be disclosed that a quorum of the Senate is present; and when a unanimous consent is thus given the same shall operate as the order of the Senate, but any unanimous consent may be revoked by another unanimous consent granted in the manner prescribed above upon one day's notice.

RULE XIII

RECONSIDERATION

1. When a question has been decided by the Senate, any Senator voting with the prevailing side or who has not voted may, on the same day or on either of the next two days of actual session thereafter, move a reconsideration; and if the Senate shall refuse to reconsider such a motion entered, or if such a motion is withdrawn by leave of the Senate, or if upon reconsideration the Senate shall affirm its first decision, no further motion to reconsider shall be in order unless by unanimous consent. Every motion to reconsider shall be decided by a majority vote, and may be laid on the table without affecting the question in reference to which the same is made, which shall be a final disposition of the motion.

2. When a bill, resolution, report, amendment, order, or message, upon which a vote has been taken, shall have gone out of the possession of the Senate and been communicated to the House of Representatives, the motion to reconsider shall be accompanied by a motion to request the House to return the same; which last motion shall be acted upon immediately, and without debate, and if determined in the negative shall be a final disposition of the motion to reconsider.

RULE XIV

JOINT RESOLUTIONS, RESOLUTIONS, AND PREAMBLES THERETO

1. Whenever a bill or joint resolution shall be offered, its introduction shall, if objected to, be postponed for one day.

2. Every bill and joint resolution shall receive three readings previous to its passage which readings on demand of any Senator shall be on three different legislative days, and the Presiding Officer shall give notice at each reading whether it be the first, second, or third: Provided, That each reading may be by title only, unless the Senate in any case shall otherwise order.

3. No bill or joint resolution shall be committed or amended until it shall have been twice read, after which it may be referred to a committee; bills and joint resolutions introduced on leave, and bills and joint resolutions from the House of Representatives, shall be read once, and may be read twice, if not objected to, on the same day for reference, but shall not be considered on that day nor debated, except for reference, unless by unanimous consent.

4. Every bill and joint resolution reported from a committee, not having previously been read, shall be read once, and twice, if not objected to, on the same day, and placed on the Calendar in the order in which the same may be reported; and every bill and joint resolution introduced on leave, and every bill and joint resolution of the House of Representatives which shall have received a first and second reading without being referred to a committee, shall, if objection be made to further proceeding thereon, be placed on the Calendar.

RULE XVI

APPROPRIATIONS AND AMENDMENTS TO GENERAL APPROPRIATIONS BILLS

1. On a point of order made by any Senator, no amendments shall be received to any general appropriation bill the effect of which will be to increase an appropriation already contained in the bill, or to add a new item of appropriation, unless it be made to carry out the provisions of some existing law, or treaty stipulation, or act or resolution previously passed by the Senate during that session; or unless the same be moved by direction of the Committee on Appropriations or of a committee of the Senate having legislative jurisdiction of the subject matter, or proposed in pursuance of an estimate submitted in accordance with law.

2. The Committee on Appropriations shall not report an appropriation bill containing amendments to such bill proposing new or general legislation or any restriction on the expenditure of the funds appropriated which proposes a limitation not authorized by law if such restriction is to take effect or cease to be effective upon the happening of a contingency, and if an appropriation bill is reported to the Senate containing amendments to such bill proposing new or general legislation or any such restriction, a point of order may be made against the bill, and if the point is sustained, the bill shall be recommitted to the Committee on Appropriations.

3. All amendments to general appropriation bills moved by direction of a committee having legislative jurisdiction of the subject matter proposing to increase an appropriation already contained in the bill, or to add new items of appropriation, shall, at least one day before they are considered, be referred to the Committee on Appropriations, and when actually proposed to the bill no amendment proposing to increase the amount stated in such amendment shall be received on a point of order made by any Senator.

4. On a point of order made by any Senator, no amendment offered by any other Senator which proposes general legislation shall be received to any general appropriation bill, nor shall any amendment not germane or relevant to the subject matter contained in the bill be received; nor shall any amendment to any item or clause of such bill be received which does not directly relate thereto; nor shall any restriction on the expenditure of the funds appropriated which proposes a limitation not authorized by law be received if such restriction is to take effect or cease to be effective upon the happening of a contingency; and all questions of relevancy of amendments under this rule, when raised, shall be submitted to the Senate and be decided without debate; and any such amendment or restriction to a general appropriation bill may be laid on the table without prejudice to the bill.

5. On a point of order made by any Senator, no amendment, the object of which is to provide for a private claim, shall be received to any general appropriation bill, unless it be to carry out the provisions of an existing law or a treaty stipulation, which shall be cited on the face of the amendment.

6. When a point of order is made against any restriction on the expenditure of funds appropriated in a general appropriation bill on the ground that the restriction violates this rule, the rule shall be construed strictly and, in case of doubt, in favor of the point of order.

7. Every report on general appropriation bills filed by the Committee on Appropriations shall identify with particularity each recommended amendment which proposes an item of appropriation which is not made to carry out the provisions of an existing law, a treaty stipulation, or an act or resolution previously passed by the Senate during that session.

8. On a point of order made by any Senator, no general appropriation bill or amendment thereto shall be received or considered if it contains a provision reappropriating unexpended balances of appropriations; except that this provision shall not apply to appropriations in continuation of appropriations for public works on which work has commenced.

RULE XIX

DEBATE

1. (a) When a Senator desires to speak, he shall rise and address the Presiding Officer, and shall not proceed until he is recognized, and the Presiding Officer shall recognize the Senator who shall first address him. No Senator shall interrupt another Senator in debate without his consent, and to obtain such consent he shall first address the Presiding Officer, and no Senator shall speak more than twice upon any one question in debate on the same legislative day without leave of the Senate, which shall be determined without debate.

(b) At the conclusion of the morning hour at the beginning of a new legislative day or after the unfinished business or any pending business has first been laid before the Senate on any calendar day, and until after the duration of three hours of actual session after such business is laid down except as determined to the contrary by unanimous consent or on motion without debate, all debate shall be germane and confined to the specific question then pending before the Senate.

2. No Senator in debate shall, directly or indirectly, by any form of words impute to another Senator or to other Senators any conduct or motive unworthy or unbecoming a Senator.

3. No Senator in debate shall refer offensively to any State of the Union.

4. If any Senator, in speaking or otherwise, in the opinion of the Presiding Officer transgress the rules of the Senate the Presiding Officer shall, either on his own motion or at the request of any other Senator, call him to order; and when a Senator shall be called to order he shall take his seat, and may not proceed without leave of the Senate, which, if granted, shall be upon motion that he be allowed to proceed in order, which motion shall be determined without debate. Any Senator directed by the Presiding Officer to take his seat, and any Senator requesting the Presiding Officer to require a Senator to take his seat, may appeal from the ruling of the Chair, which appeal shall be open to debate.

5. If a Senator be called to order for words spoken in debate, upon the demand of the Senator or of any other Senator, the exceptionable words shall be taken down in writing, and read at the table for the information of the Senate.

6. Whenever confusion arises in the Chamber or the galleries, or demonstrations of approval or disapproval are indulged in by the occupants of the galleries, it shall be the duty of the Chair to enforce order on his own initiative and without any point of order being made by a Senator.

7. No Senator shall introduce to or bring to the attention of the Senate during its sessions any occupant in the galleries of the Senate. No motion to suspend this rule shall be in order, nor may the Presiding Officer entertain any request to suspend it by unanimous consent.

8. Former Presidents of the United States shall be entitled to address the Senate upon appropriate notice to the Presiding Officer who shall thereupon make the necessary arrangements.

RULE XX

QUESTIONS OF ORDER

1. A question of order may be raised at any stage of the proceedings, except when the Senate is voting or ascertaining the presence of a quorum, and, unless submitted to the Senate, shall be decided by the Presiding Officer without debate, subject to an appeal to the Senate. When an appeal is taken, any subsequent question of order which may arise before the decision of such appeal shall be decided by the Presiding Officer without debate; and every appeal therefrom shall be decided at once, and without debate; and any appeal may be laid on the table without prejudice to the pending proposition, and thereupon shall be held as affirming the decision of the Presiding Officer.

2. The Presiding Officer may submit any question of order for the decision of the Senate.

RULE XXII

PRECEDENCE OF MOTIONS

1. When a question is pending, no motion shall be received but

> To adjourn.
>
> To adjourn to a day certain, or that when the Senate adjourn it shall be to a day certain.
>
> To take a recess.
>
> To proceed to the consideration of executive business.
>
> To lay on the table.
>
> To postpone indefinitely.
>
> To postpone to a day certain.
>
> To commit.
>
> To amend.

Which several motions shall have precedence as they stand arranged; and the motions relating to adjournment, to take a recess, to proceed to the consideration of executive business, to lay on the table, shall be decided without debate.

2. Notwithstanding the provisions of rule II or rule IV or any other rule of the Senate, at any time a motion signed by sixteen Senators, to bring to a close the debate upon any measure, motion, other matter pending before the Senate, or the unfinished business, is

presented to the Senate, the Presiding Officer, or clerk at the direction of the Presiding Officer, shall at once state the motion to the Senate, and one hour after the Senate meets on the following calendar day but one, he shall lay the motion before the Senate and direct that the clerk call the roll, and upon the ascertainment that a quorum is present, the Presiding Officer shall, without debate, submit to the Senate by a yea-and-nay vote the question:

> "Is it the sense of the Senate that the debate shall be brought to a close?" And if that question shall be decided in the affirmative by three-fifths of the Senators duly chosen and sworn—except on a measure or motion to amend the Senate rules, in which case the necessary affirmative vote shall be two-thirds of the Senators present and voting—then said measure, motion, or other matter pending before the Senate, or the unfinished business, shall be the unfinished business to the exclusion of all other business until disposed of.

Thereafter no Senator shall be entitled to speak in all more than one hour on the measure, motion, or other matter pending before the Senate, or the unfinished business, the amendments thereto, and motions affecting the same, and it shall be the duty of the Presiding Officer to keep the time of each Senator who speaks. Except by unanimous consent, no amendment shall be proposed after the vote to bring the debate to a close, unless it had been submitted in writing to the Journal Clerk by 1 o'clock p.m. on the day following the filing of the cloture motion if an amendment in the first degree, and unless it had been so submitted at least one hour prior to the beginning of the cloture vote if an amendment in the second degree. No dilatory motion, or dilatory amendment, or amendment not germane shall be in order. Points of order, including questions of relevancy, and appeals from the decision of the Presiding Officer, shall be decided without debate.

After no more than thirty hours of consideration of the measure, motion, or other matter on which cloture has been invoked, the Senate shall proceed, without any further debate on any question, to vote on the final disposition thereof to the exclusion of all amendments not then actually pending before the Senate at that time and to the exclusion of all motions, except a motion to table, or to reconsider and one quorum call on demand to establish the presence of a quorum (and motions required to establish a quorum) immediately before the final vote begins. The thirty hours may be increased by the adoption of a motion, decided without debate, by a three-fifths affirmative vote of the Senators duly chosen and sworn, and any such time thus agreed upon shall be equally divided between and controlled by the Majority and Minority Leaders or their designees. However, only one motion to extend time, specified above, may be made in any one calendar day.

If, for any reason, a measure or matter is reprinted after cloture has been invoked, amendments which were in order prior to the reprinting of the measure or matter will continue to be in order and may be conformed and reprinted at the request of the amendment's sponsor. The conforming changes must be limited to lineation and pagination.

No Senator shall call up more than two amendments until every other Senator shall have had the opportunity to do likewise.

Notwithstanding other provisions of this rule, a Senator may yield all or part of his one hour to the majority or minority floor managers of the measure, motion, or matter or to the Majority or Minority Leader, but each Senator specified shall not have more than two hours so yielded to him and may in turn yield such time to other Senators.

Notwithstanding any other provision of this rule, any Senator who has not used or yielded at least ten minutes, is, if he seeks recognition, guaranteed up to ten minutes, inclusive, to speak only.

After cloture is invoked, the reading of any amendment, including House amendments, shall be dispensed with when the proposed amendment has been identified and has been available in printed form at the desk of the Members for not less than twenty four hours.

3. If a cloture motion on a motion to proceed to a measure or matter is presented in accordance with this rule and is signed by 16 Senators, including the Majority Leader, the Minority Leader, 7 additional Senators not affiliated with the majority, and 7 additional Senators not affiliated with the minority, one hour after the Senate meets on the following calendar day, the Presiding Officer, or the clerk at the direction of the Presiding Officer, shall lay the motion before the Senate. If cloture is then invoked on the motion to proceed, the question shall be on the motion to proceed, without further debate.

RULE XXIV

APPOINTMENT OF COMMITTEES

1. In the appointment of the standing committees, or to fill vacancies thereon, the Senate, unless otherwise ordered, shall by resolution appoint the chairman of each such committee and the other members thereof. On demand of any Senator, a separate vote shall be had on the appointment of the chairman of any such committee and on the appointment of the other members thereof. Each such resolution shall be subject to amendment and to division of the question.

2. On demand of one-fifth of the Senators present, a quorum being present, any vote taken pursuant to paragraph 1 shall be by ballot.

3. Except as otherwise provided or unless otherwise ordered, all other committees, and the chairmen thereof, shall be appointed in the same manner as standing committees.

4. When a chairman of a committee shall resign or cease to serve on a committee, action by the Senate to fill the vacancy in such committee, unless specially otherwise ordered, shall be only to fill up the number of members of the committee, and the election of a new chairman.

RULE XXV

STANDING COMMITTEES

1. The following standing committees shall be appointed at the commencement of each Congress, and shall continue and have the power to act until their successors are appointed, with leave to report by bill or otherwise on matters within their respective jurisdictions:

(a)(1) Committee on Agriculture, Nutrition, and Forestry, to which committee shall be referred all proposed legislation, messages, petitions, memorials, and other matters relating primarily to the following subjects:

1. Agricultural economics and research.

2. Agricultural extension services and experiment stations.

3. Agricultural production, marketing, and stabilization of prices.

4. Agriculture and agricultural commodities.

5. Animal industry and diseases.

6. Crop insurance and soil conservation.

7. Farm credit and farm security.

8. Food from fresh waters.

9. Food stamp programs.

10. Forestry, and forest reserves and wilderness areas other than those created from the public domain.

11. Home economics.

12. Human nutrition.

13. Inspection of livestock, meat, and agricultural products.

14. Pests and pesticides.

15. Plant industry, soils, and agricultural engineering.

16. Rural development, rural electrification, and watersheds.

17. School nutrition programs.

(2) Such committee shall also study and review, on a comprehensive basis, matters relating to food, nutrition, and hunger, both in the United States and in foreign countries, and rural affairs, and report thereon from time to time.

(b) Committee on Appropriations, to which committee shall be referred all proposed legislation, messages, petitions, memorials, and other matters relating to the following subjects:

1. Appropriation of the revenue for the support of the Government, except as provided in subparagraph (e).

2. Rescission of appropriations contained in appropriation Acts (referred to in section 105 of title 1, United States Code).

3. The amount of new spending authority described in section 401(c)(2)(A) and (B) of the Congressional Budget Act of 1974 which is to be effective for a fiscal year.

4. New spending authority described in section 401(c)(2)(C) of the Congressional Budget Act of 1974 provided in bills and resolutions referred to the committee under section 401(b)(2) of that Act (but subject to the provisions of section 401(b)(3) of that Act).

(c)(1) Committee on Armed Services, to which committee shall be referred all proposed legislation, messages, petitions, memorials, and other matters relating to the following subjects:

1. Aeronautical and space activities peculiar to or primarily associated with the development of weapons systems or military operations.

2. Common defense.

3. Department of Defense, the Department of the Army, the Department of the Navy, and the Department of the Air Force, generally.

4. Maintenance and operation of the Panama Canal, including administration, sanitation, and government of the Canal Zone.

5. Military research and development.

6. National security aspects of nuclear energy.

7. Naval petroleum reserves, except those in Alaska.

8. Pay, promotion, retirement, and other benefits and privileges of members of the Armed Forces, including overseas education of civilian and military dependents.

9. Selective service system.

10. Strategic and critical materials necessary for the common defense.

(2) Such committee shall also study and review, on a comprehensive basis, matters relating to the common defense policy of the United States, and report thereon from time to time.

(d)(1) Committee on Banking, Housing, and Urban Affairs, to which committee shall be referred all proposed legislation, messages, petitions, memorials, and other matters relating to the following subjects:

1. Banks, banking, and financial institutions.

2. Control of prices of commodities, rents, and services.

3. Deposit insurance.

4. Economic stabilization and defense production.

5. Export and foreign trade promotion.

6. Export controls.

7. Federal monetary policy, including Federal Reserve System.

8. Financial aid to commerce and industry.

9. Issuance and redemption of notes.

10. Money and credit, including currency and coinage.

11. Nursing home construction.

12. Public and private housing (including veterans' housing).

13. Renegotiation of Government contracts.

14. Urban development and urban mass transit.

(2) Such committee shall also study and review, on a comprehensive basis, matters relating to international economic policy as it affects United States monetary affairs, credit, and financial institutions; economic growth, urban affairs, and credit, and report thereon from time to time.

(e)(1) Committee on the Budget, to which committee shall be referred all concurrent resolutions on the budget (as defined in section 3(a)(4) of the Congressional Budget Act of 1974) and all other matters required to be referred to that committee under titles III and IV of that Act, and messages, petitions, memorials, and other matters relating thereto.

(2) Such committee shall have the duty

(A) to report the matters required to be reported by it under titles III and IV of the Congressional Budget Act of 1974;

(B) to make continuing studies of the effect on budget outlays of relevant existing and proposed legislation and to report the results of such studies to the Senate on a recurring basis;

(C) to request and evaluate continuing studies of tax expenditures, to devise methods of coordinating tax expenditures, policies, and programs with direct budget outlays, and to report the results of such studies to the Senate on a recurring basis; and

(D) to review, on a continuing basis, the conduct by the Congressional Budget Office of its functions and duties.

(f)(1) Committee on Commerce, Science, and Transportation, to which committee shall be referred all proposed legislation, messages, petitions, memorials, and other matters relating to the following subjects:

1. Coast Guard.

2. Coastal zone management.

3. Communications.

4. Highway safety.

5. Inland waterways, except construction.

6. Interstate commerce.

7. Marine and ocean navigation, safety, and transportation, including navigational aspects of deepwater ports.

8. Marine fisheries.

9. Merchant marine and navigation.

10. Nonmilitary aeronautical and space sciences.

11. Oceans, weather, and atmospheric activities.

12. Panama Canal and interoceanic canals generally, except as provided in subparagraph (c).

13. Regulation of consumer products and services, including testing related to toxic substances, other than pesticides, and except for credit, financial services, and housing.

14. Regulation of interstate common carriers, including railroads, buses, trucks, vessels, pipelines, and civil aviation.

15. Science, engineering, and technology research and development and policy.

16. Sports.

17. Standards and measurement.

18. Transportation.

19. Transportation and commerce aspects of Outer Continental Shelf lands.

(2) Such committee shall also study and review, on a comprehensive basis, all matters relating to science and technology, oceans policy, transportation, communications, and consumer affairs, and report thereon from time to time.

(g)(1) Committee on Energy and Natural Resources, to which committee shall be referred all proposed legislation, messages, petitions, memorials, and other matters relating to the following subjects:

1. Coal production, distribution, and utilization.

2. Energy policy.

3. Energy regulation and conservation.

4. Energy related aspects of deepwater ports.

5. Energy research and development.

6. Extraction of minerals from oceans and Outer Continental Shelf lands.

7. Hydroelectric power, irrigation, and reclamation.

8. Mining education and research.

9. Mining, mineral lands, mining claims, and mineral conservation.

10. National parks, recreation areas, wilderness areas, wild and scenic rivers, historical sites, military parks and battlefields, and on the public domain, preservation of prehistoric ruins and objects of interest.

11. Naval petroleum reserves in Alaska.

12. Nonmilitary development of nuclear energy.

13. Oil and gas production and distribution.

14. Public lands and forests, including farming and grazing thereon, and mineral extraction therefrom.

15. Solar energy systems.

16. Territorial possessions of the United States, including trusteeships.

(2) Such committee shall also study and review, on a comprehensive basis, matters relating to energy and resources development, and report thereon from time to time.

(h)(1) Committee on Environment and Public Works, to which committee shall be referred all proposed legislation, messages, petitions, memorials, and other matters relating to the following subjects:

1. Air pollution.

2. Construction and maintenance of highways.

3. Environmental aspects of Outer Continental Shelf lands.

4. Environmental effects of toxic substances, other than pesticides.

5. Environmental policy.

6. Environmental research and development.

7. Fisheries and wildlife.

8. Flood control and improvements of rivers and harbors, including environmental aspects of deepwater ports.

9. Noise pollution.

10. Nonmilitary environmental regulation and control of nuclear energy.

11. Ocean dumping.

12. Public buildings and improved grounds of the United States generally, including Federal buildings in the District of Columbia.

13. Public works, bridges, and dams.

14. Regional economic development.

15. Solid waste disposal and recycling.

16. Water pollution.

17. Water resources.

(2) Such committee shall also study and review, on a comprehensive basis, matters relating to environmental protection and resource utilization and conservation, and report thereon from time to time.

(i) Committee on Finance, to which committee shall be referred all proposed legislation, messages, petitions, memorials, and other matters relating to the following subjects:

1. Bonded debt of the United States, except as provided in the Congressional Budget Act of 1974.

2. Customs, collection districts, and ports of entry and delivery.

3. Deposit of public moneys.

4. General revenue sharing.

5. Health programs under the Social Security Act and health programs financed by a specific tax or trust fund.

6. National social security.

7. Reciprocal trade agreements.

8. Revenue measures generally, except as provided in the Congressional Budget Act of 1974.

9. Revenue measures relating to the insular possessions.

10. Tariffs and import quotas, and matters related thereto.

11. Transportation of dutiable goods.

(j)(1) Committee on Foreign Relations, to which committee shall be referred all proposed legislation, messages, petitions, memorials, and other matters relating to the following subjects:

1. Acquisition of land and buildings for embassies and legations in foreign countries.

2. Boundaries of the United States.

3. Diplomatic service.

4. Foreign economic, military, technical, and humanitarian assistance.

5. Foreign loans.

6. International activities of the American National Red Cross and the International Committee of the Red Cross.

7. International aspects of nuclear energy, including nuclear transfer policy.

8. International conferences and congresses.

9. International law as it relates to foreign policy.

10. International Monetary Fund and other international organizations established primarily for international monetary purposes (except that, at the request of the Committee on Banking, Housing, and Urban Affairs, any proposed legislation relating to such subjects reported by the Committee on Foreign Relations shall be referred to the Committee on Banking, Housing, and Urban Affairs).

11. Intervention abroad and declarations of war.

12. Measures to foster commercial intercourse with foreign nations and to safeguard American business interests abroad.

13. National security and international aspects of trusteeships of the United States.

14. Oceans and international environmental and scientific affairs as they relate to foreign policy.

15. Protection of United States citizens abroad and expatriation.

16. Relations of the United States with foreign nations generally.

17. Treaties and executive agreements, except reciprocal trade agreements.

18. United Nations and its affiliated organizations.

19. World Bank group, the regional development banks, and other international organizations established primarily for development assistance purposes.

(2) Such committee shall also study and review, on a comprehensive basis, matters relating to the national security policy, foreign policy, and international economic policy as it relates to foreign policy of the United States, and matters relating to food, hunger, and nutrition in foreign countries, and report thereon from time to time.

(k)(1) Committee on Governmental Affairs, to which committee shall be referred all proposed legislation, messages, petitions, memorials, and other matters relating to the following subjects:

1. Archives of the United States.

2. Budget and accounting measures, other than appropriations, except as provided in the Congressional Budget Act of 1974.

3. Census and collection of statistics, including economic and social statistics.

4. Congressional organization, except for any part of the matter that amends the rules or orders of the Senate.

5. Federal Civil Service.

6. Government information.

7. Intergovernmental relations.

8. Municipal affairs of the District of Columbia, except appropriations therefor.

9. Organization and management of United States nuclear export policy.

10. Organization and reorganization of the executive branch of the Government.

11. Postal Service.

12. Status of officers and employees of the United States, including their classification, compensation, and benefits.

(2) Such committee shall have the duty of

(A) receiving and examining reports of the Comptroller General of the United States and of submitting such recommendations to the Senate as it deems necessary or desirable in connection with the subject matter of such reports;

(B) studying the efficiency, economy, and effectiveness of all agencies and departments of the Government;

(C) evaluating the effects of laws enacted to reorganize the legislative and executive branches of the Government; and

(D) studying the intergovernmental relationships between the United States and the States and municipalities, and between the United States and international organizations of which the United States is a member.

(l) Committee on the Judiciary, to which committee shall be referred all proposed legislation, messages, petitions, memorials, and other matters relating to the following subjects:

1. Apportionment of Representatives.

2. Bankruptcy, mutiny, espionage, and counterfeiting.

3. Civil liberties.

4. Constitutional amendments.

5. Federal courts and judges.

6. Government information.

7. Holidays and celebrations.

8. Immigration and naturalization.

9. Interstate compacts generally.

10. Judicial proceedings, civil and criminal, generally.

11. Local courts in the territories and possessions.

12. Measures relating to claims against the United States.

13. National penitentiaries.

14. Patent Office.

15. Patents, copyrights, and trademarks.

16. Protection of trade and commerce against unlawful restraints and monopolies.

17. Revision and codification of the statutes of the United States.

18. State and territorial boundary lines.

(m)(1) Committee on Health, Education, Labor and Pensions, to which committee shall be referred all proposed legislation, messages, petitions, memorials, and other matters relating to the following subjects:

1. Measures relating to education, labor, health, and public welfare.

2. Aging.

3. Agricultural colleges.

4. Arts and humanities.

5. Biomedical research and development.

6. Child labor.

7. Convict labor and the entry of goods made by convicts into interstate commerce.

8. Domestic activities of the American National Red Cross.

9. Equal employment opportunity.

10. Gallaudet College, Howard University, and Saint Elizabeths Hospital.

11. Individuals with disabilities.

12. Labor standards and labor statistics.

13. Mediation and arbitration of labor disputes.

14. Occupational safety and health, including the welfare of miners.

15. Private pension plans.

16. Public health.

17. Railway labor and retirement.

18. Regulation of foreign laborers.

19. Student loans.

20. Wages and hours of labor.

(2) Such committee shall also study and review, on a comprehensive basis, matters relating to health, education and training, and public welfare, and report thereon from time to time.

(n)(1) Committee on Rules and Administration, to which committee shall be referred all proposed legislation, messages, petitions, memorials, and other matters relating to the following subjects:

1. Administration of the Senate Office Buildings and the Senate wing of the Capitol, including the assignment of office space.

2. Congressional organization relative to rules and procedures, and Senate rules and regulations, including floor and gallery rules.

3. Corrupt practices.

4. Credentials and qualifications of Members of the Senate, contested elections, and acceptance of incompatible offices.

5. Federal elections generally, including the election of the President, Vice President, and Members of the Congress.

6. Government Printing Office, and the printing and correction of the Congressional Record, as well as those matters provided for under rule XI.

7. Meetings of the Congress and attendance of Members.

8. Payment of money out of the contingent fund of the Senate or creating a charge upon the same (except that any resolution relating to substantive matter within the jurisdiction of any other standing committee of the Senate shall be first referred to such committee).

9. Presidential succession.

10. Purchase of books and manuscripts and erection of monuments to the memory of individuals.

11. Senate Library and statuary, art, and pictures in the Capitol and Senate Office Buildings.

12. Services to the Senate, including the Senate restaurant.

13. United States Capitol and congressional office buildings, the Library of Congress, the Smithsonian Institution (and the incorporation of similar institutions), and the Botanic Gardens.

(2) Such committee shall also

(A) make a continuing study of the organization and operation of the Congress of the United States and shall recommend improvements in such organization and operation with a view toward strengthening the Congress, simplifying its operations, improving its relationships with other branches of the United States Government, and enabling it better to meet its responsibilities under the Constitution of the United States;

(B) identify any court proceeding or action which, in the opinion of the Committee, is of vital interest to the Congress as a constitutionally established institution of the Federal Government and call such proceeding or action to the attention of the Senate; and develop, implement, and update as necessary a strategy planning process and a strategic plan for the functional and technical infrastructure support of the Senate and provide oversight over plans developed by Senate officers and others in accordance with the strategic planning process.

(o)(1) Committee on Small Business, to which committee shall be referred all proposed legislation, messages, petitions, memorials, and other matters relating to the Small Business Administration.

(2) Any proposed legislation reported by such committee which relates to matters other than the functions of the Small Business Administration shall, at the request of the chairman of any standing committee having jurisdiction over the subject matter extraneous to the functions of the Small Business Administration, be considered and reported by such standing committee prior to its consideration by the Senate; and likewise measures reported by other committees directly relating to the Small Business Administration shall, at the request of the chairman of the Committee on Small Business, be referred to the Committee on Small Business for its consideration of any portions of the measure dealing with the Small Business Administration, and be reported by this committee prior to its consideration by the Senate.

(3) Such committee shall also study and survey by means of research and investigation all problems of American small business enterprises, and report thereon from time to time.

(p) Committee on Veterans' Affairs, to which committee shall be referred all proposed legislation, messages, petitions, memorials, and other matters relating to the following subjects:

　1. Compensation of veterans.

　2. Life insurance issued by the Government on account of service in the Armed Forces.

　3. National cemeteries.

　4. Pensions of all wars of the United States, general and special.

　5. Readjustment of servicemen to civil life.

　6. Soldiers' and sailors' civil relief.

　7. Veterans' hospitals, medical care and treatment of veterans.

　8. Veterans' measures generally.

　9. Vocational rehabilitation and education of veterans.

2. Except as otherwise provided by paragraph 4 of this rule, each of the following standing committees shall consist of the number of Senators set forth in the following table on the line on which the name of that committee appears:

Committee / Members

Agriculture, Nutrition, and Forestry / 18

Appropriations / 28

Armed Services / 18

Banking, Housing, and Urban Affairs / 18

Commerce, Science, and Transportation / 20

Energy and Natural Resources / 20

Environment and Public Works / 18

Finance / 20

Foreign Relations / 18

Governmental Affairs / 16

Judiciary / 18

H.E.L.P. / 18

3.(a) Except as otherwise provided by paragraph 4 of this rule, each of the following standing committees shall consist of the number of Senators set forth in the following table on the line on which the name of that committee appears:

Committee / Members

Budget / 22

Rules and Administration / 16

Veterans' Affairs / 12

Small Business / 18

(b) Each of the following committees and joint committees shall consist of the number of Senators (or Senate members, in the case of a joint committee) set forth in the following table on the line on which the name of that committee appears:

Committee / Members

Aging / 18

Intelligence / 19

Joint Economic Committee / 10

(c) Each of the following committees and joint committees shall consist of the number of Senators (or Senate members, in the case of a joint committee) set forth in the following table on the line on which the name of that committee appears:

Committee / Members

Ethics / 6

Indian Affairs / 14

Joint Committee on Taxation / 5

4.(a) Except as otherwise provided by this paragraph

(1) each Senator shall serve on two and no more committees listed in paragraph 2; and

(2) each Senator may serve on only one committee listed in paragraph 3 (a) or (b).

(b)(1) Each Senator may serve on not more than three subcommittees of each committee (other than the Committee on Appropriations) listed in paragraph 2 of which he is a member.

(2) Each Senator may serve on not more than two subcommittees of a committee listed in paragraph 3 (a) or (b) of which he is a member.

(3) Notwithstanding subparagraphs (1) and (2), a Senator serving as chairman or ranking minority member of a standing, select, or special committee of the Senate or joint committee of the Congress may serve ex officio, without vote, as a member of any subcommittee of such committee or joint committee.

(4) No committee of the Senate may establish any subunit of that committee other than a subcommittee, unless the Senate by resolution has given permission therefor. For purposes of this subparagraph, any subunit of a joint committee shall be treated as a subcommittee.

(c) By agreement entered into by the majority leader and the minority leader, the membership of one or more standing committees may be increased temporarily from time to time by such number or numbers as may be required to accord to the majority party a majority of the membership of all standing committees. When any such temporary increase is necessary to accord to the majority party a majority of the membership of all standing committees, members of the majority party in such number as may be required for that purpose may serve as members of three standing committees listed in paragraph 2. No such temporary increase in the membership of any standing committee under this subparagraph shall be continued in effect after the need therefor has ended. No standing committee may be increased in membership under this subparagraph by more than two members in excess of the number prescribed for that committee by paragraph 2 or 3(a).

(d) A Senator may serve as a member of any joint committee of the Congress the Senate members of which are required by law to be appointed from a standing committee of the Senate of which he is a member, and service as a member of any such joint committee shall not be taken into account for purposes of subparagraph (a)(2).

(e)(1) No Senator shall serve at any time as chairman of more than one standing, select, or special committee of the Senate or joint committee of the Congress, except that a Senator may serve as chairman of any joint committee of the Congress having jurisdiction with respect to a subject matter which is directly related to the jurisdiction of a standing committee of which he is chairman.

(2) No Senator shall serve at any time as chairman of more than one subcommittee of each standing, select, or special committee of the Senate or joint committee of the Congress of which he is a member.

(3) A Senator who is serving as the chairman of a committee listed in paragraph 2 may serve at any time as the chairman of only one subcommittee of all committees listed in paragraph 2 of which he is a member and may serve at any time as the chairman of only one subcommittee of each committee listed in paragraph 3 (a) or (b) of which he is a member. A Senator who is serving as the chairman of a committee listed in paragraph 3 (a) or (b) may not serve as the chairman of any subcommittee of that committee, and may serve at any time as the chairman of only one subcommittee of each committee listed in paragraph 2 of which he is a member. Any other Senator may serve as the chairman of only one subcommittee of each committee listed in paragraph 2, 3(a), or 3(b) of which he is a member.

(f) A Senator serving on the Committee on Rules and Administration may not serve on any joint committee of the Congress unless the Senate members thereof are required by law to be appointed from the Committee on Rules and Administration, or unless such Senator served on the Committee on Rules and Administration and the Joint Committee on Taxation on the last day of the Ninety-eighth Congress.

(g) A Senator who on the day preceding the effective date of title I of the Committee System Reorganization Amendments of 1977 was serving as the chairman or ranking minority member of the Committee on the District of Columbia or the Committee on Post Office and Civil Service may serve on the Committee on Governmental Affairs in addition to serving on two other standing committees listed in paragraph 2. At the request of any such Senator, he shall be appointed to serve on such committee but, while serving on such committee and two other standing committees listed in paragraph 2, he may not serve on any committee listed in paragraph 3 (a) or (b) other than the Committee on Rules and Administration. The preceding provisions of this subparagraph shall apply with respect to any Senator only so long as his service as a member of the Committee on Governmental Affairs is continuous after the date on which the appointment of the majority and minority members of the Committee on Governmental Affairs is initially completed.

RULE XXVI

COMMITTEE PROCEDURE

1. Each standing committee, including any subcommittee of any such committee, is authorized to hold such hearings, to sit and act at such times and places during the sessions, recesses, and adjourned periods of the Senate, to require by subpena or otherwise the attendance of such witnesses and the production of such correspondence, books, papers, and documents, to take such testimony and to make such expenditures out of the contingent fund of the Senate as may be authorized by resolutions of the Senate. Each such committee may make investigations into any matter within its jurisdiction, may report such hearings as may be had by it, and may employ stenographic assistance at a cost not exceeding the amount prescribed by the Committee on Rules and Administration. The expenses of the committee shall be paid from the contingent fund of the Senate upon vouchers approved by the chairman.

2. Each committee shall adopt rules (not inconsistent with the Rules of the Senate) governing the procedure of such committee. The rules of each committee shall be published in the Congressional Record not later than March 1 of the first year of each Congress, except that if any such committee is established on or after February 1 of a year, the rules of that committee during the year of establishment shall be published in the Congressional Record not later than sixty days after such establishment. Any amendment to the rules of a committee shall not take effect until the amendment is published in the Congressional Record.

3. Each standing committee (except the Committee on Appropriations) shall fix regular weekly, biweekly, or monthly meeting days for the transaction of business before the committee and additional meetings may be called by the chairman as he may deem necessary. If at least three members of any such committee desire that a special meeting of the committee be called by the chairman, those members may file in the offices of the committee their written request to the chairman for that special meeting. Immediately upon the filing of the request, the clerk of the committee shall notify the chairman of the filing of the request. If, within three calendar days after the filing of the request, the chairman does not call the requested special meeting, to be held within seven calendar days after the filing of the request, a majority of the members of the committee may file in the offices of the committee their written notice that a special meeting of the committee will be held, specifying the date and hour of that special meeting. The committee shall meet on that date and hour. Immediately upon the filing of the notice, the clerk of the committee shall notify all members of the committee that such special meeting will be held and inform them of its date and hour. If the chairman of any such committee is not present at any regular, additional, or special meeting of the committee, the ranking member of the majority party on the committee who is present shall preside at that meeting.

4. (a) Each committee (except the Committee on Appropriations and the Committee on the Budget) shall make public announcement of the date, place, and

subject matter of any hearing to be conducted by the committee on any measure or matter at least one week before the commencement of that hearing unless the committee determines that there is good cause to begin such hearing at an earlier date.

(b) Each committee (except the Committee on Appropriations) shall require each witness who is to appear before the committee in any hearing to file with the clerk of the committee, at least one day before the date of the appearance of that witness, a written statement of his proposed testimony unless the committee chairman and the ranking minority member determine that there is good cause for noncompliance. If so requested by any committee, the staff of the committee shall prepare for the use of the members of the committee before each day of hearing before the committee a digest of the statements which have been so filed by witnesses who are to appear before the committee on that day.

(c) After the conclusion of each day of hearing, if so requested by any committee, the staff shall prepare for the use of the members of the committee a summary of the testimony given before the committee on that day. After approval by the chairman and the ranking minority member of the committee, each such summary may be printed as a part of the committee hearings if such hearings are ordered by the committee to be printed.

(d) Whenever any hearing is conducted by a committee (except the Committee on Appropriations) upon any measure or matter, the minority on the committee shall be entitled, upon request made by a majority of the minority members to the chairman before the completion of such hearing, to call witnesses selected by the minority to testify with respect to the measure or matter during at least one day of hearing thereon.

5. (a) Notwithstanding any other provision of the rules, when the Senate is in session, no committee of the Senate or any subcommittee thereof may meet, without special leave, after the conclusion of the first two hours after the meeting of the Senate commenced and in no case after two o'clock postmeridian unless consent therefor has been obtained from the majority leader and the minority leader (or in the event of the absence of either of such leaders, from his designee). The prohibition contained in the preceding sentence shall not apply to the Committee on Appropriations or the Committee on the Budget. The majority leader or his designee shall announce to the Senate whenever consent has been given under this subparagraph and shall state the time and place of such meeting. The right to make such announcement of consent shall have the same priority as the filing of a cloture motion.

(b) Each meeting of a committee, or any subcommittee thereof, including meetings to conduct hearings, shall be open to the public, except that a meeting or series of meetings by a committee or a subcommittee thereof on the same subject for a period of no more than fourteen calendar days may be closed to the public on a motion made and seconded to go into closed session to discuss only whether the matters enumerated in clauses (1) through (6) would require the meeting to be closed, followed immediately by a record vote in open session by a majority of the members of the committee or subcommittee when it is determined that the matters to be discussed or the testimony to be taken at such meeting or meetings

(1) will disclose matters necessary to be kept secret in the interests of national defense or the confidential conduct of the foreign relations of the United States;

(2) will relate solely to matters of committee staff personnel or internal staff management or procedure;

(3) will tend to charge an individual with crime or misconduct, to disgrace or injure the professional standing of an individual, or otherwise to expose an individual to public contempt or obloquy, or will represent a clearly unwarranted invasion of the privacy of an individual;

(4) will disclose the identity of any informer or law enforcement agent or will disclose any information relating to the investigation or prosecution of a criminal offense that is required to be kept secret in the interests of effective law enforcement;

(5) will disclose information relating to the trade secrets of financial or commercial information pertaining specifically to a given person if

(A) an Act of Congress requires the information to be kept confidential by Government officers and employees; or

(B) the information has been obtained by the Government on a confidential basis, other than through an application by such person for a specific Government financial or other benefit, and is required to be kept secret in order to prevent undue injury to the competitive position of such person; or

(6) may divulge matters required to be kept confidential under other provisions of law or Government regulations.

(c) Whenever any hearing conducted by any such committee or subcommittee is open to the public, that hearing may be broadcast by radio or television, or both, under such rules as the committee or subcommittee may adopt.

(d) Whenever disorder arises during a committee meeting that is open to the public, or any demonstration of approval or disapproval is indulged in by any person in attendance at any such meeting, it shall be the duty of the Chair to enforce order on his own initiative and without any point of order being made by a Senator. When the Chair finds it necessary to maintain order, he shall have the power to clear the room, and the committee may act in closed session for so long as there is doubt of the assurance of order.

(e) (1) Each committee shall prepare and keep a complete transcript or electronic recording adequate to fully record the proceeding of each meeting or conference whether or not such meeting or any part thereof is closed under this paragraph, unless a majority of its members vote to forgo such a record.

(2)(A) Except with respect to meetings closed in accordance with this rule, each committee and subcommittee shall make publicly available through the internet a video recording, audio recording, or transcript of any meeting not later than 21 business days after the meeting occurs.

(B) information required by subclause (A) shall be available until the end of the Congress following the date of the meeting.

(C) The Committee on Rules and Administration may waive this clause upon request based on the inability of a committee or subcommittee to comply with this clause due to technical or logistical reasons.

6. Morning meetings of committees and subcommittees thereof shall be scheduled for one or both of the periods prescribed in this paragraph. The first period shall end at eleven o'clock antemeridian. The second period shall begin at eleven o'clock antemeridian and end at two o'clock postmeridian.

7. (a)(1) Except as provided in this paragraph, each committee, and each subcommittee thereof is authorized to fix the number of its members (but not less than one-third of its entire membership) who shall constitute a quorum thereof for the transaction of such business as may be considered by said committee, except that no measure or matter or recommendation shall be reported from any committee unless a majority of the committee were physically present.

(2) Each such committee, or subcommittee, is authorized to fix a lesser number than one-third of its entire membership who shall constitute a quorum thereof for the purpose of taking sworn testimony.

(3) The vote of any committee to report a measure or matter shall require the concurrence of a majority of the members of the committee who are present. No vote of any member of any committee to report a measure or matter may be cast by proxy if rules adopted by such committee forbid the casting of votes for that purpose by proxy; however, proxies may not be voted when the absent committee member has not been informed of the matter on which he is being recorded and has not affirmatively requested that he be so recorded. Action by any committee in reporting any measure or matter in accordance with the requirements of this subparagraph shall constitute the ratification by the committee of all action theretofore taken by the committee with respect to that measure or matter, including votes taken upon the measure or matter or any amendment thereto, and no point of order shall lie with respect to that measure or matter on the ground that such previous action with respect thereto by such committee was not taken in compliance with such requirements.

(b) Each committee (except the Committee on Appropriations) shall keep a complete record of all committee action. Such record shall include a record of the votes on any question on which a record vote is demanded. The results of rollcall votes taken in any meeting of any committee upon any measure, or any amendment thereto, shall be announced in the committee report on that measure unless previously announced by the committee, and such announcement shall include a tabulation of the votes cast in favor of and the votes cast in opposition to each such measure and amendment by each member of the committee who was present at that meeting.

(c) Whenever any committee by rollcall vote reports any measure or matter, the report of the committee upon such measure or matter shall include a tabulation of the votes cast by each member of the committee in favor of and in opposition to such measure or matter. Nothing contained in this subparagraph shall abrogate the power of any committee to adopt rules (1) providing for proxy voting on all matters other than the reporting of a measure of matter, or (2) providing in accordance with subparagraph (a) for a lesser number as a quorum for any action other than the reporting of a measure or matter.

8. (a) In order to assist the Senate in —

(1) its analysis, appraisal, and evaluation of the application, administration, and execution of the laws enacted by the Congress, and

(2) its formulation, consideration, and enactment of such modifications of or changes in those laws, and of such additional legislation, as may be necessary or appropriate, each standing committee (except the Committees on Appropriations and the Budget), shall review and study, on a continuing basis the application, administration, and execution of those laws, or parts of laws, the subject matter of which is within the legislative jurisdiction of that committee. Such committees may carry out the required analysis, appraisal, and evaluation themselves, or by contract, or may require a Government agency to do so and furnish a report thereon to the Senate. Such committees may rely on such techniques as pilot testing, analysis of costs in comparison with benefits, or provision for evaluation after a defined period of time.

(b) In each odd-numbered year, each such committee shall submit, not later than March 31, to the Senate, a report on the activities of that committee under this paragraph during the Congress ending at noon on January 3 of such year.

9. (a) Except as provided in subparagraph (b), each committee shall report one authorization resolution each year authorizing the committee to make expenditures out of the contingent fund of the Senate to defray its expenses, including the compensation of members of its staff and agency contributions related to such compensation, during the period beginning on March 1 of such year and ending on the last day of February of the following year. Such annual authorization resolution shall be reported not later than January 31 of each year, except that, whenever the designation of members of standing committees of the Senate occurs during the first session of a Congress at a date later than January 20, such resolution may be reported at any time within thirty days after the date on which the designation of such members is completed. After the annual authorization resolution of a committee for a year has been agreed to, such committee may procure authorization to make additional expenditures out of the contingent fund of the

Senate during that year only by reporting a supplemental authorization resolution. Each supplemental authorization resolution reported by a committee shall amend the annual authorization resolution of such committee for that year and shall be accompanied by a report specifying with particularity the purpose for which such authorization is sought and the reason why such authorization could not have been sought at the time of the submission by such committee of its annual authorization resolution for that year.

(b) In lieu of the procedure provided in subparagraph (a), the Committee on Rules and Administration may

(1) direct each committee to report an authorization resolution for a two-year budget period beginning on March 1 of the first session of a Congress; and

(2) report one authorization resolution containing more than one committee authorization resolution for a one-year or two-year budget period.

10. (a) All committee hearings, records, data, charts, and files shall be kept separate and distinct from the congressional office records of the Member serving as chairman of the committee; and such records shall be the property of the Senate and all members of the committee and the Senate shall have access to such records. Each committee is authorized to have printed and bound such testimony and other data presented at hearings held by the committee.

(b) It shall be the duty of the chairman of each committee to report or cause to be reported promptly to the Senate any measure approved by his committee and to take or cause to be taken necessary steps to bring the matter to a vote. In any event, the report of any committee upon a measure which has been approved by the committee shall be filed within seven calendar days (exclusive of days on which the Senate is not in session) after the day on which there has been filed with the clerk of the committee a written and signed request of a majority of the committee for the reporting of that measure. Upon the filing of any such request, the clerk of the committee shall transmit immediately to the chairman of the committee notice of the filing of that request. This subparagraph does not apply to the Committee on Appropriations.

(c) If at the time of approval of a measure or matter by any committee (except for the Committee on Appropriations), any member of the committee gives notice of intention to file supplemental, minority, or additional views, that member shall be entitled to not less than three calendar days in which to file such views, in writing, with the clerk of the committee. All such views so filed by one or more members of the committee shall be included within, and shall be a part of, the report filed by the committee with respect to that measure or matter. The report of the committee upon that measure or matter shall be printed in a single volume which

(1) shall include all supplemental, minority, or additional views which have been submitted by the time of the filing of the report, and

(2) shall bear upon its cover a recital that supplemental, minority, or additional views are included as part of the report.

This subparagraph does not preclude

(A) the immediate filing and printing of a committee report unless timely request for the opportunity to file supplemental, minority, or additional views has been made as provided by this subparagraph; or

(B) the filing by any such committee of any supplemental report upon any measure or matter which may be required for the correction of any technical error in a previous report made by that committee upon that measure or matter.

11. (a) The report accompanying each bill or joint resolution of a public character reported by any committee (except the Committee on Appropriations and the Committee on the Budget) shall contain

(1) an estimate, made by such committee, of the costs which would be incurred in carrying out such bill or joint resolution in the fiscal year in which it is reported and in each of the five fiscal years following such fiscal year (or for the authorized duration of any program authorized by such bill or joint resolution, if less than five years), except that, in the case of measures affecting the revenues, such reports shall require only an estimate of the gain or loss in revenues for a one year period; and

(2) a comparison of the estimate of costs described in subparagraph (1) made by such committee with any estimate of costs made by any Federal agency; or

(3) in lieu of such estimate or comparison, or both, a statement of the reasons why compliance by the committee with the requirements of subparagraph (1) or (2), or both, is impracticable.

(b) Each such report (except those by the Committee on Appropriations) shall also contain

(1) an evaluation, made by such committee, of the regulatory impact which would be incurred in carrying out the bill or joint resolution. The evaluation shall include (A) an estimate of the numbers of individuals and businesses who would be regulated and a determination of the groups and classes of such individuals and businesses, (B) a determination of the economic impact of such regulation on the individuals, consumers, and businesses affected, (C) a determination of the impact on the personal privacy of the individuals affected, and (D) a determination of the amount of additional paperwork that will result from the regulations to be promulgated pursuant to the bill or joint resolution, which determination may include, but need not be limited to, estimates of the amount of time and financial costs required of affected parties, showing whether the effects of the bill or joint resolution could be substantial, as well as reasonable estimates of the recordkeeping requirements that may be associated with the bill or joint resolution; or

(2) in lieu of such evaluation, a statement of the reasons why compliance by the committee with the requirements of clause (1) is impracticable.

(c) It shall not be in order for the Senate to consider any such bill or joint resolution if the report of the committee on such bill or joint resolution does not comply with the provisions of subparagraphs (a) and (b) on the objection of any Senator.

12. Whenever a committee reports a bill or a joint resolution repealing or amending any statute or part thereof it shall make a report thereon and shall include in such report or in an accompanying document (to be prepared by the staff of such committee) (a) the text of the statute or part thereof which is proposed to be repealed; and (b) a comparative print of that part of the bill or joint resolution making the amendment and of the statute or part thereof proposed to be amended, showing by strickenthrough type and italics, parallel columns, or other appropriate typographical devices the omissions and insertions which would be made by the bill or joint resolution if enacted in the form recommended by the committee. This paragraph shall not apply to any such report in which it is stated that, in the opinion of the committee, it is necessary to dispense with the requirements of this subsection to expedite the business of the Senate.

13.(a) Each committee (except the Committee on Appropriations) which has legislative jurisdiction shall, in its consideration of all bills and joint resolutions of a public character within its jurisdiction, endeavor to insure that

(1) all continuing programs of the Federal Government and of the government of the District of Columbia, within the jurisdiction of such committee or joint committee, are designed; and

(2) all continuing activities of Federal agencies, within the jurisdiction of such committee or joint committee, are carried on; so that, to the extent consistent with the nature, requirements, and objectives of those programs and activities, appropriations therefor will be made annually.

(b) Each committee (except the Committee on Appropriations) shall with respect to any continuing program within its jurisdiction for which appropriations are not made annually, review such program, from time to time, in order to ascertain whether such program could be modified so that appropriations therefore would be made annually.

RULE XXVIII

CONFERENCE COMMITTEES; REPORTS; OPEN MEETINGS

1. The presentation of reports of committees of conference shall always be in order when available on each Senator's desk, except when the Journal is being read or a question of order or a motion to adjourn is pending, or while the Senate is voting or ascertaining the presence of a quorum; and when received the question of

proceeding to the consideration of the report, if raised, shall be immediately put, and shall be determined without debate.

2. (a) When a message from the House of Representatives is laid before the Senate, it shall be in order for a single, non-divisible motion to be made that includes-

(1) a motion to disagree to a House amendment or insist upon a Senate amendment;

(2) a motion to request a committee of conference with the House or to agree to a request by the House for a committee of conference; and

(3) a motion to authorize the Presiding Officer to appoint conferees (or a motion to appoint conferees).

(b) If a cloture motion is presented on a motion made pursuant to subparagraph (a), the motion shall be debatable for no more than 2 hours, equally divided in the usual form, after which the Presiding Officer, or the clerk at the direction of the Presiding Officer, shall lay the motion before the Senate. If cloture is then invoked on the motion, the question shall be on the motion, without further debate.

3. (a) Conferees shall not insert in their report matter not committed to them by either House, nor shall they strike from the bill matter agreed to by both Houses.

(b) If matter which was agreed to by both Houses is stricken from the bill a point of order may be made against the report, and if the point of order is sustained, the report is rejected or shall be recommitted to the committee of conference if the House of Representatives has not already acted thereon.

(c) If new matter is inserted in the report, a point of order may be made against the conference report and it shall be disposed of as provided under paragraph 5.

4. (a) In any case in which a disagreement to an amendment in the nature of a substitute has been referred to conferees—

(1) it shall be in order for the conferees to report a substitute on the same subject matter;

(2) the conferees may not include in the report matter not committed to them by either House; and

(3) the conferees may include in their report in any such case matter which is a germane modification of subjects in disagreement.

(b) In any case in which the conferees violate subparagraph (a), a point of order may be made against the conference report and it shall be disposed of as provided under paragraph 5.

5. (a) A Senator may raise a point of order that one or more provisions of a conference report violates paragraph 3 or paragraph 4, as the case may be. The

Presiding Officer may sustain the point of order as to some or all of the provisions against which the Senator raised the point of order.

(b) If the Presiding Officer sustains the point of order as to any of the provisions against which the Senator raised the point of order, then those provisions against which the Presiding Officer sustains the point of order shall be stricken. After all other points of order under this paragraph have been disposed of-

(1) the Senate shall proceed to consider the question of whether the Senate should recede from its amendment to the House bill, or its disagreement to the amendment of the House, and concur with a further amendment, which further amendment shall consist of only that portion of the conference report that has not been stricken;

(2) the question in clause (1) shall be decided under the same debate limitation as the conference report; and

(3) no further amendment shall be in order.

6. (a) Any Senator may move to waive any or all points of order under paragraph 3 or 4 with respect to the pending conference report by an affirmative vote of three-fifths of the Members, duly chosen and sworn. All motions to waive under this paragraph shall be debatable collectively for not to exceed 1 hour equally divided between the Majority Leader and the Minority Leader or their designees. A motion to waive all points of order under this paragraph shall not be amendable.

(b) All appeals from rulings of the Chair under paragraph 5 shall be debatable collectively for not to exceed 1 hour, equally divided between the Majority and the Minority Leader or their designees. An affirmative vote of three-fifths of the Members of the Senate, duly chosen and sworn, shall be required in the Senate to sustain an appeal of the ruling of the Chair under paragraph 5.

7. Each report made by a committee of conference to the Senate shall be printed as a report of the Senate. As so printed, such report shall be accompanied by an explanatory statement prepared jointly by the conferees on the part of the House and the conferees on the part of the Senate. Such statement shall be sufficiently detailed and explicit to inform the Senate as to the effect which the amendments or propositions contained in such report will have upon the measure to which those amendments or propositions relate.

8. If time for debate in the consideration of any report of a committee of conference upon the floor of the Senate is limited, the time allotted for debate shall be equally divided between the majority party and the minority party.

9. Each conference committee between the Senate and the House of Representatives shall be open to the public except when managers of either the Senate or the House of Representatives in open session determine by a rollcall vote of a majority of those managers present, that all or part of the remainder of the meeting on the day of the vote shall be closed to the public.

10. (a)(1) It shall not be in order to vote on the adoption of a report of a committee of conference unless such report has been available to Members and to the general public for at least 48 hours before such vote. If a point of order is sustained under this paragraph, then the conference report shall be set aside.

(2) For purposes of this paragraph, a report of a committee of conference is made available to the general public as of the time it is posted on a publicly accessible website controlled by a Member, committee, Library of Congress, or other office of Congress, or the Government Printing Office, as reported to the Presiding Officer by the Secretary of the Senate.

(b)(1) This paragraph may be waived in the Senate with respect to the pending conference report by an affirmative vote of three-fifths of the Members, duly chosen and sworn. A motion to waive this paragraph shall be debatable for not to exceed 1 hour equally divided between the Majority Leader and the Minority Leader or their designees.

(2) An affirmative vote of three-fifths of the Members, duly chosen and sworn, shall be required to sustain an appeal of the ruling of the Chair on a point of order raised under this paragraph. An appeal of the ruling of the Chair shall be debatable for not to exceed 1 hour equally divided between the Majority and the Minority Leader or their designees.

(c) This paragraph may be waived by joint agreement of the Majority Leader and the Minority Leader of the Senate, upon their certification that such waiver is necessary as a result of a significant disruption to Senate facilities or to the availability of the Internet.

Driver's Privacy Protection Act

18 U.S.C. §§ 2721–2725 (2013)

§ 2721. Prohibition on release and use of certain personal information from State motor vehicle records

(a) In General.— A State department of motor vehicles, and any officer, employee, or contractor thereof, shall not knowingly disclose or otherwise make available to any person or entity:

(1) personal information, as defined in 18 U.S.C. 2725(3), about any individual obtained by the department in connection with a motor vehicle record, except as provided in subsection (b) of this section; or

(2) highly restricted personal information, as defined in 18 U.S.C. 2725(4), about any individual obtained by the department in connection with a motor vehicle record, without the express consent of the person to whom such information applies, except uses permitted in subsections (b)(1), (b)(4), (b)(6), and (b)(9): *Provided*, That subsection (a)(2) shall not in any way affect the use of organ donation information on an individual's driver's license or affect the administration of organ donation initiatives in the States.

(b) Permissible Uses.— Personal information referred to in subsection (a) shall be disclosed for use in connection with matters of motor vehicle or driver safety and theft, motor vehicle emissions, motor vehicle product alterations, recalls, or advisories, performance monitoring of motor vehicles and dealers by motor vehicle manufacturers, and removal of non-owner records from the original owner records of motor vehicle manufacturers to carry out the purposes of titles I and IV of the Anti Car Theft Act of 1992, the Automobile Information Disclosure Act (15 U.S.C. 1231 et seq.), the Clean Air Act (42 U.S.C. 7401 et seq.), and chapters 301, 305, and 321–331 of title 49, and, subject to subsection (a)(2), may be disclosed as follows:

(1) For use by any government agency, including any court or law enforcement agency, in carrying out its functions, or any private person or entity acting on behalf of a Federal, State, or local agency in carrying out its functions.

(2) For use in connection with matters of motor vehicle or driver safety and theft; motor vehicle emissions; motor vehicle product alterations, recalls, or advisories; performance monitoring of motor vehicles, motor vehicle parts and dealers; motor

vehicle market research activities, including survey research; and removal of non-owner records from the original owner records of motor vehicle manufacturers.

(3) For use in the normal course of business by a legitimate business or its agents, employees, or contractors, but only—

(A) to verify the accuracy of personal information submitted by the individual to the business or its agents, employees, or contractors; and

(B) if such information as so submitted is not correct or is no longer correct, to obtain the correct information, but only for the purposes of preventing fraud by, pursuing legal remedies against, or recovering on a debt or security interest against, the individual.

(4) For use in connection with any civil, criminal, administrative, or arbitral proceeding in any Federal, State, or local court or agency or before any self-regulatory body, including the service of process, investigation in anticipation of litigation, and the execution or enforcement of judgments and orders, or pursuant to an order of a Federal, State, or local court.

(5) For use in research activities, and for use in producing statistical reports, so long as the personal information is not published, redisclosed, or used to contact individuals.

(6) For use by any insurer or insurance support organization, or by a self-insured entity, or its agents, employees, or contractors, in connection with claims investigation activities, antifraud activities, rating or underwriting.

(7) For use in providing notice to the owners of towed or impounded vehicles.

(8) For use by any licensed private investigative agency or licensed security service for any purpose permitted under this subsection.

(9) For use by an employer or its agent or insurer to obtain or verify information relating to a holder of a commercial driver's license that is required under chapter 313 of title 49.

(10) For use in connection with the operation of private toll transportation facilities.

(11) For any other use in response to requests for individual motor vehicle records if the State has obtained the express consent of the person to whom such personal information pertains.

(12) For bulk distribution for surveys, marketing or solicitations if the State has obtained the express consent of the person to whom such personal information pertains.

(13) For use by any requester, if the requester demonstrates it has obtained the written consent of the individual to whom the information pertains.

(14) For any other use specifically authorized under the law of the State that holds the record, if such use is related to the operation of a motor vehicle or public safety.

(c) Resale or Redisclosure.—An authorized recipient of personal information (except a recipient under subsection (b)(11) or (12)) may resell or redisclose the information only for a use permitted under subsection (b) (but not for uses under subsection (b)(11) or (12)). An authorized recipient under subsection (b)(11) may resell or redisclose personal information for any purpose. An authorized recipient under subsection (b)(12) may resell or redisclose personal information pursuant to subsection (b)(12). Any authorized recipient (except a recipient under subsection (b)(11)) that resells or rediscloses personal information covered by this chapter must keep for a period of 5 years records identifying each person or entity that receives information and the permitted purpose for which the information will be used and must make such records available to the motor vehicle department upon request.

(d) Waiver Procedures.—A State motor vehicle department may establish and carry out procedures under which the department or its agents, upon receiving a request for personal information that does not fall within one of the exceptions in subsection (b), may mail a copy of the request to the individual about whom the information was requested, informing such individual of the request, together with a statement to the effect that the information will not be released unless the individual waives such individual's right to privacy under this section.

(e) Prohibition on Conditions.—No State may condition or burden in any way the issuance of an individual's motor vehicle record as defined in 18 U.S.C. 2725(1) to obtain express consent. Nothing in this paragraph shall be construed to prohibit a State from charging an administrative fee for issuance of a motor vehicle record.

§ 2722. Additional unlawful acts

(a) Procurement for Unlawful Purpose.—It shall be unlawful for any person knowingly to obtain or disclose personal information, from a motor vehicle record, for any use not permitted under section 2721(b) of this title.

(b) False Representation.—It shall be unlawful for any person to make false representation to obtain any personal information from an individual's motor vehicle record.

§ 2723. Penalties

(a) Criminal Fine.—A person who knowingly violates this chapter shall be fined under this title.

(b) Violations by State Department of Motor Vehicles.—Any State department of motor vehicles that has a policy or practice of substantial noncompliance with this chapter shall be subject to a civil penalty imposed by the Attorney General of not more than $5,000 a day for each day of substantial noncompliance.

§ 2724. Civil action

(a) Cause of Action.—A person who knowingly obtains, discloses or uses personal information, from a motor vehicle record, for a purpose not permitted under this chapter shall be liable to the individual to whom the information pertains, who may bring a civil action in a United States district court.

(b) Remedies. — The court may award—

(1) actual damages, but not less than liquidated damages in the amount of $2,500;

(2) punitive damages upon proof of willful or reckless disregard of the law;

(3) reasonable attorneys' fees and other litigation costs reasonably incurred; and

(4) such other preliminary and equitable relief as the court determines to be appropriate.

§ 2725. Definitions

In this chapter—

(1) "motor vehicle record" means any record that pertains to a motor vehicle operator's permit, motor vehicle title, motor vehicle registration, or identification card issued by a department of motor vehicles;

(2) "person" means an individual, organization or entity, but does not include a State or agency thereof;

(3) "personal information" means information that identifies an individual, including an individual's photograph, social security number, driver identification number, name, address (but not the 5-digit zip code), telephone number, and medical or disability information, but does not include information on vehicular accidents, driving violations, and driver's status.[1]

(4) "highly restricted personal information" means an individual's photograph or image, social security number, medical or disability information; and

(5) "express consent" means consent in writing, including consent conveyed electronically that bears an electronic signature as defined in section 106(5) of Public Law 106-229.

---

1. So in original. The period probably should be a semicolon.

Selected Legislative History: Driver's Privacy Protection Act of 1994

I

103D CONGRESS
1ST SESSION

H. R. 3365

To amend title 18, United States Code, to protect the personal privacy and safety of licensed drivers, taking into account the legitimate needs of government and business.

IN THE HOUSE OF REPRESENTATIVES

OCTOBER 26, 1993

Mr. MORAN (for himself, Mr. FRANK of Massachusetts, Ms. PELOSI, Mr. TOWNS, Mr. SCOTT, Ms. BYRNE, and Mrs. MORELLA) introduced the following bill; which was referred to the Committee on the Judiciary

---

A BILL

To amend title 18, United States Code, to protect the personal privacy and safety of licensed drivers, taking into account the legitimate needs of government and business.

1   *Be it enacted by the Senate and House of Representa-*

2 *tives of the United States of America in Congress assembled,*

3 **SECTION 1. SHORT TITLE.**

4   This Act may be cited as the "Driver's Privacy Pro-

5 tection Act of 1993".

6 **SEC. 2. PROHIBITION ON RELEASE OF CERTAIN PERSONAL**

7   **INFORMATION BY STATES.**

8   (a) IN GENERAL.—Title 18, United States Code, is

9 amended by inserting after chapter 121 the following:

2

1   "CHAPTER 123—PROHIBITION ON RELEASE OF

2   CERTAIN PERSONAL INFORMATION BY STATES

3   "§ 2721. Prohibition on release of certain personal in-

4   formation by States

5   "(a) IN GENERAL.—It shall be unlawful for any per-

6   son or other entity to disclose personal information derived

7   from an individual's motor vehicle records to any other

8   person or entity. other than to the individual, except as

9   permitted under this chapter.

10   "(b) EXCEPTIONS.   Personal information referred to

11   in subsection (a) of this section may be disclosed for any

12   of the following uses:

13   "(1) For use by any Federal or State court in

14   carrying out its functions.

15   "(2) For use by any Federal or State agency in

16   carrying out its functions.

17   "(3) For use in connection with matters of

18   automobile and driver safety, including manufactur

19   ers of motor vehicles conducting a recall of motor ve-

20   hicles.

21   "(4) For use in the normal course of business

22   by a legitimate business (including an insurer or in-

3

1   surance support organization) or its agents or em-

2   ployees or contractors, but only

3   "(A) to verify the accuracy of personal in

4   formation submitted by the individual to the

5   business; and

6   "(B) if such information as so submitted

7   was not correct, to obtain the correct informa-

8   tion, but only for the purpose of pursuing rem-

9   edies against an individual who provided false

10   information or presented a check or similar

11   item that was not honored.

12   "(5) For use in any civil or criminal proceeding

13   in any Federal or State court.

14   "(6) For use in research activities, if the motor

15   vehicle department determines that such personal in-

16   formation will not be used to solicit the individual

17   and that the individual is not identified or associated

18   with the requested information.

19   "(7) For use in marketing activities, if the

20   motor vehicle department—

21   "(A) has provided in a clear and conspicu-

22   ous manner to the individual an opportunity to

23   prohibit such disclosure;

24   "(B) has received assurances that the in-

25   formation will be used, rented, or sold solely for

4

1   a permissible use under this chapter, including

2   marketing activities; and

3   "(C) has received assurances that each en

4   tity that sells or uses the information so ob-

5   tained keeps complete records identifying each

6   purpose for which the information is used and

7   each organization that receives the information.

8   "(8) For purposes of reselling the personal in-

9   formation for a permissible use under paragraph (7)

10   of this subsection, but only if each person or other

11   entity that sells or uses the information so obtained

12   keeps complete records identifying—

13   "(A) each purpose for which the informa-

14   tion is used; and

15   "(B) each person or other entity that re-

16   ceives the information.

17   "(9) For use by any insurer or insurance sup-

18   port organization, or its employees, agents, and con

19   tractors, but only in connection with claims inves-

20   tigation activities or antifraud activities.

21   "(c) WAIVER PROCEDURES.—(1) Each State shall

22   establish and carry out procedures under which—

23   "(A) an individual to whom the information

24   pertains may authorize the agency to disclose such

25   information; and

5

1   "(B) any motor vehicle department of the State

2   may enter into an agreement with any business (in

3   cluding an insurer or insurance support organiza

4   tion) or its agents, employees, or contractors, based

5   upon a certification that the business has obtained

6   or will have obtained consent from the individual to

7   whom the information pertains, to obtain requested

8   personal information from such department.

9   "(2) Any State department of motor vehicles, upon

10 receiving a request for personal information referred to

11 in subsection (a) of this section, other than for a use re-

12 ferred to in subsection (b) of this section, shall, if such

13 request is not accompanied by a waiver in accordance with

14 paragraph (1) of this subsection, mail, within 10 days fol-

15 lowing the receipt of such request, a copy of that request

16 to the individual concerning whom the personal informa-

17 tion was requested informing such individual of the re-

18 quest, together with a statement to the effect that such

19 information will not be released unless the individual

20 waives such individual's right to confidentiality under this

21 section.

22 **"§ 2722. Additional unlawful acts**

23   "(a) PROCUREMENT FOR UNLAWFUL PURPOSE.—It

24 shall be unlawful for any person knowingly to obtain or

25 use personal information, derived from a motor vehicle

6

1   record, for any purpose not described in section 2721(b)

2   of this title.

3   "(b) FALSE REPRESENTATIONS; UNLAWFUL DIS

4   TRIBUTION.—It shall be unlawful for any person to make

5   any false representation to obtain or use any personal in-

6   formation derived from an individual's motor vehicle

7   record.

8   **"§ 2723. Penalties and remedies**

9   "(a) WILLFUL VIOLATIONS BY NON-GOVERNMENTAL

10   ENTITIES. Any person or other entity (other than a

11   State or agency thereof) that willfully violates this chapter

12   shall be fined under this title or imprisoned not more than

13   1 year, or both.

14   "(b) NONWILLFUL VIOLATIONS BY NON-GOVERN-

15   MENTAL ENTITIES.— Any person or other entity (other

16   than a State or agency thereof) that violates this chapter

17   shall be subject to a civil penalty in an amount not to

18   exceed $5,000.

19   "(c) VIOLATION BY GOVERNMENTAL ENTITIES.—If

20   a State or agency thereof willfully violates this chapter,

21   the State shall be subject to a civil penalty in the amount

22   of $10,000. Each day of continued noncompliance by the

23   State shall constitute a separate violation.

7

1 **"§ 2724. Effect on State and local law**

2   "A State or local government may prohibit conduct

3 that is permitted in the exceptions set forth in section

4 2721(b) of this title.

5 **"§ 2725. Definitions**

6   "As used in this chapter—

7   "(1) the term 'personal information' means an

8 individual's name, address, telephone number, social

9 security number, driver's identification number,

10 medical and disability information, photograph, or

11 other information that identifies a particular individ-

12 ual;

13   "(2) the term 'State' includes the District of

14 Columbia, Puerto Rico, and any other possession or

15 territory of the United States; and

16   "(3) the term 'motor vehicle record information'

17 means

18   "(A) information about who is licensed to

19   drive vehicles on the public highways, including

20   any personal information about the licensed

21   driver that is maintained as part of, or is asso-

22   ciated with, a listing of who is so licensed;

23   "(B) registration information about a

24   motor vehicle; and

25   "(C) information about violations of traffic

26   laws and similar information kept about a li-

8

1   censed driver in connection with the operations

2   of a governmental authority that controls such

3   licensing.''.

4   (B) CLERICAL AMENDMENT.—The table of chapters

5 at the beginning of part 1 of title 18, United States Code,

6 is amended by inserting after the item relating to chapter

7 121 the following new item:

"123. Prohibition on Release of Certain Personal Infor-
      mation by States .... 2721".

○

II

103D CONGRESS
1ST SESSION

S. 1589

To amend title 18, United States Code, to prohibit any State motor vehicle department from disclosing certain personal information about a person doing business with such department.

IN THE SENATE OF THE UNITED STATES

OCTOBER 26 (legislative day, OCTOBER 13), 1993

Mrs. BOXER (for herself, Mr. WARNER, Mr. DECONCINI, Mrs. FEINSTEIN, Mr. WOFFORD, Ms. MOSELEY-BRAUN, Mr. METZENBAUM, Mrs. MURRAY, Mr. HARKIN, Ms. MIKULSKI, and Mr. FEINGOLD) introduced the following bill; which was read twice and referred to the Committee on Governmental Affairs

---

A BILL

To amend title 18, United States Code, to prohibit any State motor vehicle department from disclosing certain personal information about a person doing business with such department.

1   *Be it enacted by the Senate and House of Representa-*

2   *tives of the United States of America in Congress assembled,*

3   **SECTION 1. SHORT TITLE; PURPOSE.**

4   (a) SHORT TITLE.—This Act may be cited as the

5   "Driver's Privacy Protection Act of 1993".

2

1   (b) PURPOSE.   The purpose of this Act is to protect

2   the personal privacy and safety of licensed drivers consist-

3   ent with the legitimate needs of business and government.

4   **SEC. 2. AMENDMENT TO TITLE 18, UNITED STATES CODE.**

5   Title 18 of the United States Code is amended by

6   inserting immediately after chapter 121, the following new

7   chapter:

8   **"CHAPTER   122—PROHIBITION   ON   RE-**

9   **LEASE OF CERTAIN PERSONAL INFOR-**

10   **MATION**

"Sec. 2720. Prohibition on release of certain personal information.
"Sec. 2721. Unlawful use of personal information.
"Sec. 2722. Definitions.
"Sec. 2723. Penalties.
"Sec. 2724. Effect on State and local laws.

11   **"§ 2720. Prohibition on release of certain personal in-**

12   **formation**

13   "(a) DISCLOSURE.—It is unlawful for any depart-

14   ment of motor vehicles of any State or any other person

15   or organization to disclose or obtain, except as authorized

16   by this chapter, personal information about any individual

17   obtained by such department in connection with a motor

18   vehicle operator's permit, motor vehicle title, identification

19   card, or motor vehicle registration issued by the depart

20   ment to that individual, unless such individual has author-

21   ized such disclosure.

22   "(b) EXCEPTIONS.—It is not unlawful to disclose or

23   obtain personal information, otherwise unlawful under this

3

1   chapter, for any of the following routine uses if the person

2   receiving such information has certified to the Department

3   that the information will be used only for one of the speci-

4   fied permissible purposes:

5   "(1) For the use of any Federal, State or local

6   court in carrying out its functions.

7   "(2) For the use of any Federal, State or local

8   agency in carrying out its functions, including a law

9   enforcement agency.

10   "(3) For the use in connection with matters of

11   automobile and driver safety, including manufactur-

12   ers of motor vehicles conducting a recall of motor

13   vehicles.

14   "(4) For the use in any civil or criminal pro-

15   ceeding in any Federal, State or local court, if such

16   proceeding involves a motor vehicle.

17   "(5) For use in research activities, if the motor

18   vehicle department determines that such information

19   will not be used to contact the individual and that

20   individual is not identified or associated with the re

21   quested personal information.

22   "(6) For use in marketing activities if the

23   motor vehicle department—

24   "(A) has provided the individual with re-

25   gard to whom the information is requested with

4

1   the opportunity, in a clear and conspicuous

2   manner, to prohibit a disclosure of such infor-

3   mation for marketing activities;

4   "(B) has received assurances that the in-

5   formation will be used, rented, or sold solely for

6   a permissible use under this chapter, including

7   marketing activities; and

8   "(C) has received assurances from any per-

9   son purchasing such information from a motor

10   vehicle department for marketing purposes that

11   such person will keep complete records identify-

12   ing any person to whom they sell or rent the in

13   formation and the permissible purpose for

14   which the purchaser will use the information.

15   "(7) For use by any insurer or insurance sup-

16   port organization, or their employees, agents, and

17   contractors, in connection with claims investigation

18   activities and antifraud activities.

19   "(8) For use by any organization, or its agent,

20   in connection with a business transaction, when the

21   purpose is to verify the accuracy of personal infor-

22   mation submitted to that business or agent by the

23   person to whom such information pertains, or, if the

24   information submitted is not accurate, to obtain cor-

25   rect information for the purpose of pursuing rem-

5

1   edies against a person who provided false informa

2   tion or presented a check or similar item that was

3   not honored.

4   "(9)(A) For use by any organization, if such or-

5   ganization has certified that it has obtained a state-

6   ment from the person to whom the information per-

7   tains authorizing the disclosure of such information

8   under this chapter in accordance with an agreement

9   entered into pursuant to subparagraph (B).

10   "(B) Any motor vehicle department of a State

11   is authorized to enter into an agreement with any

12   organization under subparagraph (A) pursuant to

13   which the motor vehicle department may subse-

14   quently release information to that organization on

15   the basis of a certification that the entity has ob-

16   tained or will have obtained consent from the indi-

17   vidual to whom the information pertains to obtain

18   such personal information from the State motor ve

19   hicle department.

20 **"§ 2721. Unlawful use of personal information**

21   "(a) UNLAWFUL ACTS BY STATE MOTOR VEHICLE

22 DEPARTMENTS, ORGANIZATIONS OR PERSONS.—It is un-

23 lawful for any State motor vehicle department or organiza-

24 tion or person to disclose, sell or otherwise make available,

6

1 or use personal information about any individual referred

2 to in section 2720 except in accordance with this chapter.

3   "(b) UNLAWFUL ACTS BY PERSONS OR ORGANIZA-

4 TIONS.—It is unlawful for any person or organization—

5   "(1) to make any false representation to obtain

6   personal information from a department of motor

7   vehicles of any State or other person about any indi

8   vidual referred to in section 2720; or

9   "(2) to use personal information obtained from

10   any department of motor vehicles of any State or

11   other person for any purpose other than as re-

12   quested by that person or organization, or other

13   than the purpose for which such information was

14   disclosed.

15   "(c) EXCEPTION.—The prohibition referred to in

16 subsection (a) of section 2720 and subsections (a) and (b)

17 of this section shall not apply to any person to whom the

18 information pertains.

19 "§ 2722. **Definitions**

20   "As used in this chapter:

21   "(1) The term 'personal information' includes

22   an individual's photograph, driver's identification

23   number, name, address, telephone number, social se-

24   curity number, and medical and disability informa-

25   tion. Such term does not include information on ve-

7

1 hicular accidents, driving violations, and driver's

2 status.

3   "(2) The term 'person' means any individual.

4   "(3) The term 'State' means each of the several

5 States, District of Columbia, Commonwealth of

6 Puerto Rico, Virgin Islands, Guam, American

7 Samoa, and the Commonwealth of the Northern

8 Mariana Islands.

9   "(4) The term 'organization' means any person

10 other than an individual, including but not limited

11 to, a corporation, association, institution, a car rent-

12 al agency, employer, and insurers, insurance support

13 organization, and their employees, agents, or

14 contractors.

15 **"§ 2723. Penalties**

16   "(a) WILLFUL VIOLATIONS.—

17   "(1) Any person who willfully violates this

18 chapter shall be fined under this title, or imprisoned

19 for a period not exceeding 12 months, or both.

20   "(2) Any organization who willfully violates this

21 chapter shall be fined under this title.

22   "(b) NONWILLFUL VIOLATIONS.—Any person or or-

23 ganization who violates this chapter, other than a willful

24 violation, shall be subject to a civil penalty in an amount

25 not to exceed $5,000.

8

1　"(c) Violations by State Department of

2　Motor Vehicles.—Any State department of motor vehi-

3　cles which willfully violates this chapter shall be subject

4　to a civil penalty in the amount of S10,000. Each day of

5　continued noncompliance shall constitute a separate viola-

6　tion.

7　**"§ 2724. Effect on State and local laws**

8　"The provisions of this chapter shall supersede only

9　those provisions of law of any State or local government

10　which would require or permit the disclosure or use of per-

11　sonal information which is otherwise prohibited by this

12　chapter.".

13　Sec. 3. The amendments made by this Act shall take

14　effect upon the expiration of the 270-day period following

15　the date of its enactment.

○

LEGISLATION TO PROTECT PRIVACY AND SAFETY OF LICENSED DRIVERS

HON. JAMES P. MORAN
OF VIRGINIA

IN THE HOUSE OF REPRESENTATIVES

Wednesday, November 3, 1993

Mr. MORAN. Mr. Speaker, a group of teenagers in Iowa record the license plate numbers of expensive cars they see, obtain the names and addresses of the owners, and rob their homes.

In Virginia, a woman found out the names and addresses of over 30 licensed drivers by tracing the information through their license plate numbers, claiming the drivers in question were stealing the fillings from her teeth.

In California, actress Rebecca Schaeffer was gunned down at her Los Angeles apartment, by a man who had—through a private investigator—obtained her home address from the California DMV.

What each of these incidents have in common is that they are all true and, in each case, the name and home address of the individual stalked was given out, or sold for a nominal fee, by the State department of motor vehicles.

In 34 States across the country, there are virtually no restrictions on who has access to the name and address of licensees. In fact, very few Americans realize that by registering their car or obtaining a driver's license through the DMV, they are surrendering their personal and private information to anyone who wants to obtain it. When informed that such information can be so easily obtained, most licensees are shocked and angry. According to a survey released by the National Association to Protect Individual Rights, 92 percent of Americans believe that the DMV should not sell or release personal data about them without their knowledge and approval.

Random access to personal information contained in DMV files poses a threat to every licensed driver in the Nation. In my own State of Virginia, over 127,815 requests are made every year for personal information contained in motor vehicle files. In Virginia, like most other States, licensees are not notified that their personal information has been accessed.

Balancing the interests of public disclosure with an individual's right to privacy is a delicate, but essential, task for government. The Driver Privacy Protection Act (H.R. 3365), which I introduced last week, safeguards the privacy of drivers and vehicle owners by prohibiting the release of personal information—

including a person's name and address—to anyone without a specific business-related reason for obtaining the information.

H.R. 3365 acknowledges that there are many businesses that depend on access to motor vehicle records to serve their customers, including insurance companies, financial institutions, vehicle dealers, and others. By focusing this legislation on the personal information contained within a driver file, this bill does not limit those legitimate organizations in using the information. It does, however, restrict access to all those without a legitimate purpose.

States will still be allowed to sell personal information to direct marketers, as long as they have provided every driver with the opportunity to restrict such sales. This requirement is consistent with the principles established by the Direct Marketing Association and the Privacy Act of 1974, that the unconsented use of personal data for incompatible purposes should be prevented.

By enacting this legislation, Congress will reaffirm that privacy is not a Democratic or Republican issue, but a basic human right to which every person is entitled.

This bill by itself will not stop stalking. But it will stop State government from being an accomplice to the crime.

A copy of the text of H.R. 3365 follows:

H.R. 3365

Be it enacted by the Senate and House of Representatives of the United States of America in Congress assembled,

SECTION 1. SHORT TITLE.

This Act may be cited as the "Driver's Privacy Protection Act of 1993".

SEC. 2. PROHIBITION ON RELEASE OF CERTAIN PERSONAL INFORMATION BY STATES.

(a) IN GENERAL.—Title 18, United States Code, is amended by inserting after chapter 121 the following

"CHAPTER 123—PROHIBITION ON RELEASE OF CERTAIN PERSONAL INFORMATION BY STATES

"Sec.
"2721. Prohibition on release of certain personal information by States.
"2722. Additional unlawful acts.
"2723. Penalties and remedies.
"2724. Effect on State and local law.
"2725. Definitions.

"§ 2721. Prohibition on release of certain personal information by States'

"(a) IN GENERAL.—It shall be unlawful for any person or other entity to disclose personal information derived from an individual's motor vehicle records to any other person or entity, other than to the individual, except as permitted under this chapter.

"(b) EXCEPTIONS.—Personal information referred to in subsection (a) of this section may be disclosed for any of the following uses:

"(1) For use by any Federal or State court in carrying out its functions.

"(2) For use by any Federal or State agency in carrying out its functions.

"(3) For use in connection with matters of automobile and driver safety, including manufacturers of motor vehicles conducting a recall of motor vehicles.

"(4) For use in the normal course of business by a legitimate business (including an insurer or insurance support organization) or its agents or employees or contractors, but only—

"(A) to verify the accuracy of personal information submitted by the individual to the business; and

"(B) if such information as so submitted was not correct, to obtain the correct information, but only for the purpose of pursuing remedies against an individual who provided false information or presented a check or similar item that was not honored.

"(5) For use in any civil or criminal proceeding in any Federal or State court.

"(6) For use in research activities, if the motor vehicle department determines that such personal information will not be used to solicit the individual and that the individual is not identified or associated with the requested information.

"(7) For use in marketing activities, if the motor vehicle department—

"(A) has provided in a clear and conspicuous manner to the individual an opportunity to prohibit such disclosure;

"(B) has received assurances that the information will be used, rented, or sold solely for a permissible use under this chapter, including marketing activities; and

"(C) has received assurances that each entity that sells or uses the information so obtained keeps complete records identifying each purpose for which the information is used and each organization that receives the information.

"(8) For purposes of reselling the personal information for a permissible use under paragraph (7) of this subsection, but only if each person or other entity that sells or uses the information so obtained keeps complete records identifying—

"(A) each purpose for which the information is used; and

"(B) each person or other entity that receives the information.

"(9) For use by any insurer or insurance support organization, or its employees, agents, and contractors, but only in connection with claims investigation activities or antifraud activities.

"(c) WAIVER PROCEDURES.—(1) Each State shall establish and carry out procedures under which—

"(A) an individual to whom the information pertains may authorize the agency to disclose such information; and

"(B) any motor vehicle department of the State may enter into an agreement with any business (including an insurer or insurance support organization) or its agents, employees, or contractors, based upon a certification that the business has obtained or will have obtained consent from the individual to whom the information pertains, to obtain requested personal information from such department.

"(2) Any State department of motor vehicles, upon receiving a request for personal information referred to in subsection (a) of this section, other than for a use referred to in subsection (b) of this section, shall, if such request is not accompanied by a waiver in accordance with paragraph (1) of this subsection, mail, within 10 days following the receipt of such request, a copy of that request to the individual concerning whom the personal information was requested informing such individual of the request, together with a statement to the effect that such information will not be released unless the individual waives such individual's right to confidentiality under this section.

"§ 2722. Additional unlawful acts

"(a) PROCUREMENT FOR UNLAWFUL PURPOSE.—It shall be unlawful for any person knowingly to obtain or use personal information, derived from a motor vehicle record, for any purpose not described in section 2721(b) of this title.

"(b) FALSE REPRESENTATIONS; UNLAWFUL DISTRIBUTION.—It shall be unlawful for any person to make any false representation to obtain or use any personal information derived from an individual's motor vehicle record.

"§ 2723. Penalties and remedies

"(a) WILLFUL VIOLATIONS BY NON-GOVERNMENTAL ENTITIES.—Any person or other entity (other than a State or agency thereof) that willfully violates this chapter shall be fined under this title or imprisoned not more than 1 year, or both.

"(b) NONWILLFUL VIOLATIONS BY NON-GOVERNMENTAL ENTITIES.— Any person or other entity (other than a State or agency thereof) that violates this chapter shall be subject to a civil penalty in an amount not to exceed $5,000.

"(c) VIOLATION BY GOVERNMENTAL ENTITIES.—If a State or agency thereof willfully violates this chapter, the State shall be subject to a civil penalty in the amount of $10,000. Each day of continued noncompliance by the State shall constitute a separate violation.

"§ 2724. Effect on State and local law

"A State or local government may prohibit conduct that is permitted in the exceptions set forth in section 2721(b) of this title.

"§ 2725. Definitions

"As used in this chapter—

"(1) the term 'personal information' means an individual's name, address, telephone number, social security number, driver's identification number, medical and disability information, photograph, or other information that identifies a particular individual;

"(2) the term 'State' includes the District of Columbia, Puerto Rico, and any other possession or territory of the United States; and

"(3) the term 'motor vehicle record information' means—

"(A) information about who is licensed to drive vehicles on the public highways, including any personal information about the licensed driver that is maintained as part of, or is associated with, a listing of who is so licensed;

"(B) registration information about a motor vehicle; and

"(C) information about violations of traffic laws and similar information kept about a licensed driver in connection with the operations of a governmental authority that controls such licensing.".

(B) CLERICAL AMENDMENT.—The table of chapters at the beginning of part I of title 18, United States Code, is amended by inserting after the item relating to chapter 121 the following new item:

"123. Prohibition on Release of Certain Personal Information by States .... 2721".

The term "personal information" as used in the act, is limited to the information outlined in 2725(1) of the act. Personal information shall not be interpreted to include the information included in the term "motor vehicle record information" in 2725 (3) of the act. Access to information described in 2725(3)(A), (3)(B), and 3(C) shall not be restricted by any provisions of the act or any regulations promulgated as a result of the act.

For the purpose of determining when an individual has submitted personal information to a legitimate business under new 2721(b)(4) of the act, the oral communication of personal information, or physical presentation of a driver's license or other form of personal identification, by the individual to an employee or agent of the business shall be considered to be a submission of personal information.

Mrs. BOXER. Mr. President, today I join the Senator from Virginia [Mr. WARNER] and 26 other cosponsors, to offer an amendment to protect the privacy of all Americans.

In California, actress Rebecca Schaeffer was brutally murdered in the doorway of her Los Angeles apartment by a man who had obtained her home address from my State's DMV.

In Iowa, a gang of teenagers copied down the license plate numbers of expensive cars, obtained the home addresses of the owners from the Department of Transportation, and then robbed them at night.

In Tempe, AZ, a woman was murdered by a man who had obtained her home address from that State's DMV.

And, in California, a 31-year-old man copied down the license plate numbers of five women in their early twenties, obtained their home address from the DMV and then sent them threatening letters at home. I want to briefly read from two of those letters.

I'm lonely and so I thought of you. I'll give you one week to respond or I will come looking for you.

Another one read:

I looked for you though all I knew about you was your license plate. Now I know more and yet nothing. I know you're a Libra, but I don't know what it's like to smell your hair while I'm kissing your neck and holding you in my arms.

When they apprehended him, they found in his possession a book entitled "You Can Find Anyone" which spelled out how to do just that using someone's license plate.

In 34 States, someone can walk into a State Motor Vehicle Department with your license plate number and a few dollars and walk out with your name and home address. Think about this. You might have an unlisted phone number and address. But, someone can find your name or see your car, go to the DMV and obtain the very personal information that you may have taken painful steps to restrict.

Mr. President, the American people think that this is wrong. In a recent Lou Harris survey, 80 percent of the people were uncomfortable with one person obtaining this type of information about another.

Can we afford to wait until every State has their own tragedy? That is not the way to legislate. Our Representatives are elected to lead, to think ahead and—at every turn—to find ways to protect the people they represent. In many States, police officers, public figures and other victims of these privacy abuses have been allowed to request that the DMV keep their home addresses confidential. Of course, these people deserve privacy and protection. But, so do all of our people.

Mr. HATCH. Will the Senator yield?

Mrs. BOXER. I will be delighted to yield.

Mr. HATCH. Mr. President, I appreciate my colleague from California's effort to control the disclosure of State department of motor vehicle [DMV] information. We need to comprehensively review the means by which government agencies disclose personal information to the public.

Stalking is a problem which is beginning to receive the attention of legislators at both the State and Federal level. I too share the concerns of my colleagues. Last Congress, I supported legislation authored by Senator COHEN which directed the Department of Justice to develop model anti-stalking legislation for the States. As well, I coauthored the Violence Against Women Act which provides $1.89 billion to fight violence perpetrated against women. The Senate passed this measure as an amendment to the crime bill. As well, I coauthored the Chafee-Hatch amendment to the crime bill which adds another category of offenders—stalkers—to the list of persons banned from purchasing firearms.

I believe the crime bill already does much to combat stalking. I commend my colleague for wanting to do more. However, concerns have been raised by the National Governors Association, the American Association of Motor Vehicle Administrators, the American Society of Newspaper Editors, and the Newspaper Association of America. These organizations raise legitimate points:

The bill from which this amendment is taken was introduced less than 1 month ago and there has not been an adequate amount of time to assess its impact and cost;

It places unfunded mandates on the States which may result in the States prohibiting all uses of DMV information for any purpose, including legitimate business and press purposes;

It subjects the DMV's to civil penalties for wrongful disclosure of drivers license information; and

While I support the goals of the Boxer amendment, I believe it warrants careful and studious review.

We are prepared to take the Senator's amendment but I do have to add this caveat. We are prepared to take the amendment on both sides but I have had a number of people very, very concerned about it. I would like to take it under the condition that we work on it together and see if we can perfect it somewhat between now and conference. Because I have received letters, for instance, this one from the Society of Professional Journalists, Utah Headliners Chapter, which I ask unanimous consent be printed in the RECORD at this point.

There being no objection, the letter was ordered to be printed in the RECORD, as follows:

SOCIETY OF PROFESSIONAL JOURNALISTS, UTAH HEADLINERS CHAPTER,
Salt Lake City, UT, November 16, 1993.
Hon. ORRIN G. HATCH,
Committee on the Judiciary, U.S. Senate Washington, DC.

DEAR SENATOR HATCH; the Utah Headliners Chapter of the Society of Professional Journalists has learned that there may be a vote on proposed amendments to the Crime Bill this afternoon. Among those amendments to be considered is the Boxer/Moran Driver's Privacy Protection Act of 1993. Our organization is concerned and strongly opposed to the incorporation of the measure into the Crime Bill without appropriate public hearings.

Our organization represents journalists throughout Utah and has been active in protecting the public's access to government proceedings and records. Nationally, the Society is the nation's oldest and largest journalism organization.

While we are sympathetic to the concerns about privacy connected with the proposed legislation, we believe there may be other approaches to the problem that would ensure the public's right to know while protecting against abuse of these records. For example, government could enact tough stalking laws rather than closing off records because of isolated violence associated with information gained from public records.

Consider the valuable ways journalists use driver and motor vehicle records to further the public interest. News organizations have discovered pilots, bus drivers and police officers who have DUI convictions but were still operating vehicles. In New Mexico, a series of articles based on these records, helped change the state's DUI laws and the court system's leniency with DUI convictions. Other stories have shown how dealers illegally rebuilt and resold automobile wrecks. Any Utah journalist could provide you with a list of ways reporters use these records in the public's behalf.

We also believe that this issue is better addressed on a state-by-state basis. For example, government officials, journalists and citizens recently spent five years debating Utah's new Government Records Access and Management Act. The act provides for balancing tests between the public interest and the interests of privacy. This is a much more reasonable approach than the wholesale closure of public documents. We are concerned that the Boxer/Moran legislation could be only the beginning of an unbalanced closure of records that creates double standards.

We ask for a full debate on these issues. There is a great deal of experience in Utah's government, legal and media community regarding these issues. We would be happy to use our resources to give you and your staff further information regarding this bill.

Best regards,

JOEL CAMPBELL,
*for the Utah Headliners Chapter
Board of Directors.*

Mr. HATCH. They are expressing a great deal of concern about the amendment of the distinguished Senator. I understand what the distinguished Senator from California is trying to do. I will personally work with her to try to make sure we can accomplish what she wants while still giving consideration to these professional journalists and others who feel her amendment might be damaging to the information-gathering process.

Mr. WARNER. Mr. President, will the Senator yield?

Mr. HATCH. I will be delighted to.

Mr. WARNER. This is a joint effort on behalf of the Senators from California and Virginia, and so I hope my colleague will address us jointly in terms of this somewhat unusual procedure. I urge the distinguished Senator from California be permitted to complete her opening remarks and the Senator from Virginia can provide his remarks and then we should discuss with the managers such procedures as they think appropriate to work on this amendment. Because it is my clear understanding the amendment was accepted and this is the first knowledge I had there was some contingency to that acceptance.

Mr. HATCH. If I can just remark, I apologize to the distinguished Senator from Virginia. In my zeal to accept the amendment, I failed to mention that this is the Boxer and Warner amendment and we feel very deeply about that.

Frankly, what we are trying to do is finish the bill tonight. I think the distinguished Senator from California has made an eloquent statement on this matter thus far. I will be happy to listen to the rest of it, but I think if we are willing to accept the amendment, if the Senators can summarize their statements, it would help.

Mr. WARNER. Mr. President, if the Senator will yield, we will be happy to do that. But I must tell you, I express great admiration for the Senator from California, for her diligence and months of hard work, together with her staff member, Laura Schiller, working with my staff member, George Cartagena. A lot of hard work has been put into this. I was absolutely astonished that this situation existed across the United States.

I urge the managers of the bill to provide the distinguished Senator from California a few more minutes and I will be happy to curtail my remarks to just a bare few minutes response.

The PRESIDING OFFICER (Mr. GRAHAM). The Senator from California.

Mrs. BOXER. If I may ask, is the time currently my time?

The PRESIDING OFFICER. The Senator from California controls 10 minutes 57 seconds.

Mrs. BOXER. I would say to my friends it would be my intention to finish my remarks in less than 5 minutes and yield the remainder of the time to my distinguished coauthor, the Senator from Virginia, Senator WARNER, and I would like to proceed.

I am very pleased that this amendment will be accepted. It has been 7 months of work. In 5 minutes I think I can complete my remarks. I thank the Senator from Virginia for his tremendous courtesy and assistance in this effort.

With this amendment we have an opportunity to protect the privacy and

29468   CONGRESSIONAL RECORD—SENATE   *November 16, 1993*

safety of all American. -not just the VIP's with special clout.

This area is clearly within Congress' authority to regulate. First, this is a fundamental issue of privacy. The Supreme Court has found that people have a right to be safe in their homes, that they have a right not to have the Government make public their personal data—and that Congress can use it's powers—section 5 of the 14th amendment—provide remedies for violations to constitutional rights.

What's more, with mail, cars, and harassment involved, this issue clearly has an impact on interstate commerce. As such—under article 1, section 8—this area is well within Congress' authority to regulate. We all understand that interstate commerce is severely threatened when mail is used, when people are scared to drive in their cars, when their civil rights are violated, and when they live in fear of being harassed and stalked.

The amendment that I am offering today strikes a critical balance between the legitimate governmental and business needs for this information, and the fundamental right of our people to privacy and safety. Under this amendment, personal information is defined as including a driver's name, address, phone number, and social security number. It does not include information on a driver's accidents, violations or status. Let me repeat that. Nothing in this bill will stop the press, insurance companies, employers, or anyone else from obtaining information about an individual's driving record.

This amendment allows access for all governmental agencies, courts, and law enforcement personnel. It allows full access for all automobile and driver safety purposes, including manufacturers of motor vehicles conducting a recall for any purpose. It sets up fair standards for insurance companies, employers, banks, researchers, and other organizations who routinely use this information. And, that is why we have the support from so many organizations, including the American Insurance Association, a trade organization representing more than 250 major insurance companies.

Currently, most States sell personal information to direct marketers. Our bill does not stop this. It simply says that if a State chooses to sell this information to marketers, they need to give people the opportunity to opt out and say no. This policy is fair. It is consistent with the Direct Marketing Association's own ethical guidelines and with the recommendations of the landmark 1977 Privacy Commission Report.

This amendment sets up clear guidelines and fair penalties. Under this amendment, only those people and individuals who willfully violate this chapter are subject to penalties. Under this amendment, aggrieved individuals and groups do not have a cause of action and cannot file suit. And, under this amendment, States are not liable for criminal penalties.

If you want to own or operate a car, you must register with the DMV. This amendment simply gives people more control over the disclosure of their personal information, especially for those reasons that are totally incompatible with the purpose for which the information was collected. States are free to be more restrictive with this information. This bill simply takes a national problem and gives the States broad latitude and 9 months to enact a national solution.

Mr. President, we have more than 20 business, consumer, police, physician and victims groups who have given their support to this amendment, from the Fraternal Order of Police, to the Consumer Federation of America, to the American Medical Association.

Finally, I want to again thank Senator WARNER for his strong support on this legislation, and Congressman MORAN, of Virginia, for his leadership on this issue; and my constituent from Los Angeles, Joyce Shorr, who brought this critical problem to my attention; again, the many groups that have endorsed the legislation, our 27 cosponsors.

Finally, I would like to address a couple remarks to the chairman of the Judiciary Committee, who I do not see on the floor right now but I want to pay tribute to him because he knows that I am new in the U.S. Senate. He knows how much this particular piece of legislation meant to me. Even when it looked like it was going to be controversial, he encouraged me to continue, to line up the votes and the support. We did it, and I am extremely pleased that the Senator from Virginia and I tonight will have our amendment agreed to. Of course, we will work to see that it survives the conference in a way that meets the very clear objectives: We want to protect the privacy and the safety of the people of America, and I think we will achieve that.

At this time, I yield the remainder of my time to the good Senator from Virginia, Senator WARNER.

The PRESIDING OFFICER. The Senator from Virginia has 6 minutes 56 seconds.

Mr. WARNER. Mr. President, I thank my distinguished colleague and friend, the Senator from California. I have to confess that the Senator from California and I came to the body with a somewhat different approach and philosophy. I thought to myself when I discovered this piece of legislation, largely through her efforts and the efforts of my distinguished colleague from Virginia, Congressman MORAN, who pioneered this legislation in the Congress for some several years, I thought the likelihood of a Boxer-War-

ner bill was impossible. But here we are. Impossible things do happen.

I thank my colleague for her kind remarks and for the opportunity for me and my staff to work as diligently as we could to perfect this piece of legislation.

Mr. President, I was absolutely astonished to learn that in some 30-plus States and, indeed, my own State, which has a provision that gives some restriction but people who demonstrate good reason can acquire this information. It applies to auto titles, to car registrations, to driver's licenses, auto tags—all this is open. There is a war in this country to fight for privacy. People are now fighting, and this is coming to their assistance to provide the privacy, which I and many others thought existed.

I had no idea when I went into my State to get licensed that all this information that I provided was going to be made public. Those in public life expect much of our factual data to be public but, indeed, others who are not in public life have a need to protect their privacy, and particularly women.

I shall not go into the specifics. My distinguished colleague from California cited some actual cases, but this legislation is to protect a wide range of individuals, protect them from the State agencies often for a price, a profit to the State, to release lists. Not only will the agency give out individual names and sponsors will call with an inquiry, but they give out the whole list, everybody in the State, if you want to buy it. It is somewhat expensive but you can get it. This legislation provides that, henceforth—the State is given 270 days within which to implement it—henceforth, individuals who go in to register cars, acquire permits, so forth, can clearly indicate their lack of willingness, their desire not to have that information released to marketers primarily. There are specific exceptions of course for law enforcement individuals and other areas where proven experience shows that this information should flow. But in those instances we have to presume it is somewhat protected.

The Boxer-Warner bill incorporates both the intent of the 1974 Privacy Act, which deals with the collection of personal information by Federal agencies as well as the recommendations of the landmark 1977 Privacy Protection Study Commission report. Registering with the DMV is mandatory. The Boxer bill will provide individuals with knowledge of and control over the disclosure of their personal information for uses unrelated to the purpose(s) for which it was collected.

Mr. President, the legislation will also:

Provide unlimited access for courts, law enforcement, governmental agencies, insurance companies involved in claims investigation and antifraud activities, and for other driver and automobile safety purposes;

Allow businesses to verify information provided by the licensee and to access personal information as long as the individual has waived his or her right to confidentiality. These businesses can enter into contracts with the DMV's to facilitate this process;

Not prohibit the disclosure of information on vehicular accidents or driving violations;

Provide access to this information for marketing purposes if the licensees have been given the opportunity to prohibit such disclosure. This policy is consistent with the Privacy Commission report and with the ethical guidelines of the Direct Marketing Association;

Allow States to enact tougher restrictions and gives them room to craft their own specific responses to the regulations;

Allow the DMV's to price their sale of services to fully recover any initial costs associated with implementing this legislation—most DMV's already sell this information, and costs for implementing the additional security provisions are estimated to be negligible; and

Only penalize the States when the Attorney General has found that a State's failure to comply with these regulations was willful.

This is a superb piece of legislation badly needed to protect individuals in their fight to retain privacy.

I thank the Chair and I thank my colleague.

Several Senators addressed the Chair.

The PRESIDING OFFICER. The Senator from Utah.

Mr. HATCH. Mr. President, we are prepared to accept the amendment.

Mrs. BOXER. I am very pleased. I have no further remarks.

I understand the Senator from Virginia, Senator ROBB, has come over to lend support. I would appreciate a moment or two. How much time remains?

The PRESIDING OFFICER. The Senator from California controls 3 minutes 7 seconds.

The PRESIDING OFFICER. The Senator from Virginia is recognized with 2 minutes 45 seconds remaining.

Mr. ROBB. Mr. President, I am very pleased to join my senior colleague and the Senator from California in cosponsoring this amendment.

The right to privacy, without which the Americans are not secure in their own homes, is seriously threatened. It is easy for anyone anywhere to access information as personal as your address and phone number, even if they are not listed in the telephone directory. Even your Social Security number is available, and the chief agent giving out this kind of information is the very government that is supposed to protect its citizens.

Many Americans are infuriated and, more importantly, they are vulnerable to these violations of privacy which happen in 34 States in this country every day, my own included.

Recently, a woman in Virginia was shocked to discover black balloons and antiabortion literature on her doorstep days after she had visited a health clinic that performs abortions. Apparently, someone used her license plate number to track down personal information which was used to stalk her.

In another case in Georgia, an obsessive fan obtained the home address of a fashion model from the State Department of Motor Vehicles and assaulted her in front of her apartment.

These are but two examples of how simple it is to submit a driver's license number, pay a nominal fee to the DMV and receive a person's name and address. This is no mere loophole in a system, it is a visible gap that needs to be plugged.

Luckily, we have the opportunity to close that hole by the amendment offered by the Senator from California and my distinguished senior colleague, Senator WARNER. This amendment would place safeguards on the privacy of the driver and vehicle owners by prohibiting release of personal information to anyone without a specific business-related or government-related reason for obtaining the information.

While this bill alone will not stop people from stalking, it will inhibit States from unknowingly aiding and abetting this type of crime. Easy access to personal information makes every driver in this Nation vulnerable and infringes on their right to privacy. Government's duty is to keep citizens safe and it should not, therefore, be contributing to insecurity.

I hope that our colleagues will help to restrict easy, unlimited access to personal information by supporting this amendment.

I commend the Senator from California, my senior colleague and our colleague in the House for offering it.

I yield the floor.

Mr. WARNER. Mr. President, I ask unanimous consent I may proceed for another minute-and-a-half.

The PRESIDING OFFICER. Without objection, it is so ordered. The Senator from Virginia is recognized for 90 seconds.

Mr. WARNER. Mr. President, I pose a question to my distinguished colleague. In his former capacity as a very distinguished Governor of the Commonwealth of Virginia, it is very interesting, listening to his remarks, that this was a situation that apparently was not recognized by the Governors as being so compelling as it is today during the period when he was Governor.

I wonder if the Senator might have a recollection of how the history of the need of this legislation has evolved in the intervening years since he was

Governor of the Commonwealth of Virginia.

Mr. ROBB. Mr. President, I can respond to my senior colleague by telling him, indeed, this is a problem, like many others, that has simply evolved. In recent years, it has become increasingly evident that this information was accessible and it was being used for purposes that were certainly not intended by the framers of the actual legislation that permitted its release.

This legislation is simply designed to close an important loophole that at this point restricts the privacy that I think most of our citizens believe they have but in some cases subjects them to stalking, abuse or other improper utilization of information which simply should not be in their hands.

Mr. WARNER. Mr. President, I thank my distinguished colleague. I think this is a very important part of the legislative history that we are making tonight. It has been a relatively short period of time that the urgency for such legislation as this be adopted by the Congress. It is my fervent hope and wish that it will be.

The PRESIDING OFFICER. Who yields time?

The Senator from Delaware.

Mr. BIDEN. Mr. President, I rise to not only support but compliment my friend from California. She came early on with this amendment when it did not look like anybody was likely to support it at all. And because she always cooperates, she indicated she did not want to get in the way of the passage of the bill she supports, but she felt strongly about it.

One of the things I am learning is that she is a freshman Senator, but she is no freshman like I have ever seen. She has walked into this place with significant experience in the House and is frighteningly effective. I compliment her on her pushing this amendment along. It is a very important amendment. I for one would like to compliment her and the Senator from Virginia for their calling this concern and need to the attention of the Senate and the people of the country. I think it is a good amendment.

I support the amendment of the Senator from California. This amendment would make it unlawful for States to disseminate personal information about any person or organization simply because the person seeking the information can recite a driver's or motor vehicle license number.

Too often we read, or hear on television, stories about women who suffer serious injury or death after being stalked by estranged and violent husbands and boyfriends. Stalking is a crime of terror and fear, plaguing thousands of Americans every year.

By protecting the privacy of addresses and telephone numbers—which would otherwise be available at the mere mention of a license plate or driver's license number—the amendment is another weapon against this violence.

This amendment closes a loophole in the law that permits stalkers to obtain—on demand—private, personal information about their potential victims.

Under the law in over 30 States, it is permissible to give out to any person the name, telephone number, and address of any other person if a drivers' license or vehicle plate number is provided to a State agency.

Thus, potential criminals are able to obtain private, personal information about their victims simply by making a request. These open-record policies in many States are open invitations to would-be stalkers.

In my view, this amendment makes common sense. Americans do not believe they should relinquish their legitimate expectations of privacy simply by obtaining drivers' licenses or registering their cars. Yet the laws of some States do just that by routinely providing this identifying information to all who request it.

The States should not provide the mechanism for the terror that can be unleashed through the indiscriminate release of this kind of information. Some restrictions on the dissemination of private information such as an address or telephone number are reasonable and appropriate.

This amendment is narrowly tailored in that it carefully preserves the right of States to disseminate this private information for legitimate purposes such as law enforcement, automobile safety activities, and insurance investigations.

I applaud the Senator from California for her work in this regard. She provides a reasoned and measured approach to the protection of private information and the placement of yet another roadblock in the way of would-be criminals.

When time is yielded back, I am prepared to accept the amendment and again congratulate the sponsors for their persistence and insight into this problem

The PRESIDING OFFICER. Is there further debate?

Mr. HARKIN. Mr. President, I rise in strong support of this amendment, which will ensure that the private information that drivers provide to their State licensing authorities will not be improperly disclosed to violate those drivers right to privacy. The Drivers Privacy Protection Act, of which I am an original cosponsor, strikes a fair balance between reasonable interests of the State and the public in this information, and the rights of private citizens to be left alone.

I became aware of this issue through the plight of one of my constituents, Karen Stewart. Karen was a patient of Dr. Herbert Remer, a physician who specializes in obstetrics and gynecological care in the Des Moines area. Because Dr. Remer performs abortions, his clinic has been the site of repeated protests by those who oppose women's right to choose.

But Karen was going to Dr. Remer to save her pregnancy, not to terminate it. She was experiencing complications, and went to Dr. Remer for treatment. Unfortunately, a few days after the visit, Karen suffered a miscarriage.

And then she received the letter. Extremists from Operation Rescue sent a venomous letter apparently intended to traumatize Dr. Remer's patients. The letter spoke of "God's curses for the shedding of innocent blood," and "the guilt of having killed one's own child." They got her name and address from department of transportation records, after they spotted her car parked near Dr. Remer's clinic.

This is one example of the potential for abuse of these public records, but it is far from the only one. According to the Des Moines Register of October 10, 1992, a gang of teens used State records to help them carry out their crimes. They would find cars with expensive stereos in parking lots and on the streets, take down their license numbers, and find the owners' home address through DOT records.

Most tragically, these records are used by stalkers to track down their victims. Rebecca Shaeffer, a promising young actress from California, was brutally murdered by an obsessed fan. That fan obtained her address from department of motor vehicles records through a private investigator.

I strongly believe that this legislation will provide important protection to every American's privacy. I want to congratulate Senator BOXER on her amendment, which is a well-balanced proposal that strongly protects privacy, yet accommodates a variety of important interests. I urge its adoption.

Mr. WARNER. Mr. President, I wish to join with my distinguished colleague from California in thanking the managers of this bill. It has been a somewhat difficult task to work it through, and that has been successfully done tonight with the cooperation of the managers and their excellent staffs.

So at this point in time I believe the Senator from California would urge adoption of the amendment.

Mrs. BOXER. I urge adoption of the amendment.

The PRESIDING OFFICER. The Senator from California has urged adoption of the amendment. Is there further debate? If not, the question is on agreeing to the amendment.

The amendment (No. 1203) was agreed to.

Mr. WARNER. Mr. President, I move to reconsider the vote.

Mrs. BOXER. I move to lay that motion on the table.

The motion to lay on the table was agreed to.

consent that the modifications be considered as read and printed in the RECORD.

The CHAIRMAN pro tempore. Is there objection to the request of the gentleman from Texas?

There was no objection.

The CHAIRMAN pro tempore. The Clerk will designate the amendments en bloc, as modified.

The text of the amendments en bloc, as modified, is as follows:

Amendments en bloc, as modified, offered by Mr. BROOKS, consisting of amendment No. 32 offered by Mr. BEILENSON, amendment No. 36 offered by Mr. KENNEDY, amendment No. 40 offered by Mr. MORAN, amendment No. 48 offered by Ms. PRYCE of Ohio, amendment No. 49 offered by Mr. CANADY, and amendment No. 50 offered by Mr. CANADY:

AMENDMENT OFFERED BY MR. BEILENSON

At the end insert the following new title:

TITLE XXIV—CRIMINAL ALIENS

SEC. 2401. FEDERAL INCARCERATION OF UNDOCUMENTED CRIMINAL ALIENS.

(a) FEDERAL INCARCERATION.—Section 242 of the Immigration and Nationality Act (8 U.S.C. 1252) is amended by adding at the end the following:

"(j) FEDERAL INCARCERATION.—

"(1) Subject to paragraph (2), the Attorney General shall take into the custody of the Federal Government, and shall incarcerate for a determinate sentence of imprisonment, an undocumented criminal alien if—

"(A) the chief official of the State (or, if appropriate, a political subdivision of the State) exercising authority with respect to the incarceration of the undocumented criminal alien submits a written request to the Attorney General; and

"(B) the undocumented criminal alien is sentenced to a determinate term of imprisonment.

"(2)(A) If the Attorney General determines that adequate Federal facilities are not available for the incarceration of an undocumented criminal alien under paragraph (1), the Attorney General shall enter into a contractual arrangement which provides for compensation to the State or a political subdivision of the State, as may be appropriate, with respect to the incarceration of such undocumented criminal alien for such determinate sentence of imprisonment.

"(B) Compensation under subparagraph (A) shall be determined by the Attorney General and may not exceed the median cost of incarceration of a prisoner in all maximum security facilities in the United States as determined by the Bureau of Justice Statistics.

"(3) For purposes of this subsection, the term 'undocumented criminal alien' means an alien who—

"(A) has been convicted of a felony and sentenced to a term of imprisonment, and

"(B)(i) entered the United States without inspection or at any time or place other than as designated by the Attorney General,

"(ii) was the subject of exclusion or deportation proceedings at the time he or she was taken into custody by the State or a political subdivision of the State, or

"(iii) was admitted as a nonimmigrant and at the time he or she was taken into custody by the State or a political subdivision of the State has failed to maintain the nonimmigrant status in which the alien was admitted or to which it was changed under section 248, or to comply with the conditions of any such status.

"(4)(A) In carrying out this subsection, the Attorney General shall give priority to the Federal incarceration of undocumented criminal aliens who have committed aggravated felonies.

"(B) The Attorney General shall ensure that undocumented criminal aliens incarcerated in Federal facilities pursuant to this subsection are held in facilities which provide a level of security appropriate to the crimes for which they were convicted.".

(b) EFFECTIVE DATE.—The amendments made by this section shall take effect October 1, 1996.

(c) LIMITATION.—The authority created in section 242(j) of the Immigration and Nationality Act (as added by this section) shall be subject to appropriation until October 1, 1996.

AMENDMENT OFFERED BY MR. KENNEDY

At the end of the bill add the following new title:

TITLE —NATIONAL STALKER AND DOMESTIC VIOLENCE REDUCTION

SEC. . AUTHORIZING ACCESS TO FEDERAL CRIMINAL INFORMATION DATA BASES.

(a) ACCESS.—The Attorney General shall amend existing regulations (published at 28 C.F.R. 20.33(a)) to authorize the dissemination of information from existing national crime information databases, including the National Crime Information Center and III ("Triple I"), to courts and court personnel, civil or criminal, for use in domestic violence or stalking cases. Nothing in this subsection shall be construed to permit any person or court access to criminal history record information for any other purpose or for any other civil case other than for use in a stalking or domestic violence case.

(b) ENTRY.—The Attorney General shall amend existing regulations to permit Federal and State criminal justice agencies, assigned to input information into national crime information databases, to include arrests, warrants, and orders for the protection of parties from stalking or domestic violence, whether issued by a criminal, civil, or family court. Such amendment shall include a definition of criminal history information that covers warrants, arrests, and orders for the protection of parties from stalking or domestic violence. Nothing in this subsection shall be construed to permit access to such information for any purpose which is different than the purposes described in subsection (a).

(c) PROCEDURES.—The regulations required by subsection (a) shall be proposed no later than 90 days after the date of the enactment of this Act, after appropriate consultation with the Director of the Federal Bureau of Investigation, the officials charged with managing the National Crime Information Center, and the National Crime Information Center Advisory Policy Board. Final regulations shall be issued no later than 180 days after the date of the enactment of this Act.

SEC. . NONSERIOUS OFFENSE BAIL.

The Attorney General shall amend existing regulations to specify that the term "nonserious offenses", as used in 28 C.F.R. 20.32, does not include stalking or domestic violence offenses. Nothing in this section is intended to change current regulations requiring that juvenile offenses shall be excluded from national crime information databases unless the juvenile has been tried as an adult.

SEC. . PERFORMANCE GRANT PROGRAM.

(a) IN GENERAL.—The Attorney General, through the Director of the Bureau of Justice Assistance, is authorized to provide performance grants to the States to improve

VIOLENT CRIME CONTROL AND LAW ENFORCEMENT ACT OF 1994

The SPEAKER pro tempore (Mrs. MEEK of Florida). Pursuant to House Resolution 401 and rule XXIII, the Chair declares the House in the Committee of the Whole on the State of the Union for the further consideration of the bill, H.R. 4092.

□ 1158

IN THE COMMITTEE OF THE WHOLE

Accordingly the House resolved itself into the Committee of the Whole House on the State of the Union for the further consideration of the bill (H.R. 4092) to control and prevent crime, with Mr. SPRATT (Chairman pro tempore) in the chair.

The Clerk read the title of the bill.

The CHAIRMAN pro tempore. When the Committee of the Whole rose on Tuesday, April 19, 1994, amendment No. 16 printed in part 1 of House report 103-474 offered by the gentleman from New Jersey [Mr. HUGHES] had been disposed of.

AMENDMENTS EN BLOC, AS MODIFIED, OFFERED BY MR. BROOKS

Mr. BROOKS. Mr. Chairman, I offer amendments en bloc made in order under the rule, and I ask unanimous processes for entering data about stalking and domestic violence into national crime information databases.

(b) ELIGIBILITY.—Eligible grantees under subsection (a) are States that provide, in their application, that all criminal justice agencies within their jurisdiction shall enter into the National Crime Information Center all records of (1) warrants for the arrest of persons violating civil protection orders intended to protect victims from stalking or domestic violence; (2) arrests of persons violating civil protection orders intended to protect victims from stalking or domestic violence; and (3) orders for the protection of persons from violence, including stalking and domestic violence.

(c) PERFORMANCE-BASED DISTRIBUTION.—Eligible grantees under subsection (a) shall be awarded 25 percent of their grant moneys upon application approval as "seed money" to cover start-up costs for the project funded by the grant. Upon successful completion of the performance audit provided in subsection (d), the grantees shall be awarded the remaining sums in the grant.

(d) PERFORMANCE AUDIT.—Within 6 months after the initial 25 percent of a grant is provided, the State shall report to the Federal Bureau of Investigation and the Bureau of Justice Assistance, the number of records included in national crime information databases as a result of the grant funding, including separate data for warrants, arrests, and protective orders. If the State can show a substantial increase in the number of records entered, then it shall be eligible for the entire grant amount. However, the Director shall suspend funding for an approved application if an applicant fails to submit a 6 month performance report or if funds are expended for purposes other than those set forth under this title. Federal funds may be used to supplement, not supplant, State funds.

(e) GRANT AMOUNT.—From amounts appropriated, the amount of grants under subsection (a) shall be—

(1) $75,000 to each State; and

(2) That portion of the then remaining available money to each State that results from a distribution among the States on the basis of each State's population in relation to the population of all States.

SEC. . APPLICATION REQUIREMENTS.

The application requirements provided in section 513 of the Omnibus Crime Control and Safe Streets Act of 1968 (42 U.S.C. 3711 et seq.) shall apply to grants made under this title. In addition, applications shall include documentation showing—

(1) the need for grant funds and that State funding does not already cover these operations;

(2) intended use of the grant funds, including a plan of action to increase record input; and

(3) an estimate of expected results from the use of the grant funds.

SEC. . DISBURSEMENT.

(a) GENERAL RULE.—No later than 30 days after the receipt of an application under this title, the Director shall either disburse the appropriate sums provided for under this title or shall inform the applicant why the application does not conform to the terms of section 513 of the Omnibus Crime Control and Safe Streets Act of 1968 or to the requirements of section of this title.

(b) REGULATIONS.—In disbursing moneys under this title, the Director of the Bureau of Justice Assistance shall issue regulations to ensure that grantees give priority to the areas with the greatest showing of need.

SEC. . FEDERAL NONMONETARY ASSISTANCE.

In addition to the assistance provided under the performance grant program, the Attorney General may direct any Federal agency, with or without reimbursement, to use its authorities and the resources granted to it under Federal law (including personnel, equipment, supplies, facilities, and managerial, technical, and advisory services) in support of State and local law enforcement efforts to combat stalking and domestic violence.

SEC. . AUTHORIZATION.

There are authorized to be appropriated for each of the fiscal years 1994, 1995, and 1996, $2,000,000 to carry out the purposes of the Performance Grant Program under this title.

SEC. . TRAINING PROGRAMS FOR JUDGES.

The National Institute of Justice, in conjunction with a nationally recognized nonprofit organization expert in stalking and domestic violence cases, shall conduct training programs for judges to ensure that any judge issuing an order in stalking or domestic violence cases has all available criminal history and other information, whether from State or Federal sources.

SEC. . RECOMMENDATIONS ON INTRASTATE COMMUNICATION.

The National Institute of Justice, after consulting a nationally recognized nonprofit associations expert in data sharing among criminal justice agencies and familiar with the issues raised in stalking and domestic violence cases, shall recommend proposals about how State courts may increase intrastate communication between family courts, juvenile courts, and criminal courts.

SEC. . INCLUSION IN NATIONAL INCIDENT-BASED REPORTING SYSTEM.

Not later than 2 years after the date of enactment of this Act, the Attorney General, in coordination with the Federal Bureau of Investigation and the States, shall compile data regarding stalking civil protective orders and other forms of domestic violence as part of the National Incident-Based Reporting System (NIBRS).

SEC. . REPORT TO CONGRESS.

The Attorney General shall submit to the Congress an annual report, beginning one year after the date of the enactment of this Act, that reports information on the incidence of stalking and other forms of domestic violence, and evaluates the effectiveness of State anti-stalking efforts and legislation.

SEC. . DEFINITIONS.

As used in this title—

(1) the term "national crime information databases" refers to the National Crime Information Center and its incorporated criminal history databases, including III ("Triple I");

(2) the term "stalking" includes any conduct that would, if proven, justify the issuance of an order of protection under the stalking, or other, laws of the State in which it occurred; and

(3) the term "domestic violence" includes any conduct that would, if proven, justify the issuance of an order of protection under the domestic violence, or other, laws of the State in which it occurred.

AMENDMENT OFFERED BY MR. MORAN

At the end, add the following:

TITLE —PROTECTING THE PRIVACY OF INFORMATION IN STATE MOTOR VEHICLE RECORDS.

SEC. . SHORT TITLE.

This title may be cited as the "Driver's Privacy Protection Act of 1994".

SEC. . PROHIBITION ON RELEASE AND USE OF CERTAIN PERSONAL INFORMATION FROM STATE MOTOR VEHICLE RECORDS.

Title 18, United States Code, is amended by inserting after chapter 121 the following:

"CHAPTER 123—PROHIBITION ON RELEASE AND USE OF CERTAIN PERSONAL INFORMATION FROM STATE MOTOR VEHICLE RECORDS

"§ 2721. Prohibition on release and use of certain personal information from State motor vehicle records

"(a) IN GENERAL.—Except as provided in subsection (b), a State department of motor vehicles, and any officer, employee, or contractor thereof, shall not knowingly disclose or otherwise make available to any person or entity personal information about any individual obtained by the department in connection with a motor vehicle record.

"(b) PERMISSIBLE USES.—Personal information referred to in subsection (a) of this section shall be disclosed for paragraphs (1) and (2) to carry out the purpose of the Automobile Information Disclosure Act, the Motor Vehicle Information and Cost Saving Act, the National Traffic and Motor Vehicle Safety Act of 1966, the Anti-Car Theft Act of 1992, and the Clean Air Act, and may be disclosed for paragraphs (3) through (14), as follows:

"(1) For use by any Federal, State, or local agency, including any court or law enforcement agency, in carrying out its functions, or any private person or entity acting on behalf of a Federal, State, or local agency in carrying out its functions.

"(2) For use in connection with matters of motor vehicle or driver safety and theft, motor vehicle emissions, motor vehicle product alteration, recall or advisory, and motor vehicle customer satisfaction.

"(3) For use in the normal course of business by a legitimate business or its agents, employees, or contractors, but only—

"(A) to verify the accuracy of personal information submitted by the individual to the business or its agents, employees, or contractors; and

"(B) if such information as so submitted is not correct or is no longer correct, to obtain the correct information, but only for the purposes of preventing fraud by, pursuing legal remedies against, or recovering on a debt or security interest against, the individual.

"(4) For use in connection with any civil, criminal, administrative, or arbitral proceeding in any Federal, State, or local court or agency or before any self-regulatory body, including the service of process, investigation in anticipation of litigation, and the execution or enforcement of judgments and orders, or pursuant to an order of a Federal, State, or local court

"(5) For use in research activities, including survey research, and for use in producing statistical reports, provided that the personal information is not published or redisclosed and provided that the personal information is not used to direct solicitations or marketing offers at the individuals whose personal information is disclosed under this paragraph.

"(6) For use by any insurer or insurance support organization, or by a self insured entity, or its agents, employees, or contractors, in connection with claims investigation activities, antifraud activities, rating or underwriting.

"(7) For the purpose of providing notice to the owners of towed or impounded vehicles.

"(8) For use by any licensed private investigative agency or licensed security service for any purpose permitted under this subsection.

"(9) For use by an employer or its agent or insurer to obtain or verify information relating to a holder of a commercial driver's license that is required under the Commercial Motor Vehicle Safety Act of 1986 (49 U.S.C. App. 2710 et seq.).

"(10) For use in connection with the operation of private toll transportation facilities.

"(11) For any other purpose in response to requests for individual motor vehicle records if the motor vehicle department has provided in a clear and conspicuous manner to the individual to whom the information pertains an opportunity to prohibit such disclosures.

"(12) For bulk distribution for marketing or solicitations if the motor vehicle department has implemented methods and procedures to ensure—

"(A) that individuals are provided an opportunity, in a clear and conspicuous manner, to prohibit such disclosure; and

"(B) that the information will be used, rented, or sold solely for bulk distribution for marketing and solicitations, and that such solicitations will not be directed at those individuals who have requested in a timely fashion that they not be directed at them.

'Methods and procedures' includes the motor vehicle department's use of a mail preference list to remove from its records before bulk distribution the names and personal information of those individuals who have requested that solicitations not be directed at them.

"(13) For use by any requestor, if the requestor demonstrates it has obtained the written consent of the individual to whom the information pertains.

"(14) For any other purpose specifically authorized under the law of the State that holds the record, if such purpose is related to the operation of a motor vehicle or public safety.

"(c) RESALE OR REDISCLOSURE.—Any authorized recipient of personal information may resell or redisclose the information for any use permitted under subsection (b). Any authorized recipient (except a recipient under subsections (b)(11) or (12)) that resells or rediscloses personal information covered by this title must keep for a period of 5 years records identifying each person or entity that receives the information and the permitted purpose for which the information will be used.

"(d) WAIVER PROCEDURES.—A State motor vehicle department may establish and carry out procedures under which the department or its agents, upon receiving a request for personal information that does not fall within one of the exceptions in subsection (b), may mail a copy of the request to the individual about whom the information was requested, informing such individual of the request, together with a statement to the effect that the information will not be released unless the individual waives such individual's right to privacy under this section.

§2722. Additional unlawful acts

"(a) PROCUREMENT FOR UNLAWFUL PURPOSE.—It shall be unlawful for any person knowingly to obtain or disclose personal information, from a motor vehicle record, for any purpose not permitted under section 2721(b) of this title.

"(b) FALSE REPRESENTATIONS.—It shall be unlawful for any person to make false representation to obtain any personal information from an individual's motor vehicle record.

§2723. Criminal penalty

"Any person that knowingly violates this chapter shall be fined under this title.

§2724. Civil Action

"(a) CAUSE OF ACTION.—A person who knowingly obtains, discloses or uses personal information, derived from a motor vehicle record, for a purpose not permitted under this chapter shall be liable to the individual to whom the information pertains, who may bring a civil action in a United States district court.

"(b) REMEDIES.—The court may award—

"(1) actual damages, but not less than liquidated damages in the amount of $2,500;

"(2) punitive damages upon proof of willful or reckless disregard of the law;

"(3) reasonable attorneys' fees and other litigation costs reasonably incurred; and

"(4) such other preliminary and equitable relief as the court determines to be appropriate.

§2725. Definitions

"As used in this chapter—

"(1) "motor vehicle record" means any record that pertains to a motor vehicle operator's permit, motor vehicle title, motor vehicle registration, or identification card issued by a department of motor vehicles;

"(2) "personal information" means information that identifies an individual, including an individual's photograph, social security number, driver identification number, name, address (but not the 5-digit zip code), telephone number, and medical or disability information. Such term does not include information on vehicular accidents, driving violations, and driver's status; and

"(3) "person" means an individual, organization or entity, but does not include a State or agency thereof.".

SEC. . EFFECTIVE DATE.

This title shall take effect 3 years after the date of enactment. In the interim, personal information covered by this title may be released consistent with State law or practice.

AMENDMENT OFFERED BY MR. CANADY

At the end of the bill insert the following:

TITLE —CIVIL RIGHTS OF INSTITUTIONALIZED PERSONS ACT

SEC. . EXHAUSTION REQUIREMENT.

Section 8 of the Civil Rights of Institutionalized Persons Act (42 U.S.C. 1997e) is amended—

(1) in subsection (a)—

(A) in paragraph (1)—

(i) by striking "in any action brought" and inserting "no action shall be brought";

(ii) by striking "the court shall" and all that follows through "require exhaustion of" and insert "until"; and

(iii) by inserting "are exhausted" after "available"; and

(B) in paragraph (2), by inserting "or are otherwise fair and effective" before the period at the end.

SEC. . FRIVOLOUS ACTIONS.

Section 8(a) of the Civil Rights of Institutionalized Persons Act (42 U.S.C. 1997e(a)) is amended by adding at the end the following:

"(3) The court shall on its own motion or on motion of a party dismiss any action brought pursuant to section 1979 of the Revised Statutes of the United States by an adult convicted of a crime and confined in any jail, prison, or other correctional facility if the court is satisfied that the action fails to state a claim upon which relief can be granted or is frivolous or malicious.

SEC. . MODIFICATION OF REQUIRED MINIMUM STANDARDS.

Section 8(b)(2) of the Civil Rights of Institutionalized Persons Act (42 U.S.C.

1997e(b)(2)) is amended by striking subparagraph (A) and redesignating subparagraphs (B) through (E) as subparagraphs (A) through (D), respectively.

SEC. . REVIEW AND CERTIFICATION PROCEDURE CHANGES.

Section 8(c) of the Civil Rights of Institutionalized Persons Act (42 U.S.C. 1997e(c)) is amended—

(1) in paragraph (1), by inserting "or are otherwise fair and effective" before the period at the end; and

(2) in paragraph (2), by inserting "or is no longer fair and effective" before the period at the end.

SEC. . PROCEEDINGS IN FORMA PAUPERIS.

(a) DISMISSAL.—Section 1915(d) of title 28, United States Code, is amended—

(1) by inserting "at any time" after "counsel and may"; and

(2) by striking "and may" and inserting "and shall";

(3) by inserting "fails to state a claim upon which relief may be granted or" after "that the action"; and

(4) by inserting "even if partial failing fees have been imposed by the court" before the period.

(b) PRISONER'S STATEMENT OF ASSETS.—Section 1915 of title 28, United States Code, is amended by adding at the end the following:

"(f) If a prisoner in a correctional institution files an affidavit in accordance with subsection (a) of this section, such prisoner shall include in that affidavit a statement of all assets such prisoner possesses. The court shall make inquiry of the correctional institution in which the prisoner is incarcerated for information available to that institution relating to the extent of the prisoner's assets. The court shall require full or partial payment of filing fees according to the prisoner's ability to pay.".

AMENDMENT OFFERED BY MR. CANADY

At the end of the bill insert the following:

TITLE —PRISON OVERCROWDING

SEC. . APPROPRIATE REMEDIES FOR PRISON OVERCROWDING.

(a) AMENDMENT OF TITLE 18, UNITED STATES CODE.—Subchapter C of chapter 229 of part 2 of title 18, United States Code, is amended by adding at the end the following.

"§3626. Appropriate remedies with respect to prison crowding

"(a) REQUIREMENT OF SHOWING WITH RESPECT TO THE PLAINTIFF IN PARTICULAR.—

"(1) HOLDING.—A Federal court shall not hold prison or jail crowding unconstitutional under the eighth amendment except to the extent that an individual plaintiff inmate proves that the crowding causes the infliction of cruel and unusual punishment of that inmate.

"(2) RELIEF.—The relief in a case described in paragraph (1) shall extend no further than necessary to remove the conditions that are causing the cruel and unusual punishment of the plaintiff inmate.

"(b) INMATE POPULATION CEILINGS.—

"(1) REQUIREMENT OF SHOWING WITH RESPECT TO PARTICULAR PRISONERS.—A Federal court shall not place a ceiling on the inmate population of any Federal, State, or local detention facility as an equitable remedial measure for conditions that violate the eighth amendment unless crowding is inflicting cruel and usual punishment on particular identified prisoners.

"(2) RULE OF CONSTRUCTION.—Paragraph (1) of this subsection shall not be construed to have any effect on Federal judicial power to issue equitable relief other than that described in paragraph (1) of this subsection, including the requirement of improved medical or health care and the imposition of civil contempt fines or damages, where such relief is appropriate.

"(c) PERIODIC REOPENING.—Each Federal court order or consent decree seeking to remedy an eighth amendment violation shall be reopened at the behest of a defendant for recommended modification at a minimum of 2-year intervals.".

(b) APPLICATION OF AMENDMENT.—Section 3626 of title 18, United States Code, as added by paragraph (1), shall apply to all outstanding court orders on the date of enactment of this Act. Any State or municipality shall be entitled to seek modification of any outstanding eighth amendment decree pursuant to that section.

(c) CLERICAL AMENDMENT.—The table of sections at the beginning of subchapter C of chapter 229 of title 18, United States Code, is amended by adding at the end the following new item:

"3626. Appropriate remedies with respect to prison crowding.".

(d) SUNSET PROVISION.—This section and the amendments made by this section are repealed effective as of the date that is 5 years after the date of enactment of this Act.

AMENDMENT OFFERED BY MS. PRYCE OF OHIO:

Add at the end the following:

TITLE —PRISON SECURITY
ENHANCEMENT

SEC. . PRISON SECURITY.

(a) IN GENERAL.—Chapter 303 of title 18, United States Code, is amended by adding at the end the following new section:

"§4017. Strength-training of prisoners prohibited

"The Bureau of Prisons shall take care that—

"(1) prisoners under its jurisdiction do not engage in any activities designed to increase their physical strength or their fighting ability; and

"(2) that all equipment designed for this purpose be removed from Federal correctional facilities."

(b) CLERICAL AMENDMENT.—The table of sections at the beginning of chapter 303 of title 18, United States Code, is amended by adding at the end the following new item:

"4017. Strength-training of prisoners prohibited.".

The CHAIRMAN pro tempore. Pursuant to the rule, the gentleman from Texas [Mr. BROOKS] will be recognized for 5 minutes, and the gentleman from Florida [Mr. McCOLLUM] will be recognized for 5 minutes.

The Chair recognizes the gentleman from Texas [Mr. BROOKS].

MODIFICATION TO AMENDMENTS EN BLOC, AS MODIFIED, OFFERED BY MR. BROOKS

Mr. BROOKS. Mr. Chairman, I ask unanimous consent that the Beilenson amendment, as modified, be that which is at the desk now.

The CHAIRMAN pro tempore. Is there objection to the request of the gentleman from Texas?

There was no objection.

The Clerk will report the modification.

The Clerk read as follows:

Amendment No. 32, as modified, offered by Mr. BEILENSON:

At the end insert the following new title:

TITLE XXIV–CRIMINAL ALIENS

SEC. 2401. INCARCERATION OF UNDOCUMENTED CRIMINAL ALIENS.

(a) INCARCERATION.—Section 242 of the Immigration and Nationality Act (8 U.S.C. 1252) is amended by adding at the end the following:

"(j) INCARCERATION.—

"(1) If the chief official of the State (or, if appropriate, a political subdivision of the State) exercising authority with respect to the incarceration of an undocumented criminal alien (sentenced to a determinate term of imprisonment) submits a written request to the Attorney General, the Attorney General shall, as determined by the Attorney General—

"(A) enter into a contractual arrangement which provides for compensation to the State of a political subdivision of the State, as may be appropriate, with respect to the incarceration of such undocumented criminal alien for such determinate sentence of imprisonment, or

"(B) take the undocumented criminal alien into the custody of the Federal Government and incarcerate such alien for such determinate sentence of imprisonment.

"(2) Compensation under paragraph (1)(A) shall be determined by the Attorney General and may not exceed the median cost of incarceration of a prisoner in all maximum security facilities in the United States as determined by the Bureau of Justice Statistics.

"(3) For purposes of this subsection, the term 'undocumented criminal alien' means an alien who—

"(A) has been convicted of a felony and sentenced to a term of imprisonment, and

"(B)(i) entered the United States without inspection or at any time or place other than as designated by the Attorney General,

"(ii) was the subject of exclusion or deportation proceedings at the time he or she was taken into custody by the State or a political subdivision of the State, or

"(iii) was admitted as a nonimmigrant and at the time he or she was taken into custody by the State or a political subdivision of the State has failed to maintain the nonimmigrant status in which the alien was admitted or to which it was changed under section 248, or to comply with the conditions of any such status.

"(4)(A) In carrying out paragraph (1), the Attorney General shall give priority to the Federal incarceration of undocumented criminal aliens who have committed aggravated felonies.

"(B) The Attorney General shall ensure that undocumented criminal aliens incarcerated in Federal facilities pursuant to this subsection are held in facilities which provide a level of security appropriate to the crimes for which they were convicted."

(b) EFFECTIVE DATE.—The amendments made by this section shall take effect October 1, 1994.

(c) LIMITATION.—The authority created in section 242(j) of the Immigration and Nationality Act (as added by subsection (a)) shall be subject to appropriation until October 1, 1998.

Mr. BROOKS (during the reading). Mr. Chairman, I ask unanimous consent that the amendment, as modified, be considered as read and printed in the RECORD.

The CHAIRMAN pro tempore. Is there objection to the request of the gentleman from Texas?

There was no objection.

☐ 1200

The CHAIRMAN pro tempore (Mr. SPRATT). The Chair recognizes the gentleman from Texas [Mr. BROOKS].

Mr. BROOKS. Mr. Chairman, I yield myself such time as I may consume.

Mr. Chairman, in the interest of moving this legislation toward completion, I am at this time offering a second en block amendment consisting of six provisions made in order under the rule. They are the Beilenson-Berman-Condit-Thurman amendment requiring the Federal Government to incarcerate or to reimburse States and localities for the costs of incarcerating undocumented aliens; the Kennedy amendment to provide criminal history information for use in stalking and domestic violence cases; the Moran amendment protecting the privacy of information provided to State motor vehicle departments; the Canady amendment requiring State prison inmates to exhaust the prison's administrative remedies prior to filing an action in Federal court; the Canady-Geren amendment on prison overcrowding; and finally the Pryce amendment on strength training for prisoners.

These amendments are discussed in the subject matter addressed. And, while I strongly support the Beilenson, Kennedy, and Moran amendments, I have concerns about some of the others. I offer these Democratic and Republican amendments now simply to move this important legislation forward to passage, conference, and enactment into law.

Mr. Chairman, I reserve the balance of my time.

Mr. McCOLLUM. Mr. Chairman, I yield myself such time as I may consume.

Mr. Chairman, I wish to first of all say that I support all of these amendments that are out here today that are being offered. I think that they are a good set of amendments.

They are being done en bloc so we will not have a lot of time to discuss all of them. I certainly support the Beilenson, Berman, Condit, Thurman amendment. It deals with reimbursing the States and paying for costs of housing undocumented aliens in our State prisons. My State of Florida is affected deeply by that.

I do not think it goes far enough. I think the date for its actual enactment ought to be moved up from 1999 so we get this process going on much closer, and I hope we have some opportunity to do that in this process.

I also particularly support the two Canady amendments, the Canady No. 49, and the Canady-Geren amendment. They go a great deal of the distance we need to go toward trying to help alleviate the problems Federal courts have created for prison overcrowding by making rulings that are not always consistent with the way that most of us would think would be the norm for

Mr. BROOKS. Mr. Chairman, I yield 30 seconds to the gentleman from Virginia [Mr. MORAN], the distinguished author of the Moran amendment.

Mr. MORAN. Mr. Chairman, the first thing we are going to do is yield to the subcommittee chairman, the gentleman from California [Mr. EDWARDS], who helped us on this bill that may provide more protection to the individual citizen than virtually any other amendment we have in this bill.

Very few people realize that anybody can write down the license plate number of your spouse and daughter and find out where they live and their name and their Social Security number in many States; it should not be allowed to continue.

Mr. Chairman, I want to thank the Rules Committee for making this amendment in order and to particularly thank the chairman of the Judiciary Subcommittee on Civil and Constitutional Rights, Congressman DON EDWARDS, for holding very constructive hearings on the Driver's Privacy Protection Act, which helped to strengthen and improve this amendment. Congressman EDWARDS is a credit to this institution and he will be sorely missed after his retirement at the end of this session.

The amendment that I am offering today will close a loophole in State law that allows anyone, for any reason, to gain access to personal information—defined as a driver's name, address, and Social Security number—in your DMV file. Currently, in 34 States across the country anyone can walk into a DMV office with your tag number, pay a small fee, and get your name, address, phone number and other personal information—no questions asked. Think about that. A total stranger can obtain personal information about you without knowing anything more about you than your license plate number and you are helpless to stop it.

You may have gone to the trouble of getting an unlisted phone number and address, but the DMV will sell it anyway, to anyone who asks. That's what happened in California to Rebecca Schaeffer, promising young star of the television show "My Sister Sam." Although she had an unlisted home number and address, Ms. Schaeffer was shot to death by an obsessed fan who obtained her name and address through the DMV. In Iowa, a gang of thieves copied down the license plate numbers of expensive cars they saw, found out the names and addresses of the owners and robbed their homes at night. In Virginia, a woman regularly wrote to the DMV, provided the license plate numbers of drivers and asked for the names and addresses of the owners who she claimed were stealing the fillings from her teeth at night.

In each of these cases, the drivers whose personal information was released were never notified of the request or the subsequent release of their information. By selling personal information from DMV records without providing a name removal option, States are violating requirements for procedural fairness and the "due process principles," reflected in the Constitution.

The amendment I am offering simply gives drivers the ability to restrict release of personal information for reasons that are totally incompatible for the reasons it was collected. In doing so, it strikes a critical balance between an individual's fundamental right to privacy and safety and the legitimate governmental and business needs for this information.

The amendment authorizes unlimited access to personal information for courts, law enforcement, governmental agencies, and for other driver and automobile safety purposes. It authorizes access to businesses to verify information provided by the driver and to access personal information if that information is incorrect or outdated. Licensed private detectives could access the information for any purpose authorized in the amendment.

Marketers use DMV lists to do targeted mailings and other types of marketing. This amendment will allow them to continue to do so, as long as they agree not to market drivers who object to their personal information being used for marketing purposes. Eight States have already instituted opt-out systems which allow drivers to restrict the use of their name for marketing purposes. This amendment will not alter those opt-out systems.

My intent is for this provision to furnish States that proceed with opt-out systems with substantial flexibility in the operation of these systems, including the flexibility to furnish multi-purpose users with a single list of license holders. Any driver that had notified the State that he/she did not want to receive direct mail solicitations would still be on that list, but the State would have to clearly identify to the purchaser the individuals to whom solicitations should not be directed and the purchaser would have to agree not to direct solicitation to that driver. In addition, if the multipurpose user resold the file to a third party that only used the information for marketing purposes, the multipurpose user would have to delete all of the names of those individuals that did not want to receive solicitations before the sale of that file. To the extent that the possibility of confusion exists on this issue, I would welcome appropriate changes to the language in conference that would clarify my intention.

The amendment would also allow any non-authorized person to access DMV information, as long as the DMV provides all drivers the opportunity to restrict the sale of their personal information for non-authorized purposes. The basic presumption is that personal information in DMV records will be open unless a licensee specifically restricts access for non-authorized purposes. If drivers choose to restrict access to their file, someone coming in off the street, without a permissible purpose could not gain access to that person's file. However, insurance companies, law enforcement professionals, attorneys, and all other authorized users would continue to have access to this information.

This particular provision was added after hearings were held on the Driver's Privacy Protection Act and the press raised concerns that they would not have access to personal information held by the DMV. Although my staff tried to come up with language to specifically authorize access by the press, they didn't want it, claiming they didn't want to be treated any differently than the general public. So, in order to accommodate them, we changed the bill to allow access to all personal information unless a licensee specifically restricts it. Press groups support this approach.

It is very important to note that the amendment in no way affects access to accident information about the car or driver. Nothing in this bill would stop anyone from finding out another person's driving record, accidents, or status.

In addition, the amendment only penalizes individuals who knowingly obtain, disclose or use personal information for a purpose not permitted under the amendment. Individual drivers aggrieved by such illegal release could sue for damages in district court.

The amendment before the House today reflects many comments and suggestions received during hearings held by the Subcommittee on Civil and Constitutional Rights. Changes were made to the Driver's Privacy Protection Act as a result of those hearings that make this amendment very different than the amendment that was offered to the crime bill by Senator BOXER. Unlike the Boxer amendment, my amendment allows greater access for private detectives and the press and more flexibility to the States in allowing additional uses of personal information.

Another aspect of this legislation which received considerable attention at the hearings was the potential impact of the Driver's Privacy Protection Act on access rules applying to other kinds of public records held by State and local governments. The key difference between DMV records and other public records comes from the license plate, through which every vehicle on the public highways can be linked to a specific individual. Anyone with access to data linking license plates with vehicle ownership has the ability to ascertain the name and address of the person who owns that vehicle. Other public records are not vulnerable to abuse in the same way.

Unlike with license plate numbers, people concerned about privacy can usually take reasonable steps to withhold their names and addresses from strangers, and thus limit their access to personally identifiable information. By contrast, no one is free to conceal his or her license plate while traveling by automobile.

Recognizing this distinction, this amendment applies only to specified categories of personal information contained in motor vehicle records. It does not apply to any other systems of public records maintained by States or local governments.

There are many organizations and businesses specifically concerned about easy access to DMV information. That's why this amendment is strongly supported by over 20 organizations, including the standard-making body for all State DMVs, the American Association of Motor Vehicle Administrators, the National Consumers League, the Fraternal Order of Police, the American Insurance Association, and other business, consumer, police, physician, and victim's groups.

I urge my colleagues to support this amendment and protect the privacy of all Americans.

Mr. BROOKS. Mr. Chairman, I yield 30 seconds to the gentleman from California [Mr. EDWARDS].

Mr. EDWARDS of California. Mr. Chairman, the gentleman from Virginia [Mr. MORAN] worked very closely with the subcommittee I chair. We held 2 days of hearings on his amendment to this bill. It is a good bill.

The gentleman from Virginia [Mr. MORAN] was very skillful in writing the bill and very cooperative in working with the subcommittee, and we are looking forward to having the Moran proposal becoming law.

Mr. Chairman, this amendment requires States to adopt an opt-out when information about vehicle registrants or drivers is disclosed in bulk for use in marketing and solicitation.

Our intent is to give States that proceed with opt-out systems flexibility in the operation of these systems, including the flexibility to furnish multi-purpose users with a single list as long as the State ensures that solicitations are not directed at individuals who have requested of the DMV in a timely fashion that solicitations not be directed at them based on their motor vehicle records.

One means of accomplishing this would be for the State to flag or otherwise identify to the list purchaser the individuals to whom solicitations should not be directed. This is a common practice in the States that currently have an opt-out system in place. It is our intent that this amendment permit the continuation of this method and procedure in those States and in other States wishing to implement an opt-out system. Such multipurpose users may redisseminate lists of drivers or registrants only after they have excluded the flagged names.

Indeed, one of the advantages of this flagging type of procedure is that it may be more effective than a suppression procedure in ensuring that individuals how have opted-out in fact not have solicitations directed at them. These individuals most probably already are on various solicitation lists previously compiled from information obtained from motor vehicle records and other sources. The list users update their data with information obtained from motor vehicle departments. If the updates simply skip over the names and addresses of individuals who have opted out, the desire of these individuals to opt-out will not be disclosed to the list users who in turn will leave undisturbed the names and addresses of these individuals in their historical lists. Consequently, without flagged names and addresses, the list users probably would continue soliciting these households based on the earlier record they compiled, eventually stopping years later when the data becomes obsolete. By comparison, flagging names and addresses permits the opt-out to go into effect immediately because it enables the list purchaser to match these individuals against all name and address outputs to ensure that a flagged record is not released.

To the extent that the possibility of confusion exists on this issue, we may make further changes to the language in conference that would clarify my intention.

One other aspect of this legislation which received considerable attention at the subcommittee's hearings deserves further discussion: The potential precedential impact of the Driver's Privacy Protection Act on access rules applying to other kinds of public records held by State and local governments. These governments collect and maintain large quantities of records that have traditionally been open to broad public access, including land transaction and ownership records, voter registration rolls, court records, and corporate legal filings, among others. The testimony before the subcommittee underscored the need to maintain the public record character of this data, even if it is necessary to impose restrictions on access to some personal data held by State motor vehicle administrations.

There are key differences between DMV records and other public records. There was no evidence before the subcommittee that other public records are vulnerable to abuse in the same way that DMV records have been abused. Unlike with license plate numbers, people concerned about privacy can usually take reasonable steps to withhold their names and address from strangers, and thus limit their access to personally identifiable information contained in voter registration lists, court records, or land records. By contrast, no one is free to conceal his or her license plate while traveling by automobile.

Recognizing this distinction, this legislation applies only to specified categories of personal information contained in motor vehicle records. It does not apply to any other systems of public records maintained by States or local governments. There was testimony before the subcommittee that these records should remain publicly accessible in accordance with applicable State law. Broad public access to such records remains enormously important to our society, for preservation of a free press, for government accountability, and for a number of valuable economic and business applications.

Mr. BROOKS. Mr. Chairman, I yield such time as he may consume to the gentleman from Texas [Mr. PETE GEREN].

TITLE 18 U.S. Code, Part I, Chapter 73

OBSTRUCTION OF JUSTICE

§ 1501. Assault on process server

Whoever knowingly and willfully obstructs, resists, or opposes any officer of the United States, or other person duly authorized, in serving, or attempting to serve or execute, any legal or judicial writ or process of any court of the United States, or United States magistrate judge; or

Whoever assaults, beats, or wounds any officer or other person duly authorized, knowing him to be such officer, or other person so duly authorized, in serving or executing any such writ, rule, order, process, warrant, or other legal or judicial writ or process—

Shall, except as otherwise provided by law, be fined under this title or imprisoned not more than one year, or both.

§ 1502. Resistance to extradition agent

Whoever knowingly and willfully obstructs, resists, or opposes an extradition agent of the United States in the execution of his duties, shall be fined under this title or imprisoned not more than one year, or both.

§ 1503. Influencing or injuring officer or juror generally

(a) Whoever corruptly, or by threats or force, or by any threatening letter or communication, endeavors to influence, intimidate, or impede any grand or petit juror, or officer in or of any court of the United States, or officer who may be serving at any examination or other proceeding before any United States magistrate judge or other committing magistrate, in the discharge of his duty, or injures any such grand or petit juror in his person or property on account of any verdict or indictment assented to by him, or on account of his being or having been such juror, or injures any such officer, magistrate judge, or other committing magistrate in his person or property on account of the performance of his official duties, or corruptly or by threats or force, or by any threatening letter or communication, influences, obstructs, or impedes, or endeavors to influence, obstruct, or impede, the due administration of justice, shall be punished as provided in subsection (b). If the offense under this section occurs in connection with a trial of a criminal case, and the act in violation of this section involves the threat of physical force or physical force, the maximum term of imprisonment which may be imposed for the offense shall be the higher of that otherwise provided by law or the maximum term that could have been imposed for any offense charged in such case.

(b) The punishment for an offense under this section is—

(1) in the case of a killing, the punishment provided in sections 1111 and 1112;

(2) in the case of an attempted killing, or a case in which the offense was committed against a petit juror and in which a class A or B felony was charged, imprisonment for not more than 20 years, a fine under this title, or both; and

(3) in any other case, imprisonment for not more than 10 years, a fine under this title, or both.

§ 1504. Influencing juror by writing

Whoever attempts to influence the action or decision of any grand or petit juror of any court of the United States upon any issue or matter pending before such juror, or before the jury of which he is a member, or pertaining to his duties, by writing or sending to him any written communication, in relation to such issue or matter, shall be fined under this title or imprisoned not more than six months, or both.

Nothing in this section shall be construed to prohibit the communication of a request to appear before the grand jury.

§ 1505. Obstruction of proceedings before departments, agencies, and committees

Whoever, with intent to avoid, evade, prevent, or obstruct compliance, in whole or in part, with any civil investigative demand duly and properly made under the Antitrust Civil Process Act, willfully withholds, misrepresents, removes from any place, conceals, covers up, destroys, mutilates, alters, or by other means falsifies any documentary material, answers to written interrogatories, or oral testimony, which is the subject of such demand; or attempts to do so or solicits another to do so; or

Whoever corruptly, or by threats or force, or by any threatening letter or communication influences, obstructs, or impedes or endeavors to influence, obstruct, or impede the due and proper administration of the law under which any pending proceeding is being had before any department or agency of the United States, or the due and proper exercise of the power of inquiry under which any inquiry or investigation is being had by either House, or any committee of either House or any joint committee of the Congress—

Shall be fined under this title, imprisoned not more than 5 years or, if the offense involves international or domestic terrorism (as defined in section 2331), imprisoned not more than 8 years, or both.

§ 1506. Theft or alteration of record or process; false bail

Whoever feloniously steals, takes away, alters, falsifies, or otherwise avoids any record, writ, process, or other proceeding, in any court of the United States, whereby any judgment is reversed, made void, or does not take effect; or

Whoever acknowledges, or procures to be acknowledged in any such court, any recognizance, bail, or judgment, in the name of any other person not privy or consenting to the same—

Shall be fined under this title or imprisoned not more than five years, or both.

§ 1507.   Picketing or parading

Whoever, with the intent of interfering with, obstructing, or impeding the administration of justice, or with the intent of influencing any judge, juror, witness, or court officer, in the discharge of his duty, pickets or parades in or near a building housing a court of the United States, or in or near a building or residence occupied or used by such judge, juror, witness, or court officer, or with such intent uses any sound-truck or similar device or resorts to any other demonstration in or near any such building or residence, shall be fined under this title or imprisoned not more than one year, or both.

Nothing in this section shall interfere with or prevent the exercise by any court of the United States of its power to punish for contempt.

§ 1508.   Recording, listening to, or observing proceedings of grand or petit juries while deliberating or voting

Whoever knowingly and willfully, by any means or device whatsoever—

(a) records, or attempts to record, the proceedings of any grand or petit jury in any court of the United States while such jury is deliberating or voting; or

(b) listens to or observes, or attempts to listen to or observe, the proceedings of any grand or petit jury of which he is not a member in any court of the United States while such jury is deliberating or voting—

shall be fined under this title or imprisoned not more than one year, or both.

Nothing in paragraph (a) of this section shall be construed to prohibit the taking of notes by a grand or petit juror in any court of the United States in connection with and solely for the purpose of assisting him in the performance of his duties as such juror.

§ 1509.   Obstruction of court orders

Whoever, by threats or force, willfully prevents, obstructs, impedes, or interferes with, or willfully attempts to prevent, obstruct, impede, or interfere with, the due exercise of rights or the performance of duties under any order, judgment, or decree of a court of the United States, shall be fined under this title or imprisoned not more than one year, or both.

No injunctive or other civil relief against the conduct made criminal by this section shall be denied on the ground that such conduct is a crime.

§ 1510.   Obstruction of criminal investigations

(a) Whoever willfully endeavors by means of bribery to obstruct, delay, or prevent the communication of information relating to a violation of any criminal statute of the United States by any person to a criminal investigator shall be fined under this title, or imprisoned not more than five years, or both.

(b)(1) Whoever, being an officer of a financial institution, with the intent to obstruct a judicial proceeding, directly or indirectly notifies any other person about the existence or contents of a subpoena for records of that financial institution, or information that has been furnished in response to that subpoena, shall be fined under this title or imprisoned not more than 5 years, or both.

(2) Whoever, being an officer of a financial institution, directly or indirectly notifies—

(A) a customer of that financial institution whose records are sought by a subpoena for records; or

(B) any other person named in that subpoena;

about the existence or contents of that subpoena or information that has been furnished in response to that subpoena, shall be fined under this title or imprisoned not more than one year, or both.

(3) As used in this subsection—

(A) the term "an officer of a financial institution" means an officer, director, partner, employee, agent, or attorney of or for a financial institution; and

(B) the term "subpoena for records" means a Federal grand jury subpoena or a Department of Justice subpoena (issued under section 3486 of title 18), for customer records that has been served relating to a violation of, or a conspiracy to violate—

(i) section 215, 656, 657, 1005, 1006, 1007, 1014, 1344, 1956, 1957, or chapter 53 of title 31; or

(ii) section 1341 or 1343 affecting a financial institution.

(c) As used in this section, the term "criminal investigator" means any individual duly authorized by a department, agency, or armed force of the United States to conduct or engage in investigations of or prosecutions for violations of the criminal laws of the United States.

(d)(1) Whoever—

(A) acting as, or being, an officer, director, agent or employee of a person engaged in the business of insurance whose activities affect interstate commerce, or

(B) is engaged in the business of insurance whose activities affect interstate commerce or is involved (other than as an insured or beneficiary under a policy of insurance) in a transaction relating to the conduct of affairs of such a business, with intent to obstruct a judicial proceeding, directly or indirectly notifies any other person about the existence or contents of a subpoena for records of that person engaged in such business or information that has been furnished to a Federal grand jury in response to that subpoena, shall be fined as provided by this title or imprisoned not more than 5 years, or both.

(2) As used in paragraph (1), the term "subpoena for records" means a Federal grand jury subpoena for records that has been served relating to a violation of, or a conspiracy to violate, section 1033 of this title.

(e) Whoever, having been notified of the applicable disclosure prohibitions or confidentiality requirements of section 2709(c)(1) of this title, section 626(d)(1) or 627(c)(1) of the Fair Credit Reporting Act (15 U.S.C. 1681u(d)(1) or 1681v(c)(1)), section 1114(a)(3)(A) or 1114(a)(5)(D)(i) of the Right to Financial Privacy Act [1] (12 U.S.C. 3414(a)(3)(A) or 3414(a)(5)(D)(i)), or section 802(b)(1) of the National Security Act of 1947 (50 U.S.C. 436(b)(1)), knowingly and with the intent to obstruct an investigation or judicial proceeding violates such prohibitions or requirements applicable by law to such person shall be imprisoned for not more than five years, fined under this title, or both.

§ 1511.   Obstruction of State or local law enforcement

(a) It shall be unlawful for two or more persons to conspire to obstruct the enforcement of the criminal laws of a State or political subdivision thereof, with the intent to facilitate an illegal gambling business if —

(1) one or more of such persons does any act to effect the object of such a conspiracy;

(2) one or more of such persons is an official or employee, elected, appointed, or otherwise, of such State or political subdivision; and

(3) one or more of such persons conducts, finances, manages, supervises, directs, or owns all or part of an illegal gambling business.

(b) As used in this section —

(1) "illegal gambling business" means a gambling business which —

(i) is a violation of the law of a State or political subdivision in which it is conducted;

(ii) involves five or more persons who conduct, finance, manage, supervise, direct, or own all or part of such business; and

(iii) has been or remains in substantially continuous operation for a period in excess of thirty days or has a gross revenue of $2,000 in any single day.

(2) "gambling" includes but is not limited to pool-selling, bookmaking, maintaining slot machines, roulette wheels, or dice tables, and conducting lotteries, policy, bolita or numbers games, or selling chances therein.

(3) "State" means any State of the United States, the District of Columbia, the Commonwealth of Puerto Rico, and any territory or possession of the United States.

---

1. So in original. Probably should be followed by "of 1978".

(c) This section shall not apply to any bingo game, lottery, or similar game of chance conducted by an organization exempt from tax under paragraph (3) of subsection (c) of section 501 of the Internal Revenue Code of 1986, as amended, if no part of the gross receipts derived from such activity inures to the benefit of any private shareholder, member, or employee of such organization, except as compensation for actual expenses incurred by him in the conduct of such activity.

(d) Whoever violates this section shall be punished by a fine under this title or imprisonment for not more than five years, or both.

§ 1512.   Tampering with a witness, victim, or an informant

(a)(1) Whoever kills or attempts to kill another person, with intent to —

(A) prevent the attendance or testimony of any person in an official proceeding;

(B) prevent the production of a record, document, or other object, in an official proceeding; or

(C) prevent the communication by any person to a law enforcement officer or judge of the United States of information relating to the commission or possible commission of a Federal offense or a violation of conditions of probation, parole, or release pending judicial proceedings;

shall be punished as provided in paragraph (3).

(2) Whoever uses physical force or the threat of physical force against any person, or attempts to do so, with intent to —

(A) influence, delay, or prevent the testimony of any person in an official proceeding;

(B) cause or induce any person to —

(i) withhold testimony, or withhold a record, document, or other object, from an official proceeding;

(ii) alter, destroy, mutilate, or conceal an object with intent to impair the integrity or availability of the object for use in an official proceeding;

(iii) evade legal process summoning that person to appear as a witness, or to produce a record, document, or other object, in an official proceeding; or

(iv) be absent from an official proceeding to which that person has been summoned by legal process; or

(C) hinder, delay, or prevent the communication to a law enforcement officer or judge of the United States of information relating to the commission or possible commission of a Federal offense or a violation of conditions of probation, supervised release, parole, or release pending judicial proceedings;

shall be punished as provided in paragraph (3).

(3) The punishment for an offense under this subsection is —

(A) in the case of a killing, the punishment provided in sections 1111 and 1112;

(B) in the case of —

(i) an attempt to murder; or

(ii) the use or attempted use of physical force against any person; imprisonment for not more than 30 years; and

(C) in the case of the threat of use of physical force against any person, imprisonment for not more than 20 years.

(b) Whoever knowingly uses intimidation, threatens, or corruptly persuades another person, or attempts to do so, or engages in misleading conduct toward another person, with intent to —

(1) influence, delay, or prevent the testimony of any person in an official proceeding;

(2) cause or induce any person to —

(A) withhold testimony, or withhold a record, document, or other object, from an official proceeding;

(B) alter, destroy, mutilate, or conceal an object with intent to impair the object's integrity or availability for use in an official proceeding;

(C) evade legal process summoning that person to appear as a witness, or to produce a record, document, or other object, in an official proceeding; or

(D) be absent from an official proceeding to which such person has been summoned by legal process; or

(3) hinder, delay, or prevent the communication to a law enforcement officer or judge of the United States of information relating to the commission or possible commission of a Federal offense or a violation of conditions of probation supervised release,, parole, or release pending judicial proceedings;

shall be fined under this title or imprisoned not more than 20 years, or both.

(c) Whoever corruptly —

(1) alters, destroys, mutilates, or conceals a record, document, or other object, or attempts to do so, with the intent to impair the object's integrity or availability for use in an official proceeding; or

(2) otherwise obstructs, influences, or impedes any official proceeding, or attempts to do so, shall be fined under this title or imprisoned not more than 20 years, or both.

(d) Whoever intentionally harasses another person and thereby hinders, delays, prevents, or dissuades any person from —

(1) attending or testifying in an official proceeding;

(2) reporting to a law enforcement officer or judge of the United States the commission or possible commission of a Federal offense or a violation of conditions of probation[1] supervised release,,[1] parole, or release pending judicial proceedings;

(3) arresting or seeking the arrest of another person in connection with a Federal offense; or

(4) causing a criminal prosecution, or a parole or probation revocation proceeding, to be sought or instituted, or assisting in such prosecution or proceeding;

or attempts to do so, shall be fined under this title or imprisoned not more than 3 years, or both.

(e) In a prosecution for an offense under this section, it is an affirmative defense, as to which the defendant has the burden of proof by a preponderance of the evidence, that the conduct consisted solely of lawful conduct and that the defendant's sole intention was to encourage, induce, or cause the other person to testify truthfully.

(f) For the purposes of this section—

(1) an official proceeding need not be pending or about to be instituted at the time of the offense; and

(2) the testimony, or the record, document, or other object need not be admissible in evidence or free of a claim of privilege.

(g) In a prosecution for an offense under this section, no state of mind need be proved with respect to the circumstance—

(1) that the official proceeding before a judge, court, magistrate judge, grand jury, or government agency is before a judge or court of the United States, a United States magistrate judge, a bankruptcy judge, a Federal grand jury, or a Federal Government agency; or

(2) that the judge is a judge of the United States or that the law enforcement officer is an officer or employee of the Federal Government or a person authorized to act for or on behalf of the Federal Government or serving the Federal Government as an adviser or consultant.

(h) There is extraterritorial Federal jurisdiction over an offense under this section.

(i) A prosecution under this section or section 1503 may be brought in the district in which the official proceeding (whether or not pending or about to be instituted) was intended to be affected or in the district in which the conduct constituting the alleged offense occurred.

(j) If the offense under this section occurs in connection with a trial of a criminal case, the maximum term of imprisonment which may be imposed for the offense shall be the higher of that otherwise provided by law or the maximum term that could have been imposed for any offense charged in such case.

---

1. So in original.

(k) Whoever conspires to commit any offense under this section shall be subject to the same penalties as those prescribed for the offense the commission of which was the object of the conspiracy.

§ 1513.　Retaliating against a witness, victim, or an informant

(a)(1) Whoever kills or attempts to kill another person with intent to retaliate against any person for—

　　(A) the attendance of a witness or party at an official proceeding, or any testimony given or any record, document, or other object produced by a witness in an official proceeding; or

　　(B) providing to a law enforcement officer any information relating to the commission or possible commission of a Federal offense or a violation of conditions of probation, supervised release, parole, or release pending judicial proceedings,

shall be punished as provided in paragraph (2).

(2) The punishment for an offense under this subsection is—

　　(A) in the case of a killing, the punishment provided in sections 1111 and 1112; and

　　(B) in the case of an attempt, imprisonment for not more than 30 years.

(b) Whoever knowingly engages in any conduct and thereby causes bodily injury to another person or damages the tangible property of another person, or threatens to do so, with intent to retaliate against any person for—

　　(1) the attendance of a witness or party at an official proceeding, or any testimony given or any record, document, or other object produced by a witness in an official proceeding; or

　　(2) any information relating to the commission or possible commission of a Federal offense or a violation of conditions of probation, supervised release, parole, or release pending judicial proceedings given by a person to a law enforcement officer;

or attempts to do so, shall be fined under this title or imprisoned not more than 20 years, or both.

(c) If the retaliation occurred because of attendance at or testimony in a criminal case, the maximum term of imprisonment which may be imposed for the offense under this section shall be the higher of that otherwise provided by law or the maximum term that could have been imposed for any offense charged in such case.

(d) There is extraterritorial Federal jurisdiction over an offense under this section.

(e) Whoever knowingly, with the intent to retaliate, takes any action harmful to any person, including interference with the lawful employment or livelihood of any person, for providing to a law enforcement officer any truthful information relating to the commission or possible commission of any Federal offense, shall be fined under this title or imprisoned not more than 10 years, or both.

(f) Whoever conspires to commit any offense under this section shall be subject to the same penalties as those prescribed for the offense the commission of which was the object of the conspiracy.

(g) A prosecution under this section may be brought in the district in which the official proceeding (whether pending, about to be instituted, or completed) was intended to be affected, or in which the conduct constituting the alleged offense occurred.

§ 1514. Civil action to restrain harassment of a victim or witness

[Omitted]

§ 1514A. Civil action to protect against retaliation in fraud cases

(a) Whistleblower Protection for Employees of Publicly Traded Companies.—No company with a class of securities registered under section 12 of the Securities Exchange Act of 1934 (15 U.S.C. 78l), or that is required to file reports under section 15(d) of the Securities Exchange Act of 1934 (15 U.S.C. 78o(d)) including any subsidiary or affiliate whose financial information is included in the consolidated financial statements of such company, or nationally recognized statistical rating organization (as defined in section 3(a) of the Securities Exchange Act of 1934 (15 U.S.C. 78c),[1] or any officer, employee, contractor, subcontractor, or agent of such company or nationally recognized statistical rating organization, may discharge, demote, suspend, threaten, harass, or in any other manner discriminate against an employee in the terms and conditions of employment because of any lawful act done by the employee—

(1) to provide information, cause information to be provided, or otherwise assist in an investigation regarding any conduct which the employee reasonably believes constitutes a violation of section 1341, 1343, 1344, or 1348, any rule or regulation of the Securities and Exchange Commission, or any provision of Federal law relating to fraud against shareholders, when the information or assistance is provided to or the investigation is conducted by—

(A) a Federal regulatory or law enforcement agency;

(B) any Member of Congress or any committee of Congress; or

(C) a person with supervisory authority over the employee (or such other person working for the employer who has the authority to investigate, discover, or terminate misconduct); or

---

1. So in original. Another closing parenthesis probably should precede the comma.

(2) to file, cause to be filed, testify, participate in, or otherwise assist in a proceeding filed or about to be filed (with any knowledge of the employer) relating to an alleged violation of section 1341, 1343, 1344, or 1348, any rule or regulation of the Securities and Exchange Commission, or any provision of Federal law relating to fraud against shareholders.

(b) Enforcement Action.—

(1) In general.—A person who alleges discharge or other discrimination by any person in violation of subsection (a) may seek relief under subsection (c), by—

(A) filing a complaint with the Secretary of Labor; or

(B) if the Secretary has not issued a final decision within 180 days of the filing of the complaint and there is no showing that such delay is due to the bad faith of the claimant, bringing an action at law or equity for de novo review in the appropriate district court of the United States, which shall have jurisdiction over such an action without regard to the amount in controversy.

(2) Procedure.—

(A) In general.—An action under paragraph (1)(A) shall be governed under the rules and procedures set forth in section 42121(b) of title 49, United States Code.

(B) Exception.—Notification made under section 42121(b)(1) of title 49, United States Code, shall be made to the person named in the complaint and to the employer.

(C) Burdens of proof.—An action brought under paragraph (1)(B) shall be governed by the legal burdens of proof set forth in section 42121(b) of title 49, United States Code.

(D) Statute of limitations.—An action under paragraph (1) shall be commenced not later than 180 days after the date on which the violation occurs, or after the date on which the employee became aware of the violation.

(E) Jury trial.—A party to an action brought under paragraph (1)(B) shall be entitled to trial by jury.

(c) Remedies.—

(1) In general.—An employee prevailing in any action under subsection (b)(1) shall be entitled to all relief necessary to make the employee whole.

(2) Compensatory damages.—Relief for any action under paragraph (1) shall include—

(A) reinstatement with the same seniority status that the employee would have had, but for the discrimination;

(B) the amount of back pay, with interest; and

(C) compensation for any special damages sustained as a result of the discrimination, including litigation costs, expert witness fees, and reasonable attorney fees.

(d) Rights Retained by Employee.—Nothing in this section shall be deemed to diminish the rights, privileges, or remedies of any employee under any Federal or State law, or under any collective bargaining agreement.

(e) Nonenforceability of Certain Provisions Waiving Rights and Remedies or Requiring Arbitration of Disputes.—

(1) Waiver of rights and remedies.—The rights and remedies provided for in this section may not be waived by any agreement, policy form, or condition of employment, including by a predispute arbitration agreement.

(2) Predispute arbitration agreements.—No predispute arbitration agreement shall be valid or enforceable, if the agreement requires arbitration of a dispute arising under this section.

§ 1515.   Definitions for certain provisions; general provision

(a) As used in sections 1512 and 1513 of this title and in this section—

(1) the term "official proceeding" means—

(A) a proceeding before a judge or court of the United States, a United States magistrate judge, a bankruptcy judge, a judge of the United States Tax Court, a special trial judge of the Tax Court, a judge of the United States Court of Federal Claims, or a Federal grand jury;

(B) a proceeding before the Congress;

(C) a proceeding before a Federal Government agency which is authorized by law; or

(D) a proceeding involving the business of insurance whose activities affect interstate commerce before any insurance regulatory official or agency or any agent or examiner appointed by such official or agency to examine the affairs of any person engaged in the business of insurance whose activities affect interstate commerce;

(2) the term "physical force" means physical action against another, and includes confinement;

(3) the term "misleading conduct" means—

(A) knowingly making a false statement;

(B) intentionally omitting information from a statement and thereby causing a portion of such statement to be misleading, or intentionally concealing a material fact, and thereby creating a false impression by such statement;

(C) with intent to mislead, knowingly submitting or inviting reliance on a writing or recording that is false, forged, altered, or otherwise lacking in authenticity;

(D) with intent to mislead, knowingly submitting or inviting reliance on a sample, specimen, map, photograph, boundary mark, or other object that is misleading in a material respect; or

(E) knowingly using a trick, scheme, or device with intent to mislead;

(4) the term "law enforcement officer" means an officer or employee of the Federal Government, or a person authorized to act for or on behalf of the Federal Government or serving the Federal Government as an adviser or consultant—

(A) authorized under law to engage in or supervise the prevention, detection, investigation, or prosecution of an offense; or

(B) serving as a probation or pretrial services officer under this title;

(5) the term "bodily injury" means—

(A) a cut, abrasion, bruise, burn, or disfigurement;

(B) physical pain;

(C) illness;

(D) impairment of the function of a bodily member, organ, or mental faculty; or

(E) any other injury to the body, no matter how temporary; and

(6) the term "corruptly persuades" does not include conduct which would be misleading conduct but for a lack of a state of mind.

(b) As used in section 1505, the term "corruptly" means acting with an improper purpose, personally or by influencing another, including making a false or misleading statement, or withholding, concealing, altering, or destroying a document or other information.

(c) This chapter does not prohibit or punish the providing of lawful, bona fide, legal representation services in connection with or anticipation of an official proceeding.

§ 1516.   Obstruction of Federal audit

(a) Whoever, with intent to deceive or defraud the United States, endeavors to influence, obstruct, or impede a Federal auditor in the performance of official duties relating to a person, entity, or program receiving in excess of $100,000, directly or indirectly, from the United States in any 1 year period under a contract or subcontract, grant, or cooperative agreement, or relating to any property that is security for a mortgage note that is insured, guaranteed, acquired, or held by the Secretary of Housing and Urban Development pursuant to any Act administered by the Secretary, or relating to any property that is security for a loan that is made or guaranteed under title V of the Housing Act of 1949, shall be fined under this title, or imprisoned not more than 5 years, or both.

(b) For purposes of this section—

(1) the term "Federal auditor" means any person employed on a full- or part-time or contractual basis to perform an audit or a quality assurance inspection for or on behalf of the United States; and

(2) the term "in any 1 year period" has the meaning given to the term "in any one-year period" in section 666.

§ 1517.   Obstructing examination of financial institution

Whoever corruptly obstructs or attempts to obstruct any examination of a financial institution by an agency of the United States with jurisdiction to conduct an examination of such financial institution shall be fined under this title, imprisoned not more than 5 years, or both.

§ 1518.   Obstruction of criminal investigations of health care offenses

(a) Whoever willfully prevents, obstructs, misleads, delays or attempts to prevent, obstruct, mislead, or delay the communication of information or records relating to a violation of a Federal health care offense to a criminal investigator shall be fined under this title or imprisoned not more than 5 years, or both.

(b) As used in this section the term "criminal investigator" means any individual duly authorized by a department, agency, or armed force of the United States to conduct or engage in investigations for prosecutions for violations of health care offenses.

§ 1519.   Destruction, alteration, or falsification of records in Federal investigations and bankruptcy

Whoever knowingly alters, destroys, mutilates, conceals, covers up, falsifies, or makes a false entry in any record, document, or tangible object with the intent to impede, obstruct, or influence the investigation or proper administration of any matter within the jurisdiction of any department or agency of the United States or any case filed under title 11, or in relation to or contemplation of any such matter or case, shall be fined under this title, imprisoned not more than 20 years, or both.

§ 1520.   Destruction of corporate audit records

(a)(1) Any accountant who conducts an audit of an issuer of securities to which section 10A(a) of the Securities Exchange Act of 1934 (15 U.S.C. 78j–1(a)) applies, shall maintain all audit or review workpapers for a period of 5 years from the end of the fiscal period in which the audit or review was concluded.

(2) The Securities and Exchange Commission shall promulgate, within 180 days, after adequate notice and an opportunity for comment, such rules and regulations, as are reasonably necessary, relating to the retention of relevant records such as workpapers, documents that form the basis of an audit or review, memoranda, correspondence, communications, other documents, and records (including electronic records) which are created, sent, or received in connection with an audit or review and contain conclusions, opinions, analyses, or financial data relating to such

an audit or review, which is conducted by any accountant who conducts an audit of an issuer of securities to which section 10A(a) of the Securities Exchange Act of 1934 (15 U.S.C. 78j–1(a)) applies. The Commission may, from time to time, amend or supplement the rules and regulations that it is required to promulgate under this section, after adequate notice and an opportunity for comment, in order to ensure that such rules and regulations adequately comport with the purposes of this section.

(b) Whoever knowingly and willfully violates subsection (a)(1), or any rule or regulation promulgated by the Securities and Exchange Commission under subsection (a)(2), shall be fined under this title, imprisoned not more than 10 years, or both.

(c) Nothing in this section shall be deemed to diminish or relieve any person of any other duty or obligation imposed by Federal or State law or regulation to maintain, or refrain from destroying, any document.

§ 1521. Retaliating against a Federal judge or Federal law enforcement officer by false claim or slander of title

Whoever files, attempts to file, or conspires to file, in any public record or in any private record which is generally available to the public, any false lien or encumbrance against the real or personal property of an individual described in section 1114, on account of the performance of official duties by that individual, knowing or having reason to know that such lien or encumbrance is false or contains any materially false, fictitious, or fraudulent statement or representation, shall be fined under this title or imprisoned for not more than 10 years, or both.

Selected Legislative History:
The Civil Rights Attorney's Fees
Awards Act of 1976

[121 Cong. Rec. S 14975 (daily ed., Aug. 1, 1975)]

By Mr. TUNNEY:

S. 2278. A bill entitled "The Civil Rights Attorneys' Fees Awards Act of 1975." Referred to the Committee on the Judiciary.

CIVIL RIGHTS ATTORNEYS' FEES AWARDS ACT

Mr. TUNNEY. Mr. President, today I am introducing a bill which would allow a court, in its discretion, to award attorney's fees to a prevailing party in suits brought to enforce the civil rights acts which Congress has passed since 1866.

This bill is identical to a provision in S. 1279, the Senate version of the Voting Rights Act extension, which was reported favorably by the Subcommittee on Constitutional Rights by a vote of 8 to 2, and by the full Judiciary Committee by a vote of 10 to 4. As you know, the time pressure created by the August 6th expiration date of the Voting Rights Act prevented the Senate from considering its own version of the extension. Even though I felt strongly about this attorney's fees provision that was in the Senate version, as floor manager I urged passage of the House version without substantial modification because I felt that the need to get a Voting Rights Act passed before its expiration was an overriding consideration. As a result, this provision of S. 1279 was never taken up by the full Senate. I introduce it today as a separate bill in the hope that it can receive the swift consideration of this body.

The purpose and effect of this bill is simple—it is to allow the courts to provide the traditional remedy of reasonable counsel fee awards to private citizens who must go to court to vindicate their rights under our civil rights statutes. The Supreme Court's recent Alyeska decision has required specific statutory authorization if Federal courts are to continue previous policies of awarding fees under all Federal civil rights statutes. This bill simply applies the type of "fee-shifting" provision already contained in titles II and VII of the 1964 Civil Rights Act to the other civil rights statutes which do not already specifically authorize fee awards. It therefore restores to the Federal courts authority which they had exercised for years until a little over 2 months ago.

In the typical case that arises under these statutes the citizen whose rights have been violated has little or no money with which to hire a lawyer, and there is often no damage claim from which an attorney could draw his fee. If private citizens are to be able to assert their rights under these laws—if those who violate these most basic human freedoms are not to proceed with impunity—then citizens must have the opportunity to recover what it costs them to vindicate these rights in court.

Congress recognized this need when it made specific provision for such fee-shifting in titles II and VII of the Civil Rights Act of 1964,

(3)

4

which apply to discrimination in public accommodations and employment. This sort of provision is equally appropriate in other civil rights statutes, because there, as in employment and public accommodations cases, Congress depends heavily on private enforcement.

Mr. President, the reason why this legislation specifically authorizing fee awards under all our civil rights laws was not introduced years ago is simply that, until very recently, it was widely believed and held that the courts already had the power to award counsel fees in all civil rights cases as part of their inherent equity power. Before May 12 of this year, when the Supreme Court issued its opinion in Alyeska Pipeline Service Co. against Wilderness Society, many lower Federal courts had followed the congressional fee-shifting policies of titles II and VII of the 1964 act and had awarded fees to prevailing plaintiffs in suits brought under these other civil rights laws without requiring specific statutory authorization.

However, in the Alyeska case the Court held that Federal courts did not have the power to grant fees to prevailing parties without such specific statutory authorization.

I should emphasize here that the Alyeska court did not disapprove of these attorney's fee awards. On the contrary, Justice White, speaking for the majority, noted that it was—

apparent from our national experience that the encouragement of private action to implement public policy has been viewed as desirable in a variety of circumstances.

The Court's holding merely reflected its belief that it is powerless to proceed with such beneficial fee awards until Congress "gives the word"—in a bill such as this one.

However, even though the Alyeska decision turned on a question of judicial power and not on the merits of fee awards—and even though Alyeska was an environmental case and not a civil rights case—its effect was to create an unexpected and anomalous gap in our civil rights laws whereby awards of fees are suddenly unavailable in the most fundamental civil rights cases. For instance, fees are now authorized in an employment discrimination suit under title VII of the 1964 Civil Rights Act, but not in the same suit brought under 42 U.S.C. 1981, which protects similar rights but involves fewer technical prerequisites to the filing of an action. Fees are allowed in a suit under title II of the 1964 act challenging discrimination in a private restaurant, but not in suits under 42 U.S.C. 1983 redressing violations of the Federal Constitution or laws by officials sworn to uphold the laws.

This bill would remedy these gaps in the statutory language by providing the specific authorization required by the Court in Alyeska. It would thus return to Federal judges the beneficial power to award counsel fees to the victims of violations of our most basic civil rights statutes.

Of course, since citizens would only recover fees under this bill if they were successful in their suits, this act would do nothing to encourage frivolous or bad faith litigation. In fact, by allowing assessment of fees against a "bad faith" plaintiff, it would have exactly the opposite effect.

Mr. President, if our civil rights laws are not to become mere hollow pronouncements, which the average citizen cannot enforce, we must

5

maintain the traditionally effective remedy of fee-shifting in these cases. This bill, then, contains no startling new remedy—it only meets the technical requirements that the Supreme Court has laid down if the Federal courts are to continue the practice of awarding attorney's fees which had been going on for years prior to the Court's May decision. It does not change the statutory provisions regarding the protection of civil rights except as it provides the fee awards which are necessary if citizens are to be able to effectively secure compliance with these existing statutes. This provision has already received the favorable recommendation of the full Judiciary Committee, and I urge its speedy passage by the full Senate.

Mr. President, I ask unanimous consent that the text of the bill be printed in the Record.

There being no objection, the bill was ordered to be printed in the Record, as follows:

S. 2278

Be it enacted by the Senate and House of Representatives of the United States of America in Congress assembled, Revised Statutes Section 722 (42 U.S.C. Sec. 1988) is amended by adding the following: "In any action or proceeding to enforce a provision of section 1977, 1978, 1979, 1980 and 1981 of the Revised Statutes, or Title VI of the Civil Rights Act of 1964, the court, in its discretion, may allow the prevailing party, other than the United States, a reasonable attorney's fee as part of the costs".

Calendar No. 955

94TH CONGRESS *2d Session*	SENATE	REPORT No. 94-1011

CIVIL RIGHTS ATTORNEYS' FEES AWARDS ACT

JUNE 29 (legislative day, JUNE 18), 1976.—Ordered to be printed

Mr. TUNNEY, from the Committee on the Judiciary,
submitted the following

REPORT

[To accompany S. 2278]

The Committee on the Judiciary, to which was referred the bill
(S. 2278) to amend Revised Statutes section 722 (42 U.S.C. § 1988)
to allow a court, in its discretion, to award attorneys' fees to a prevailing party in suits brought to enforce certain civil rights acts, having
considered the same, reports favorably thereon and recommends that
the bill do pass.

The text of S. 2278 is as follows:

S. 2278

Revised Statutes section 722 (42 U.S.C. Sec. 1988) is
amended by adding the following: "In any action or proceeding to enforce a provision of sections 1977, 1978, 1979,
1980 and 1981 of the Revised Statutes, or Title VI of the Civil
Rights Act of 1964, the court, in its discretion, may allow the
prevailing party, other than the United States, a reasonable
attorney's fee as part of the costs.".

PURPOSE

This amendment to the Civil Rights Act of 1866, Revised Statutes
Section 722, gives the Federal courts discretion to award attorneys'
fees to prevailing parties in suits brought to enforce the civil rights
acts which Congress has passed since 1866. The purpose of this amendment is to remedy anomalous gaps in our civil rights laws created by
the United States Supreme Court's recent decision in *Alyeska Pipeline
Service Co.* v. *Wilderness Society*, 421 U.S. 240 (1975), and to achieve
consistency in our civil rights laws.

57–010

2

HISTORY OF THE LEGISLATION

The bill grows out of six days of hearings on legal fees held before the Subcommittee on the Representation of Citizen Interests of this Committee in 1973. There were more than thirty witnesses, including Federal and State public officials, scholars, practicing attorneys from many areas of expertise, and private citizens. Those who did not appear were given the opportunity to submit material for the record, and many did so, including the representatives of the American Bar Association and the Bar Associations of 22 States and the District of Columbia. The hearings, when published, included not only the testimony and exhibits, but numerous statutory provisions, proposed legislation, case reports and scholarly articles.

In 1975, the provisions of S. 2278 were incorporated in a proposed amendment to S. 1279, extending the Voting Rights Act of 1965.

The Subcommittee on Constitutional Rights specifically approved the amendment on June 11, 1975, by a vote of 8–2, and the full Committee favorably reported it on July 18, 1975, as part of S. 1279. Because of time pressure to pass the Voting Rights Amendments, the Senate took action on the House-passed version of the legislation. S. 1279 was not taken up on the Senate floor; hence, the attorneys' fees amendment was never considered.

On July 31, 1975, Senator Tunney introduced S. 2278, which is identical to the amendment to S. 1279 which was reported favorably by this Committee last summer.

Shortly thereafter, similar legislation was introduced in the House of Representatives, including H.R. 9552, which is identical to S. 2278 except for one minor technical difference. The Subcommittee on Courts, Civil Liberties and the Administration of Justice of the House Judiciary Committee has conducted three days of hearings at which the witnesses have generally confirmed the record presented to this Committee in 1973. H.R. 9552, the counterpart of S. 2278, has received widespread support by the witnesses appearing before the House Subcommittee.

STATEMENT

The purpose and effect of S. 2278 are simple—it is designed to allow courts to provide the familiar remedy of reasonable counsel fees to prevailing parties in suits to enforce the civil rights acts which Congress has passed since 1866. S. 2278 follows the language of Titles II and VII of the Civil Rights Act of 1964, 42 U.S.C. §§ 2000a–3(b) and 2000e–5(k), and section 402 of the Voting Rights Act Amendments of 1975, 42 U.S.C. § 1973l(e). All of these civil rights laws depend heavily upon private enforcement, and fee awards have proved an essential remedy if private citizens are to have a meaningful opportunity to vindicate the important Congressional policies which these laws contain.

In many cases arising under our civil rights laws, the citizen who must sue to enforce the law has little or no money with which to hire a lawyer. If private citizens are to be able to assert their civil rights, and if those who violate the Nation's fundamental laws are not to proceed with impunity, then citizens must have the opportunity to recover what it costs them to vindicate these rights in court.

3

Congress recognized this need when it made specific provision for such fee shifting in Titles II and VII of the Civil Rights Act of 1964:

> When a plaintiff brings an action under [Title II] he cannot recover damages. If he obtains an injunction, he does so not for himself alone but also as a "private attorney general," vindicating a policy that Congress considered of the highest priority. If successful plaintiffs were routinely forced to bear their own attorneys' fees, few aggrieved parties would be in a position to advance the public interest by invoking the injunctive powers of the Federal courts. Congress therefore enacted the provision for counsel fees—* * * to encourage individuals injured by racial discrimination to seek judicial relief under Title II." *Newman* v. *Piggie Park Enterprises, Inc.*, 390 U.S. 400, 402 (1968).

The idea of the "private attorney general" is not a new one, nor are attorneys' fees a new remedy. Congress has commonly authorized attorneys' fees in laws under which "private attorneys general" play a significant role in enforcing our policies. We have, since 1870, authorized fee shifting under more than 50 laws, including, among others, the Securities Exchange Act of 1934, 15 U.S.C. §§ 78i(c) and 78r(a), the Servicemen's Readjustment Act of 1958, 38 U.S.C. § 1822(b), the Communications Act of 1934, 42 U.S.C. § 206, and the Organized Crime Control Act of 1970, 18 U.S.C. § 1964(c). In cases under these laws, fees are an integral part of the remedy necessary to achieve compliance with our statutory policies. As former Justice Tom Clark found, in a union democracy suit under the Labor-Management Reporting and Disclosure Act (Landrum-Griffin),

> Not to award counsel fees in cases such as this would be tantamount to repealing the Act itself by frustrating its basic purpose. * * * Without counsel fees the grant of Federal jurisdiction is but an empty gesture * * *. *Hall* v. *Cole*, 412 U.S. 1 (1973), quoting 462 F. 2d 777, 780-81 (2d Cir. 1972).

The remedy of attorneys' fees has always been recognized as particularly appropriate in the civil rights area, and civil rights and attorneys' fees have always been closely interwoven. In the civil rights area, Congress has instructed the courts to use the broadest and most effective remedies available to achieve the goals of our civil rights laws.[1] The very first attorneys' fee statute was a civil rights law, the Enforcement Act of 1870, 16 Stat. 140, which provided for attorneys' fees in three separate provisions protecting voting rights.[2]

Modern civil rights legislation reflects a heavy reliance on attorneys' fees as well. In 1964, seeking to assure full compliance with the Civil Rights Act of that year, we authorized fee shifting for private suits establishing violations of the public accommodations and equal employment provisions. 42 U.S.C. §§ 2000a-3(b) and 2000e-5(k). Since 1964, every major civil rights law passed by the Congress has included, or has been amended to include, one or more fee provisions.

---

[1] For example, the Civil Rights Act of 1866 directed Federal courts to "use that combination of Federal law, common law and State law as will be best adapted to the object of the civil rights laws." *Brown* v. *City of Meridian, Mississippi*, 356 F. 2d 602, 605 (5th Cir. 1966). See 42 U.S.C. § 1988; *Lefton* v. *City of Hattiesburg, Mississippi*, 333 F. 2d 280 (5th Cir. 1964).

[2] The causes of action established by these provisions were eliminated in 1894. 28 Stat. 36.

4

E.g., Title VIII of the Civil Rights Act of 1968, 42 U.S.C. § 3612(c); the Emergency School Aid Act of 1972, 20 U.S.C. § 1617; the Equal Employment Amendments of 1972, 42 U.S.C. § 2000e–16(b); and the Voting Rights Act Extension of 1975, 42 U.S.C. § 1973*l*(e).

These fee shifting provisions have been successful in enabling vigorous enforcement of modern civil rights legislation, while at the same time limiting the growth of the enforcement bureaucracy. Before May 12, 1975, when the Supreme Court handed down its decision in *Alyeska Pipeline Service Co.* v. *Wilderness Society*, 421 U.S. 240 (1975), many lower Federal courts throughout the Nation had drawn the obvious analogy between the Reconstruction Civil Rights Acts and these modern civil rights acts, and, following Congressional recognition in the newer statutes of the "private attorney general" concept, were exercising their traditional equity powers to award attorneys' fees under early civil rights laws as well.[3]

These pre-*Alyeska* decisions remedied a gap in the specific statutory provisions and restored an important historic remedy for civil rights violations. However, in *Alyeska*, the United States Supreme Court, while referring to the desirability of fees in a variety of circumstances, ruled that only Congress, and not the courts, could specify which laws were important enough to merit fee shifting under the "private attorney general" theory. The Court expressed the view, in dictum, that the Reconstruction Acts did not contain the necessary congressional authorization. This decision and dictum created anomalous gaps in our civil rights laws whereby awards of fees are, according to *Alyeska*, suddenly unavailable in the most fundamental civil rights cases. For instance, fees are now authorized in an employment discrimination suit under Title VII of the 1964 Civil Rights Act, but not in the same suit brought under 42 U.S.C. § 1981, which protects similar rights but involves fewer technical prerequisites to the filing of an action. Fees are allowed in a housing discrimination suit brought under Title VIII of the Civil Rights Act of 1968, but not in the same suit brought under 42 U.S.C. § 1982, a Reconstruction Act protecting the same rights. Likewise, fees are allowed in a suit under Title II of the 1964 Civil Rights Act challenging discrimination in a private restaurant, but not in suits under 42 U.S.C. § 1983 redressing violations of the Federal Constitution or laws by officials sworn to uphold the laws.

This bill, S. 2278, is an appropriate response to the *Alyeska* decision. It is limited to cases arising under our civil rights laws, a category of cases in which attorneys fees have been traditionally regarded as appropriate. It remedies gaps in the language of these civil rights laws by providing the specific authorization required by the Court in *Alyeska*, and makes our civil rights laws consistent.

It is intended that the standards for awarding fees be generally the same as under the fee provisions of the 1964 Civil Rights Act. A party seeking to enforce the rights protected by the statutes covered by S. 2278, if successful, "should ordinarily recover an attorney's fee unless special circumstances would render such an award unjust." *Newman* v. *Piggie Park Enterprises, Inc.*, 390 U.S. 400, 402 (1968).[4]

---

[3] These civil rights cases are too numerous to cite here. See, e.g., *Sims* v. *Amos* 340 F. Supp. 691 (M.D. Ala. 1972), aff'd, 409 U.S. 942 (1972); *Stanford Daily* v. *Zurcher*, 366 F. Supp. 18 (N.D. Cal. 1973); and cases cited in *Alyeska Pipeline, supra*, at n. 46. Many of the relevant cases are collected in "Hearings on the Effect of Legal Fees on the Adequacy of Representation Before the Subcom. on Representation of Citizen Interests of the Senate Comm. on the Judiciary," 93d Cong., 1st sess., pt. III, at pp. 888–1024, and 1060–62.

[4] In the large majority of cases the party or parties seeking to enforce such rights will be the plaintiffs and/or plaintiff-intervenors. However, in the procedural posture of some cases, the parties seeking to enforce such rights may be the defendants and/or defendant-intervenors. See, e.g., *Shelley* v. *Kraemer*, 334 U.S. 1 (1948).

5

Such "private attorneys general" should not be deterred from bringing good faith actions to vindicate the fundamental rights here involved by the prospect of having to pay their opponent's counsel fees should they lose. *Richardson* v. *Hotel Corporation of America*, 332 F. Supp. 519 (E.D. La. 1971), aff'd, 468 F. 2d 951 (5th Cir. 1972). (A fee award to a defendant's employer, was held unjustified where a claim of racial discrimination, though meritless, was made in good faith.) Such a party, if unsuccessful, could be assessed his opponent's fee only where it is shown that his suit was clearly frivolous, vexatious, or brought for harassment purposes. *United States Steel Corp.* v. *United States*, 385 F. Supp. 346 (W.D. Pa. 1974), aff'd, 9 E.P.D. ¶ 10,225 (3d Cir. 1975). This bill thus deters frivolous suits by authorizing an award of attorneys' fees against a party shown to have litigated in "bad faith" under the guise of attempting to enforce the Federal rights created by the statutes listed in S. 2278. Similar standards have been followed not only in the Civil Rights Act of 1964, but in other statutes providing for attorneys' fees. E.g., the Water Pollution Control Act, 1972 U.S. Code Cong. & Adm. News 3747; the Marine Protection Act, Id. at 4249–50; and the Clean Air Act, Senate Report No. 91–1196, 91st Cong., 2d Sess., p. 483 (1970). See also *Hutchinson* v. *William Barry, Inc.*, 50 F. Supp. 292, 298 (D. Mass. 1943) (Fair Labor Standards Act).

In appropriate circumstances, counsel fees under S. 2278 may be awarded pendente lite. See *Bradley* v. *School Board of the City of Richmond*, 416 U.S. 696 (1974). Such awards are especially appropriate where a party has prevailed on an important matter in the course of litigation, even when he ultimately does not prevail on all issues. See *Bradley, supra; Mills* v. *Electric Auto-Lite Co.*, 396 U.S. 375 (1970). Moreover, for purposes of the award of counsel fees, parties may be considered to have prevailed when they vindicate rights through a consent judgment or without formally obtaining relief. *Kopet* v. *Esquire Realty Co.*, 523 F. 2d 1005 (2d Cir. 1975), and cases cited therein; *Parham* v. *Southwestern Bell Telephone Co.*, 433 F. 2d 421 (8th Cir. 1970); *Richards* v. *Griffith Rubber Mills*, 300 F. Supp. 338 (D. Ore. 1969); *Thomas* v. *Honeybrook Mines, Inc.*, 428 F. 2d 981 (3d Cir. 1970); *Aspira of New York, Inc.* v. *Board of Education of the City of New York*, 65 F.R.D. 541 (S.D.N.Y. 1975).

In several hearings held over a period of years, the Committee has found that fee awards are essential if the Federal statutes to which S. 2278 applies are to be fully enforced.[5] We find that the effects of such fee awards are ancillary and incident to securing compliance with these laws, and that fee awards are an integral part of the remedies necessary to obtain such compliance. Fee awards are therefore provided in cases covered by S. 2278 in accordance with Congress' powers under, inter alia, the Fourteenth Amendment, Section 5. As with cases brought under 20 U.S.C. § 1617, the Emergency School Aid Act of 1972, defendants in these cases are often State or local bodies or State or local officials. In such cases it is intended that the attorneys' fees, like other items of costs,[6] will be collected either directly from the official, in his official capacity,[7] from funds of his agency or under his control, or from the State or local government (whether or not the agency or government is a named party).

---

[5] See, e.g., "Hearings on the Effect of Legal Fees," supra.
[6] *Fairmont Creamery Co.* v. *Minnesota*, 275 U.S. 168 (1927).
[7] Proof that an official had acted in bad faith could also render him liable for fees in his individual capacity, under the traditional bad faith standard recognized by the Supreme Court in *Alyeska*. See *Class* v. *Norton*, 505 F. 2d 123 (2d Cir. 1974); *Doe* v. *Poelker*, 515 F. 2d 541 (8th Cir. 1975).

6

It is intended that the amount of fees awarded under S. 2278 be governed by the same standards which prevail in other types of equally complex Federal litigation, such as antitrust cases and not be reduced because the rights involved may be nonpecuniary in nature. The appropriate standards, see *Johnson* v. *Georgia Highway Express*, 488 F. 2d 714 (5th Cir. 1974), are correctly applied in such cases as *Stanford Daily* v. *Zurcher*, 64 F.R.D. 680 (N.D. Cal. 1974); *Davis* v. *County of Los Angeles*, 8 E.P.D. ¶ 9444 (C.D. Cal. 1974); and *Swann* v. *Charlotte-Mecklenburg Board of Education*, 66 F.R.D. 483 (W.D.N.C. 1975). These cases have resulted in fees which are adequate to attract competent counsel, but which do not produce windfalls to attorneys. In computing the fee, counsel for prevailing parties should be paid, as is traditional with attorneys compensated by a fee-paying client, "for all time reasonably expended on a matter." *Davis, supra; Stanford Daily, supra,* at 684.

This bill creates no startling new remedy—it only meets the technical requirements that the Supreme Court has laid down if the Federal courts are to continue the practice of awarding attorneys' fees which had been going on for years prior to the Court's May decision. It does not change the statutory provisions regarding the protection of civil rights except as it provides the fee awards which are necessary if citizens are to be able to effectively secure compliance with these existing statutes. There are very few provisions in our Federal laws which are self-executing. Enforcement of the laws depends on governmental action and, in some cases, on private action through the courts. If the cost of private enforcement actions becomes too great, there will be no private enforcement. If our civil rights laws are not to become mere hollow pronouncements which the average citizen cannot enforce, we must maintain the traditionally effective remedy of fee shifting in these cases.

CHANGES IN EXISTING LAW MADE BY THE BILL ARE ITALICIZED

REVISED STATUTES § 722, 42 U.S.C. § 1988

"The jurisdiction in civil and criminal matters conferred on the district courts by the provisions of this chapter and Title 18, for the protection of all persons in the United States in their civil rights, and for their vindication, shall be exercised and enforced in conformity with the laws of the United States, so far as such laws are suitable to carry the same into effect; but in all cases where they are not adapted to the object, or are deficient in the provisions necessary to furnish suitable remedies and punish offenses against law, the common law, as modified and changed by the constitution and statutes of the State wherein the court having jurisdiction of such civil or criminal cause is held, so far as the same is not inconsistent with the Constitution and laws of the United States, shall be extended to and govern the said courts in the trial and disposition of the cause, and, if it is of a criminal nature, in the infliction of punishment on the party found guilty." *In any action or proceeding to enforce a provision of sections 1977, 1978, 1979, 1980 and 1981 of the Revised Statutes, or Title VI of the Civil Rights Act of 1964, the court, in its discretion, may allow the prevailing party, other than the United States, a reasonable attorney's fee as part of the costs.*

S.R. 1011

7

Cost of Legislation

The Congressional Budget Office, in a letter dated March 1, 1976, has advised the Judiciary Committee that: "Pursuant to Section 403 of the Congressional Budget Act of 1974, the Congressional Budget Office has reviewed S. 2278, a bill to award attorneys' fees to prevailing parties in civil rights suits.

"Based on this review, it appears that no additional costs to the government would be incurred as a result of the enactment of this bill."

O

94TH CONGRESS } HOUSE OF REPRESENTATIVES {   REPORT
  2d Session }   { No. 94-1558

THE CIVIL RIGHTS ATTORNEY'S FEES AWARDS ACT
OF 1976

SEPTEMBER 15, 1976.—Committed to the Committee of the Whole House on the
State of the Union and ordered to be printed

Mr. DRINAN, from the Committee on the Judiciary,
submitted the following

REPORT

[Including cost estimate of the Congressional Budget Office]

[To accompany H.R. 15460]

The Committee on the Judiciary, to whom was referred the bill
(H.R. 15460) to allow the awarding of attorney's fees in certain civil
rights cases, having considered the same, report favorably thereon
without amendment and recommend that the bill do pass.

PURPOSE OF THE BILL

H.R. 15460, the Civil Rights Attorney's Fees Awards Act of 1976,
authorizes the courts to award reasonable attorney fees to the prevailing party in suits instituted under certain civil rights acts. Under
existing law, some civil rights statutes contain counsel fee provisions,
while others do not. In order to achieve uniformity in the remedies
provided by Federal laws guaranteeing civil and constitutional rights,
it is necessary to add an attorney fee authorization to those civil rights
acts which do not presently contain such a provision.

The effective enforcement of Federal civil rights statutes depends
largely on the efforts of private citizens. Although some agencies of
the United States have civil rights responsibilities, their authority and
resources are limited. In many instances where these laws are violated,
it is necessary for the citizen to initiate court action to correct the
illegality. Unless the judicial remedy is full and complete, it will
remain a meaningless right. Because a vast majority of the victims
of civil rights violations cannot afford legal counsel, they are unable
to present their cases to the courts. In authorizing an award of reasonable attorney's fees, H.R. 15460 is designed to give such persons
effective access to the judicial process where their grievances can be
resolved according to law.

57-006

2

STATEMENT

A. NEED FOR THE LEGISLATION

In *Alyeska Pipeline Service Corp* v. *Wilderness Society*, 421 U.S. 240 (1975), the Supreme Court held that federal courts do not have the power to award attorney's fees to a prevailing party unless an Act of Congress expressly authorizes it.[1] In the *Alyeska* case, the plaintiffs sought to prevent the construction of the Alaskan pipeline because of the damage it would cause to the environment. Although the plaintiffs succeeded in the early stages of the litigation, Congress later overturned that result by legislation permitting the construction of the pipeline. Nonetheless the lower federal courts awarded the plaintiffs their attorney's fees because of the service they had performed in the public interest. The Supreme Court reversed that award on the basis of the "American Rule": that each litigant, victorious or otherwise, must pay for its own attorney.

Although the *Alyeska* case involved only environmental concerns, the decision barred attorney fee awards in a wide range of cases, including civil rights. In fact the Supreme Court, in footnote 46 of the *Alyeska* opinion, expressly disapproved a number of lower court decisions involving civil rights which had awarded fees without statutory authorization. Prior to *Alyeska*, such courts had allowed fees on the theory that civil rights plaintiffs act as "private attorneys general" in eliminating discriminatory practices adversely affecting all citizens, white and non-white. In 1968, the Supreme Court had approved the "private attorney general" theory when it gave a generous construction to the attorney fee provision in Title II of the Civil Rights Act of 1964. *Newman* v. *Piggie Park Enterprises, Inc.*, 390 U.S. 400 (1968).[2] The Court stated:

> If (the plaintiff) obtains an injunction, he does so not for himself alone but also as a "private attorney general," vindicating a policy that Congress considered of the highest importance. *Id.* at 402.

However, the Court in *Alyeska* rejected the application of that theory to the award of counsel fees in the absence of statutory authorization. It expressly reaffirmed, however, its holding in *Newman* that, in civil rights cases where counsel fees are allowed by Congress, "the award should be made to the successful plaintiff absent exceptional circumstances." *Alyeska* case, *supra* at 262.

In the hearings conducted by the Subcommittee on Courts, Civil Liberties, and the Administration of Justice, the testimony indicated that civil rights litigants were suffering very severe hardships because of the *Alyeska* decision. Thousands of dollars in fees were automatically lost in the immediate wake of the decision. Representatives of the Lawyers Committee for Civil Rights Under Law, the Council

---

[1] The Court in *Alyeska* recognized three very narrow exceptions to the rule: (1) where a "common fund" is involved; (2) where the litigant's conduct is vexatious, harassing, or in bad faith; and (3) where a court order is willfully disobeyed.

[2] In *Trafficante* v. *Metropolitan Life Insurance Co.*, 409 U.S. 205 (1972), the Supreme Court applied the "private attorney general" theory in according broad "standing" to persons injured by discriminatory housing practices under the Federal Fair Housing Act. 42 U.S.C. 3601–3619.

ȝ

for Public Interest Law, the American Bar Association Special Committee on Public Interest Practice, and witnesses practicing in the field testified to the devastating impact of the case on litigation in the civil rights area. Surveys disclosed that such plaintiffs were the hardest hit by the decision.[3] The Committee also received evidence that private lawyers were refusing to take certain types of civil rights cases because the civil rights bar, already short of resources, could not afford to do so. Because of the compelling need demonstrated by the testimony, the Committee decided to report a bill allowing fees to prevailing parties in certain civil rights cases.

It should be noted that the United States Code presently contains over fifty provisions for attorney fees in a wide variety of statutes. See Appendix A. In the past few years, the Congress has approved such allowances in the areas of antitrust, equal credit, freedom of information, voting rights, and consumer product safety. Although the recently enacted civil rights statutes contain provisions permitting the award of counsel fees, a number of the older statutes do not. It is to these provisions that much of the testimony was directed.

B. HISTORY OF H.R. 15460

At the time of the Subcomittee hearings on October 6 and 8, and Dec. 3, 1975, three bills were pending which dealt expressly with counsel fees in civil rights cases: H.R. 7828 (same as H.R. 8220); H.R. 7969 (same as H.R. 8742); and H.R. 9552. H.R. 7828 and H.R. 9552 would allow attorney fees to be awarded in cases brought under specific provisions of the United States Code, while H.R. 7969 would permit such awards in any case involving civil or constitutional rights, no matter what the source of the claim. H.R. 7828 was stated in mandatory terms; H.R. 9552 and H.R. 7969 allowed discretionary awards. The Justice Department, through its representative, Assistant Attorney General Rex Lee of the Civil Division, expressed its support of H.R. 9552. Hearings held in 1973 by the Senate Judiciary Subcommittee on the Representation of Citizen Interests also highlighted the need of the public for legal assistance in this and other areas.

In August, 1976, the Judiciary Subcommittee on Courts, Civil Liberties, and the Administration of Justice concluded that a bill to allow counsel fees in certain civil rights cases should be reported favorably in view of the pressing need. On August 26, 1976, the Subcommittee approved H.R. 9552 with an amendment in the nature of a substitute because it was similar to S. 2278, which had cleared the Senate Judiciary Committee and was awaiting action by the full Senate. The amendment in the nature of a substitute sought to conform H.R. 9552 technically to S. 2278; no substantive changes were made. It was then reported unanimously by the Subcommittee.

On September 2, 1976, the full Committee approved H.R. 9552, as amended, with an amendment offered by Congresswoman Holtzman and accepted by the Committee. That amendment added title IX of Public Law 92–318 to the substantive provisions under which successful litigants could be awarded counsel fees. The Committee then

---

[3] See, *Balancing the Scales of Justice: Financing Public Interest Law in America* (Council for Public Interest Law, 1976), pp. 238, 364, D–2).

4

ordered that a clean bill be reported to the House. H.R. 15460, the clean bill, was introduced on September 8 and approved pro forma by the Committee on September 9, 1976.[4]

C. SCOPE OF THE BILL

H.R. 15460, the Civil Rights Attorney's Fees Awards Act of 1976, would amend Section 722 (42 U.S.C. 1988) of the Revised Statutes to allow the award of fees in certain civil rights cases.[5] It would apply to actions brought under seven specific sections of the United States Code.[6] Those provisions are: Section 1981, 1982, 1983, 1985, 1986, and 2000d et seq. of Title 42; and Section 1681 et seq. of Title 20. See Appendix B for full texts. The affected sections of Title 42 generally prohibit denial of civil and constitutional rights in a variety of areas, while the referenced sections of Title 20 deal with discrimination on account of sex, blindness, or visual impairment in certain education programs and activities.[7]

More specifically, Section 1981 is frequently used to challenge employment discrimination based on race or color. *Johnson* v. *Railway Express Agency, Inc.*, 421 U.S. 454 (1975).[8] Under that section the Supreme Court recently held that whites as well as blacks could bring suit alleging racially discriminatory employment practices. *McDonald* v. *Santa Fe Trail Transportation Co.*, —— U.S. ——, 96 S. Ct. 2574 (1976). Section 1981 has also been cited to attack exclusionary admissions policies at recreational facilities. *Tillman* v. *Wheaton-Haven Recreation Ass'n, Inc.*, 410 U.S. 431 (1973). Section 1982 is regularly used to attack discrimination in property transactions, such as the purchase of a home. *Jones* v. *Alfred H. Mayer Co.*, 392 U.S. 409 (1968).[9]

Section 1983 is utilized to challenge official discrimination, such as racial segregation imposed by law. *Brown* v. *Board of Education*, 347 U.S. 483 (1954). It is ironic that, in the landmark *Brown* case challenging school segregation, the plaintiffs could not recover their attorney's fees, despite the significance of the ruling to eliminate officially

---

[4] Apart from the addition of Title IX of Public Law 92–318, the only difference between H.R. 9552 and the clean bill (H.R. 15460) are technical, not affecting the substance, made on advice of the House Parliamentarian and staff and legislative counsel.

[5] The bill amends the Revised Statutes rather than the United States Code because Title 42 is not codified, and thus is not "the law of the United States."

[6] In accordance with applicable decisions of the Supreme Court, the bill is intended to apply to all cases pending on the date of enactment as well as all future cases. *Bradley* v. *Richmond School Board*, 416 U.S. 696 (1974).

[7] To the extent a plaintiff joins a claim under one of the statutes enumerated in H.R. 15460 with a claim that does not allow attorney fees, that plaintiff, if it prevails on the non-fee claim, is entitled to a determination on the other claim for the purpose of awarding counsel fees. *Morales* v. *Haines*, 486 F. 2d 880 (7th Cir. 1973). In some instances, however, the claim with fees may involve a constitutional question which the courts are reluctant to resolve if the non-constitutional claim is dispositive. *Hagans* v. *Lavine*, 415 U.S. 528 (1974). In such cases, if the claim for which fees may be awarded meets the "substantiality" test, *see Hagans* v. *Lavine, supra*; *United Mine Workers* v. *Gibbs*, 383 U.S. 715 (1966), attorney's fees may be allowed even though the court declines to enter judgment for the plaintiff on that claim, so long as the plaintiff prevails on the non-fee claim arising out of a "common nucleus of operative fact." *United Mine Workers* v. *Gibbs, supra* at 725.

[8] With respect to the relationship between Section 1981 and Title VII of the Civil Rights Act of 1964, the House Committee on Education and Labor has noted that "the remedies available to the individual under Title VII are co-extensive with the individual's right to sue under the provisions of the Civil Rights Act of 1866, 42 U.S.C. § 1981, and that the two procedures augment each other and are not mutually exclusive." H.R. Rept. No. 92–238, p. 19 (92nd Cong. 1st Sess. 1971). That view was adopted by the Supreme Court in *Johnson* v. *Railway Express Agency, supra*.

[9] As with Section 1981 and Title VII, Section 1982 and Title VIII of the Civil Rights Act of 1968 are complementary remedies, with similarities and differences in coverage and enforcement mechanism. See *Jones* v. *Mayer Co., supra*.

5

imposed segregation. Section 1983 has also been employed to challenge unlawful official action in non-racial matters. For example, in *Harper* v. *Virginia State Board of Elections*, 383 U.S. 663 (1966), indigent plaintiffs successfully challenged as unconstitutional the imposition of a poll tax in state and local elections. In *Monroe* v. *Pape*, 365 U.S. 167 (1961), a private citizen sought damages against local officials for an unconstitutional search of a private residence. See also *Elrod* v. *Burns*, —— U.S. ——, 96 S. Ct. 2673 (June 28, 1976) (discrimination on account of political affiliation in public employment); *O'Connor* v. *Donaldson*, 422 U.S. 563 (1975) (terms and conditions of institutional confinement).

Section 1985 and 1986 are used to challenge conspiracies, either public or private, to deprive individuals of the equal protection of the laws. See *Griffin* v. *Breckenridge*, 403 U.S. 88 (1971). The bill also covers suits brought under Title IX of Public Law 92–318, the Education Amendments of 1972, 20 U.S.C. 1681–1686. Title IX forbids specific kinds of discrimination on account of sex, blindness, or visual impairment in certain federally assisted programs and activities relating to education. Finally H.R. 15460 would also apply to actions arising under Title VI of the Civil Rights Act of 1964, 42 U.S.C. 2000d–2000d–6.[10]

Title VI prohibits the discriminatory use of Federal funds, requiring recipients to administer such assistance without regard to race, color, or national origin. *Lau* v. *Nichols*, 414 U.S. 563 (1974); *Hills* v. *Gautreaux*, —— U.S. ——, 96 S. Ct. 1538 (April 20, 1976); *Adams* v. *Richardson*, 480 F. 2d 1159 (D.C. Cir. 1973); *Bossier Parish School Board* v. *Lemon*, 370 F. 2d 847 (5th Cir.), *cert. denied*, 388 U.S. 911 (1967); *Laufman* v. *Oakley Building and Loan Co.*, 408 F. Supp. 489 (S.D. Ohio 1976).

D. DESCRIPTION OF H.R. 15460

As noted earlier, the United States Code presently contains over fifty provisions for the awarding of attorney fees in particular cases. They may be placed generally into four categories: (1) mandatory awards only for a prevailing plaintiff; (2) mandatory awards for any prevailing party; (3) discretionary awards for a prevailing plaintiff; and (4) discretionary awards for any prevailing party. Existing statutes allowing fees in certain civil rights cases generally fall into the fourth category. Keeping with that pattern, H.R. 15460 tracks the language of the counsel fee provisions of Titles II and VII of the Civil Rights Act of 1964,[11] and Section 402 of the Voting Rights Act Amendments of 1975.[12] The substantive section of H.R. 15460 reads as follows:

> In any action or proceeding to enforce a provision of sections 1977, 1978, 1979, 1980, and 1981 of the Revised Statutes, title IX of Public Law 92–318, or title VI of the Civil Rights Act of 1964, the court, in its discretion, may allow the prevailing party, other than the United States, a reasonable attorney's fee as part of the costs.

---

[10] Title VI of the Civil Rights Act of 1964 is the only substantive title of that Act which does not contain a provision for attorney fees.
[11] 42 U.S.C. 2000a–3(b) (Title II) ; 42 U.S.C. 2000e–5(k) (Title VII).
[12] 42 U.S.C. 1973(e) (Section 402).

θ

The three key features of this attorney's fee provision are: (1) that awards may be made to any "prevailing party"; (2) that fees are to be allowed in the discretion of the court; and (3) that awards are to be "reasonable". Because other statutes follow this approach, the courts are familiar with these terms and in fact have reviewed, examined, and interpreted them at some length.

1. Prevailing party

Under H.R. 15460, either a prevailing plaintiff or a prevailing defendant is eligible to receive an award of fees. Congress has not always been that generous. In about two-thirds of the existing statutes, such as the Clayton Act and the Packers and Stockyards Act, only prevailing plaintiffs may recover their counsel fees.[13] This bill follows the more modest approach of other civil rights acts.

It should be noted that when the Justice Department testified in support of H.R. 9552, the precedessor to H.R. 15460, it suggested an amendment to allow recovery only to prevailing plaintiffs. Assistant Attorney General Lee thought the phrase "prevailing party" might have a "chilling effect" on civil rights plaintiffs, discouraging them from initiating law suits. The Committee was very concerned with the potential impact such a phrase might have on persons seeking to vindicate these important rights under Federal law. In light of existing case law under similar provisions, however, the Committee concluded that the application of current standards to this bill will significantly reduce the potentially adverse affect on the victims of unlawful conduct who seek to assert their federal claims.

On two occasions, the Supreme Court has addressed the question of the proper standard for allowing fees in civil rights cases. In *Newman* v. *Piggie Park Enterprises, Inc.*, 390 U.S. 400, 402 (1968) (per curiam), a case involving racial discrimination in a place of public accommodation, the Court held that a prevailing plaintiff "should ordinarily recover an attorney's fee unless special circumstances would render such an award unjust."

Five years later, the Court applied the same standard to the attorney's fee provision contained in Section 718 of the Emergency School Aid Act of 1972, 20 U.S.C. 1617. *Northcross* v. *Memphis Board of Education*, 412 U.S. 427 (1973) (per curiam). The rationale of the rule rests upon the recognition that nearly all plaintiffs in these suits are disadvantaged persons who are the victims of unlawful discrimination or unconstitutional conduct. It would be unfair to impose upon them the additional burden of counsel fees when they seek to invoke the jurisdiction of the federal courts. "If successful plaintiffs were routinely forced to bear their own attorneys' fees, few aggrieved parties would be in a position to advance the public interest by invoking the injunctive powers of the federal courts." *Newman* v. *Piggie Park Enterprises, Inc., supra* at 402.

Consistent with this rationale, the courts have developed a different standard for awarding fees to prevailing defendants because they do "not appear before the court cloaked in a mantle of public interest." *United States Steel Corp.* v. *United States*, 519 F.2d 359, 364 (3rd Cir. 1975). As noted earlier such litigants may, in proper circum-

---

[13] 15 U.S.C. 15 (Clayton Act); 7 U.S.C. 210(f) (Packers and Stockyards Act).

7

stances, recover their counsel fees under H.R. 15460. To avoid the potential "chilling effect" noted by the Justice Department and to advance the public interest articulated by the Supreme Court, however, the courts have developed another test for awarding fees to prevailing defendants. Under the case law, such an award may be made only if the action is vexatious and frivolous, or if the plaintiff has instituted it solely "to harass or embarrass" the defendant. *United States Steel Corp.* v. *United States, supra* at 364. If the plaintiff is "motivated by malice and vindictiveness," then the court may award counsel fees to the prevailing defendant. *Carrion* v. *Yeshiva University,* 535 F.2d 722 (2d Cir. 1976). Thus if the action is not brought in bad faith, such fees should not be allowed. See, *Wright* v. *Stone Container Corp.* 524 F.2d 1058 (8th Cir. 1975) ; see also *Richardson* v. *Hotel Corp of America,* 332 F. Supp. 519 (E.D.La. 1971), *aff'd without published opinion,* 468 F.24 951 (5th Cir. 1972). This standard will not deter plaintiffs from seeking relief under these statutes, and yet will prevent their being used for clearly unwarranted harassment purposes.

With respect to the awarding of fees to prevailing defendants, it should further be noted that governmental officials are frequently the defendants in cases brought under the statutes covered by H.R. 15460. See, *e.g., Brown* v. *Board of Education, supra; Gautreaux* v. *Hills, supra; O'Connor* v. *Donaldson, supra.* Such governmental entities and officials have substantial resources available to them through funds in the common treasury, including the taxes paid by the plaintiffs themselves. Applying the same standard of recovery to such defendants would further widen the gap between citizens and government officials and would exacerbate the inequality of litigating strength. The greater resources available to governments provide an ample base from which fees can be awarded to the prevailing plaintiff in suits against governmental officials or entities.[14]

The phrase "prevailing party" is not intended to be limited to the victor only after entry of a final judgment following a full trial on the merits. It would also include a litigant who succeeds even if the case is concluded prior to a full evidentiary hearing before a judge or jury. If the litigation terminates by consent decree, for example, it would be proper to award counsel fees. *Incarcerated Men of Allen County* v. *Fair,* 507 F.2d 281 (6th Cir. 1974) ; *Parker* v. *Matthews.* 411 F. Supp. 1059 (D.D.C. 1976) ; *Aspira of New York, Inc.,* v. *Board of Education of the City of New York,* 65 F.R.D. 541 (S.D.N.Y. 1975). A "prevailing" party should not be penalized for seeking an out-of-court settlement, thus helping to lessen docket congestion. Similarly, after a complaint is filed, a defendant might voluntarily cease the unlawful practice. A court should still award fees even though it might conclude, as a matter of equity, that no formal relief, such as an injunction, is needed. *E.g., Parham* v. *Southwestern Bell Telephone Co.,* 433 F.2d 421 (8th Cir. 1970) ; *Brown* v. *Gaston County Dyeing Machine Co.,* 457 F.2d 1377 (4th Cir.), *cert denied,* 409 U.S. 982 (1972) : see also *Lea* v. *Cone Mills Corp.,* 438 F.2d 86 (4th Cir. 1971) ; *Evers* v. *Dwyer,* 358 U.S. 202 (1958).

A prevailing defendant may also recover its fees when the plaintiff seeks and obtains a voluntary dismissal of a groundess complaint,

---

[14] Of course, the 11th Amendment is not a bar to the awarding of counsel fees against state governments. *Fitzpatrick v. Bitzer,* ——U.S.——, 96 S.Ct. 2666 (June 28, 1976).

8

Corcoran v. *Columbia Broadcasting System*, 121 F.2d 575 (9th Cir. 1941), as long as the other factors, noted earlier, governing awards to defendants are met. Finally the courts have also awarded counsel fees to a plaintiff who successfully concludes a class action suit even though that individual was not granted any relief. *Parham* v. *Southwestern Bell Telephone Co., supra; Reed* v. *Arlington Hotel Co., Inc.*, 476 F.2d 721 (8th Cir. 1973).

Furthermore, the word "prevailing" is not intended to require the entry of a *final* order before fees may be recovered. "A district court must have discretion to award fees and costs incident to the final disposition of interim matters." *Bradley* v. *Richmond School Board*, 416 U.S. 696, 723 (1974); see also *Mills* v. *Electric Auto-Lite Co.*, 396 U.S. 375 (1970). Such awards pendente lite are particularly important in protracted litigation, where it is difficult to predicate with any certainty the date upon which a final order will be entered. While the courts have not yet formulated precise standards as to the appropriate circumstances under which such interim awards should be made, the Supreme Court has suggested some guidelines. "(T)he entry of any order that determines substantial rights of the parties may be an appropriate occasion upon which to consider the propriety of an award of counsel fees. . . ." *Bradley* v. *Richmond School Board, supra* at 722 n. 28.

2. *Judicial discretion*

The second key feature of the bill is its mandate that fees are only to be allowed in the discretion of the court. Congress has passed many statutes *requiring* that fees be awarded to a prevailing party.[15] Again the Committee adopted a more moderate approach here by leaving the matter to the discretion of the judge, guided of course by the case law interpreting similar attorney's fee provisions. This approach was supported by the Justice Department on Dec. 31, 1975. The Committee intends that, at a minimum, existing judicial standards, to which ample reference is made in this report, should guide the courts in construing H.R. 15460.

3. *Reasonable fees*

The third principal element of the bill is that the prevailing party is entitled to "reasonable" counsel fees. The courts have enumerated a number of factors in determining the reasonableness of awards under similarly worded attorney's fee provisions. In *Johnson* v. *Georgia Highway Express, Inc.*, 488 F.2d 714 (5th Cir. 1974), for example, the court listed twelve factors to be considered, including the time and labor required, the novelty and difficulty of the questions involved, the skill needed to present the case, the customary fee for similar work, and the amount received in damages, if any. *Accord: Evans* v. *Sheraton Park Hotel*, 503 F.2d 177 (D.C. Cir. 1974); see also *United States Steel Corp.* v. *United States, supra.*

Of course, it should be noted that the mere recovery of damages should not preclude the awarding of counsel fees.[16] Under the anti-

---

[15] E.g., 7 U.S.C. 499g(b) (Perishable Agricultural Commodities Act); 15 U.S.C. 1640(a) (Truth-in-Lending Act); 46 U.S.C. 1277 (Merchant Marine Act of 1936); 47 U.S.C. 206 (Communications Act of 1934).

[16] Similarly, a prevailing party is entitled to counsel fees even if represented by an organization or if the party is itself an organization. *Incarcerated Men of Allen County* v. *Fair, supra; Torres* v. *Sachs*, 69 F.R.D. 343 (S.D.N.Y. 1975), aff'd. —— F.2d —— (2d Cir., June 25, 1976); *Fairley* v. *Patterson*, 493 F2d 598 (5th Cir. 1974).

9

trust laws, for example, a plaintiff may recover treble damages and still the court is required to award attorney fees. The same principle should apply here as civil rights plaintiffs should not be singled out for different and less favorable treatment. Furthermore, while damages are theoretically available under the statutes covered by H.R. 15460, it should be observed that, in some cases, immunity doctrines and special defenses, available only to public officials, preclude or severely limit the damage remedy.[17] Consequently awarding counsel fees to prevailing plaintiffs in such litigation is particularly important and necessary if Federal civil and constitutional rights are to be adequately protected. To be sure, in a large number of cases brought under the provisions covered by H.R. 15460, only injunctive relief is sought, and prevailing plaintiffs should ordinarily recover their counsel fees. *Newman* v. *Piggie Park Enterprises, Inc., supra; Northcross* v. *Memphis Board of Education, supra.*

The application of these standards will insure that reasonable fees are awarded to attract competent counsel in cases involving civil and constitutional rights, while avoiding windfalls to attorneys. The effect of H.R. 15460 will be to promote the enforcement of the Federal civil rights acts, as Congress intended, and to achieve uniformity in those statutes and justice for all citizens.

OVERSIGHT

Oversight of the administration of justice in the federal court system is the responsibility of the Committee on the Judiciary. The hearings on October 6 and 8 and Dec. 3, 1975, focused on specific pending legislation. However, they did have an oversight purpose, as well, since the impact of the Supreme Court's *Alyeska* decision on the public and the related issue of equal access to the courts were subjects of the hearing.

COMMITTE VOTE

H.R. 15460 was reported favorably by a voice vote of the Committee on September 9, 1976. Twenty-seven members of the Committee were present.

STATEMENT OF THE COMMITTE ON GOVERNMENT OPERATIONS

No statement has been received on the legislation from the House Committee on Government Operations.

STATEMENT OF THE CONGRSSIONAL BUDGET OFFICE

Pursuant to clause 7, rule XIII of the Rules of the House of Representatives and section 403 of the Congressional Budget Act of 1974, the Committee estimates there will be no cost to the federal government.

---

[17] *Wood* v. *Strickland,* 420 U.S. 308 (1975) ; *Scheuer* v. *Rhodes,* 416 U.S. 232 (1974) ; *Pierson* v. *Ray,* 386 U.S. 547 (1967).

10

CONGRESS OF THE UNITED STATES,
CONGRESSIONAL BUDGET OFFICE,
Washington, D.C., September 7, 1976.

Hon. PETER W. RODINO,
*Chairman, Committee on the Judiciary, U.S. House of Representatives,
Rayburn House Office Building, Washington, D.C.*

DEAR MR. CHAIRMAN: Pursuant to Section 403 of the Congressional Budget Act of 1974, the Congressional Budget Office has reviewed the Civil Rights Attorney's Fees Award Act of 1976, a bill to award attorney's fees to prevailing parties in civil rights suits to enforce Sections 1977, 1978, 1979, 1980 and 1981 of the Revised Statutes, Title IX of P.L. 92–318 or Title VI of the Civil Rights Act of 1964.

Based on this review, it appears that no additional cost to the government would be incurred as a result of enactment of this bill.

Sincerely,

ALICE M. RIVLIN,
Director.

INFLATIONARY IMPACT STATEMENT

The legislation will have no foreseeable inflationary impact on prices or costs in the operation of the national economy.

SECTION-BY-SECTION ANALYSIS

Section 1

Section 1 merely recites the short title of the legislation, "The Civil Rights Attorney's Fees Awards Act of 1976".

Section 2

Section 2 amends section 722 (42 U.S.C. 1988) of the Revised Statutes by adding at the end of that section the following language:

> In any action or proceeding to enforce a provision of sections 1977, 1978, 1979, 1980, 1981 of the Revised Statutes, title IX of Public Law 92–318, or title VI of the Civil Rights Act of 1964, the court, in its discretion, may allow the prevailig party, other than the United States, a reasonable attorney's fee as part of the costs.

CHANGES IN EXISTING LAW MADE BY THE BILL, AS REPORTED

In compliance with clause 3 of rule XIII of the Rules of the House of Representatives, changes in existing law made by the bill, as reported, are shown as follows (new matter is printed in italic, existing law in which no change is proposed is shown in roman):

SECTION 722 OF THE REVISED STATUTES

SEC. 722. The jurisdiction in civil and criminal matters conferred on the district and circuit courts by the provisions of this Title, and of Title "CIVIL RIGHTS," and of Title "CRIMES," for the protection of all persons in the United States in their civil rights, and for their vindi-

11

cation, shall be exercised and enforced in conformity with the laws of the United States, so far as such laws are suitable to carry the same into effect; but in all cases where they are not adapted to the object, or are deficient in the provisions necessary to furnish suitable remedies and punish offenses against law, the common law, as modified and changed by the constitution and statutes of the State wherein the court having jurisdiction of such civil or criminal cause is held, so far as the same is not inconsistent with the Constitution and laws of the United States, shall be extended to and govern the said courts in the trial and disposition of the cause, and, if it is of a criminal nature, in the infliction of punishment on the party found guilty. *In any action or proceeding to enforce a provision of sections 1977, 1978, 1979, 1980, and 1981 of the Revised Statutes, title IX of Public Law 92–318, or title VI of the Civil Rights Act of 1964, the court, in its discretion, may allow the prevailing party, other than the United States, a reasonable attorney's fee as part of the costs.*

Appendix A[1]

FEDERAL STATUTES AUTHORIZING THE AWARD OF ATTORNEY FEES

1. Federal Contested Election Act, 2 U.S.C. 396.
2. Freedom of Information Act, 5 U.S.C. 552(a)(4)(E).
3. Privacy Act, 5 U.S.C. 552a(g)(3)(B).
4. Federal Employment Compensation For Work Injuries, 5 U.S.C. 8127.
5. Packers and Stockyards Act, 7 U.S.C. 210(f).
6. Perishable Agricultural Commodities Act, 7 U.S.C. 499g (b), (c).
7. Agricultural Unfair Trade Practices Act, 7 U.S.C. 2305 (a), (c).
8. Plant Variety Act, 7 U.S.C. 2565.
9. Bankruptcy Act, 11 U.S.C. 104(a)(1).
10. Railroad Reorganization Act of 1935, 11 U.S.C. 205(c)(12).
11. Corporate Reorganization Act, 11 U.S.C. 641, 642, 643, and 644.
12. Federal Credit Union Act, 12 U.S.C. 1786(O).
13. Bank Holding Company Act, 12 U.S.C. 1975.
14. Clayton Act, 15 U.S.C. 15.
15. Unfair Competition Act (FTC), 15 U.S.C. 72.
16. Securities Act of 1933, 15 U.S.C. 77k(e).
17. Trust Indenture Act, 15 U.S.C. 77www(a).
18. Securities Exchange Act of 1934, 15 U.S.C. 78i(e), 78r(a).
19. Jewelers Hall-Mark Act, 15 U.S.C. 298 (b), (c) and (d).
20. Truth-in-Lending Act (Fair Credit Billing Amendments), 15 U.S.C. 1640(a).
21. Fair Credit Reporting Act, 15 U.S.C. 1681(n).
22. Motor Vehicle Information and Cost Savings Act, 15 U.S.C. 1918(a), 1989(a)(2).
23. Consumer Product Safety Act, 15 U.S.C. 2072, 2073.
24. Federal Trade Improvements Act (Amendments), 15 U.S.C. 2310(a)(5)(d)(2).
25. Copyright Act, 17 U.S.C. 1116.
26. Organized Crime Control Act of 1970, 18 U.S.C. 1964(c).
27. Education Amendments of 1972, 20 U.S.C. 1617.
28. Mexican American Treaty Act of 1950, 22 U.S.C. 277d–21.
29. International Claim Settlement Act, 22 U.S.C. 1623(f).
30. Federal Tort Claim Act, 28 U.S.C. 2678.
31. Norris-LaGuardia Act, 29 U.S.C. 107.
32. Fair Labor Standards Act, 29 U.S.C. 216(b).
33. Employees Retirement Income Security Act, 29 U.S.C. 1132(g).
34. Labor Management Reporting and Disclosure Act, 29 U.S.C. 431(c), 501(b).
35. Longshoremen and Harbor Workers Compensation Act, 33 U.S.C. 928.

[1] This list is compiled from information submitted to the Subcommittee by the Council for Public Interest La wand the Attorneys' Fee Project of the Lawyers' Committee for Civil Rights Under Law.

14

36. Water Pollution Prevention and Control Act, 33 U.S.C. 1365(d).

37. Ocean Dumping Act, 33 U.S.C. 1415(g)(4).

38. Deepwater Ports Act of 1974, 33 U.S.C. 1515.

39. Patent Infringement Act, 35 U.S.C. 285.

40. Servicemen's Group Life Insurance Act, 38 U.S.C. 784(g).

41. Servicemen's Readjustment Act, 38 U.S.C. 1822(b).

42. Veterans Benefit Act, 38 U.S.C. 3404(c).

43. Safe Drinking Water Act, 42 U.S.C. 300j-8(d).

44. Social Security Act (Amendments of 1965), 42 U.S.C. 406(b).

45. Clean Air Act (Amendments of 1970), 42 U.S.C. 1857h-2.

46. Civil Rights Act of 1964, Title II, 42 U.S.C. 2000a-3(b).

47. Civil Rights Act of 1964, Title VII, 42 U.S.C. 2000e-5(k).

48. Legal Services Corporation Act, 42 U.S.C. 2996e(f).

49. Fair Housing Act of 1968, 42 U.S.C. 3612(c).

50. Noise Control Act of 1972, 42 U.S.C. 4911(d).

51. Railway Labor Act, 45 U.S.C. 153(p).

52. Merchant Marine Act of 1936, 46 U.S.C. 1227.

53. Communications Act of 1934, 47 U.S.C. 206.

54. Interstate Commerce Act, 49 U.S.C. 8, 16(2), 908(b), 908(e), and 1017(b)(2).

APPENDIX B

STATUTES COVERED OR AMENDED BY H.R. 15460

1. Revised Statutes § 1977 (42 U.S.C. § 1981).

§ 1981. Equal rights under the law

All persons within the jurisdiction of the United States shall have the same right in every State and Territory to make and enforce contracts, to sue, be parties, give evidence, and to the full and equal benefit of all laws and proceedings for the security of persons and property as is enjoyed by white citizens, and shall be subject to like punishment, pains, penalties, taxes, licenses, and exactions of every kind, and to no other.
R.S. § 1977.

2. Revised Statutes § 1978 (42 U.S.C. § 1982).

§ 1982. Property rights of citizens

All citizens of the United States shall have the same right, in every State and Territory, as is enjoyed by white citizens thereof to inherit, purchase, lease, sell, hold, and convey real and personal property.
R.S. § 1978.

3. Revised Statutes § 1979 (42 U.S.C. § 1983).

§ 1983. Civil action for deprivation of rights

Every person who, under color of any statute, ordinance, regulation, custom, or usage, of any State or Territory, subjects, or causes to be subjected, any citizen of the United States or other person within the jurisdiction thereof to the deprivation of any rights, privileges, or immunities secured by the Constitution and laws, shall be liable to the party injured in an action at law, suit in equity, or other proper proceeding for redress.
R.S. § 1979.

4. Revised Statutes § 1980 (42 U.S.C. § 1985).

§ 1985. Conspiracy to interfere with civil rights—Preventing officer from performing duties

(1) If two or more persons in any State or Territory conspire to prevent, by force, intimidation, or threat, any person from accepting or holding any office, trust, or place of confidence under the United States, or from discharging any duties thereof; or to induce by like means any officer of the United States to leave any State, district, or place, where his duties as an officer are required to be performed, or to injure him in his person or property on account of his lawful discharge of the duties of his office, or while engaged in the lawful discharge thereof, or to injure his property so as to molest, interrupt, hinder, or impede him in the discharge of his official duties;

(15)

16

Obstructing justice; intimidating party, witness, or juror

(2) If two or more persons in any State or Territory conspire to deter, by force, intimidation, or threat, any party or witness in any court of the United States from attending such court, or from testifying to any matter pending therein, freely, fully, and truthfully, or to injure such party or witness in his person or property on account of his having so attended or testified, or to influence the verdict, presentment, or indictment of any grand or petit juror in any such court, or to injure such juror in his person or property on account of any verdict, presentment, or indictment lawfully assented to by him, or of his being or having been such juror; or if two or more persons conspire for the purpose of impeding, hindering, obstructing, or defeating, in any manner, the due course of justice in any State or Territory, with intent to deny to any citizen the equal protection of the laws, or to injure him or his property for lawfully enforcing, or attempting to enforce, the right of any person, or class of persons, to the equal protection of the laws;

Depriving persons of rights or privileges

(3) If two or more persons in any State or Territory conspire or go in disguise on the highway or on the premises of another, for the purpose of depriving, either directly or indirectly, any person or class of persons of the equal protection of the laws, or of equal privileges and immunities under the laws; or for the purpose of preventing or hindering the constituted authorities of any State or Territory from giving or securing to all persons within such State or Territory the equal protection of the laws; or if two or more persons conspire to prevent by force, intimidation, or threat, any citizen who is lawfully entitled to vote, from giving his support or advocacy in a legal manner, toward or in favor of the election of any lawfully qualified person as an elector for President or Vice President, or as a Member of Congress of the United States; or to injure any citizen in person or property on account of such support or advocacy; in any case of conspiracy set forth in this section, if one or more persons engaged therein do, or cause to be done, any act in furtherance of the object of such conspiracy, whereby another is injured in his person or property, or deprived of having and exercising any right or privilege of a citizen of the United States, the party so injured or deprived may have an action for the recovery of damages, occasioned by such injury or deprivation, against any one of more of the conspirators.

R.S. § 1980.

5. Revised Statutes § 198 (42 U.S.C. § 1986).

§ 1986. Same; action for neglect to prevent

Every person who, having knowledge that any of the wrongs conspired to be done, and mentioned in section 1985 of this title, are about to be committed, and having power to prevent or aid in preventing the commission of the same, neglects or refuses so to do, if such wrongful act be committed, shall be liable to the party injured, or his legal representatives, for all damages caused by such wrongful act, which such person by reasonable diligence could have prevented; and such damages may be recovered in an action on the case; and

17

any number of persons guilty of such wrongful neglect or refusal may be joined as defendants in the action; and if the death of any party be caused by any such wrongful act and neglect, the legal representatives of the deceased shall have such action therefor, and may recover not exceeding $5,000 damages therein, for the benefit of the widow of the deceased, if there be one, and if there be no widow, then for the benefit of the next of kin of the deceased. But no action under the provisions of this section shall be sustained which is not commenced within one year after the cause of action has accrued.

R.S. § 1981.

6. Revised Statutes § 722 (42 U.S.C. § 1988).

§ 1988.   Proceedings in vindication of civil rights

The jurisdiction in civil and criminal matters conferred on the district courts by the provisions of this chapter and Title 18, for the protection of all persons in the United States in their civil rights, and for their vindication, shall be exercised and enforced in conformity with the laws of the United States, so far as such laws are suitable to carry the same into effect; but in all cases where they are not adapted to the object, or are deficient in the provisions necessary to furnish suitable remedies and punish offenses against law, the common law, as modified and changed by the constitution and statutes of the State wherein the court having jurisdiction of such civil or criminal cause is held, so far as the same is not inconsistent with the Constitution and laws of the United States, shall be extended to and govern the said courts in the trial and disposition of the cause, and, if it is of a criminal nature, in the infliction of punishment on the party found guilty.

R.S. § 722.

7. Title IX of Public Law 92–318 (20 U.S.C. § 1681–1686), as amended.

§ 1681.   Sex—Prohibition against discrimination; exceptions

(a) No person in the United States shall, on the basis of sex, be excluded from participation in, be denied the benefits of, or be subjected to discrimination under any education program or activity receiving Federal financial assistance, except that:

Classes of Educational Institutions Subject to Prohibition

(1) in regard to admissions to educational institutions, this section shall apply only to institutions of vocational education, professional education, and graduate higher education, and to public institutions of undergraduate higher education;

Educational Institutions Commencing Planned Change in Admissions

(2) in regard to admissions to educational institutions, this section shall not apply (A) for one year from June 23, 1972, nor for six years after June 23, 1972, in the case of an educational institution which has begun the process of changing from being an institution which admits only students of one sex to being an institution which admits students of both sexes, but only if it is carrying out a plan for such a change

18

which is approved by the Commissioner of Education or (B) for seven years from the date an educational institution begins the process of changing from being an institution which admits only students of only one sex to being an institution which admits students of both sexes, but only if it is carrying out a plan for such a change which is approved by the Commissioner of Education, whichever is the later;

Educational institutions of religious organizations with contrary religious tenets

(3) this section shall not apply to an educational institution which is controlled by a religious organization if the application of this subsection would not be consistent with the religious tenets of such organization;

Educational institutions training individuals for military services or merchant marine

(4) this section shall not apply to an educational institution whose primary purpose is the training of individuals for the military services of the United States, or the merchant marine;

Public educational institutions with traditional and continuing admissions policy

(5) in regard to admissions this section shall not apply to any public institution of undergraduate higher education which is an institution that traditionally and continually from its establishment has had a policy of admitting only students of one sex; and

Social fraternities or sororities; voluntary youth service organizations

(6) This section shall not apply to membership practices—
(A) of a social fraternity or social sorority which is exempt from taxation under section 501(a) of Title 26, the active membership of which consists primarily of students in attendance at an institution of higher education, or
(B) of the Young Men's Christian Association, Young Women's Christian Association, Girl Scouts, Boy Scouts, Camp Fire Girls, and voluntary youth service organizations which are so exempt, the membership of which has traditionally been limited to persons of one sex and principally to persons of less than nineteen years of age.

Preferential or disparate treatment because of imbalance in participation or receipt of Federal benefits; statistical evidence of imbalance

(b) Nothing contained in subsection (a) of this section shall be interpreted to require any educational institution to grant preferential or disparate treatment to the members of one sex on account of an imbalance which may exist with respect to the total number or percentage of persons of that sex participating in or receiving the benefits of any federally supported program or activity, in comparison

19

with the total number or percentage of persons of that sex in any community. State, section, or other area: *Provided.* That this subsection shall not be construed to prevent the consideration in any hearing or proceeding under this chapter of statistical evidence tending to show that such an imbalance exists with respect to the participation in, or receipt of the benefits of, any such program or activity by the members of one sex.

Educational Institution Defined

(c) For purposes of this chapter an educational institution means any public or private preschool, elementary, or secondary school, or any institution of vocational, professional, or higher education, except that in the case of an educational institution composed of more than one school, college, or department which are administratively separate units, such terms means each such school, college, or department.

§ 1682. Federal administrative enforcement; report to congressional committees

Each Federal department and agency which is empowered to extend Federal financial assistance to any education program or activity, by way of grant, loan, or contract other than a contract of insurance or guaranty, is authorized and directed to effectuate the provisions of section 1681 of this title with respect to such program or activity by issuing rules, regulations, or orders of general applicability which shall be consistent with achievement of the objectives of the statute authorizing the financial assistance in connection with which the action is taken. No such rule, regulation, or order shall become effective unless and until approved by the President. Compliance with any requirement adopted pursuant to this section may be effected (1) by the termination of or refusal to grant or to continue assistance under such program or activity to any recipient as to whom there has been an express finding on the record, after opportunity for hearing, of a failure to comply with such requirement, but such termination or refusal shall be limited to the particular political entity, or part thereof, or other recipient as to whom such a finding has been made, and shall be limited in its effect to the particular program, or part thereof, in which such noncompliance has been so found, or (2) by any other means authorized by law: *Provided, however,* That no such action shall be taken until the department or agency concerned has advised the appropriate person or persons of the failure to comply with the requirement and has determined that compliance cannot be secured by voluntary means. In the case of any action terminating, or refusing to grant or continue, assistance because of failure to comply with a requirement imposed pursuant to this section, the head of the Federal department or agency shall file with the committees of the House and Senate having legislative jurisdiction over the program or activity involved a full written report of the circumstances and the grounds for such action. No such action shall become effective until thirty days have elapsed after the filing of such report.

20

Public Law 92–318, Title IX, § 902, June 23, 1972, 86 Stat. 374.

§ 1683. Judicial review

Any department or agency action taken pursuant to section 1682 of this title shall be subject to such judicial review as may otherwise be provided by law for similar action taken by such department or agency on other grounds. In the case of action, not otherwise subject to judicial review, terminating or refusing to grant or to continue financial assistance upon a finding of failure to comply with any requirement imposed pursuant to section 1682 of this title, any person aggrieved (including any State or political subdivision thereof and any agency of either) may obtain judicial review of such action in accordance with chapter 7 of Title 5, and such action shall not be deemed committed to unreviewable agency discretion within the meaning of section 701 of that Title.

Public Law 92–318, Title IX, § 903, June 23, 1972, 86 Stat. 374.

§ 1684. Blindness or visual impairment; prohibition against discriminaton

No person in the United States shall, on the ground of blindness or severely impaired vision, be denied admission in any course of study by a recipient of Federal financial assistance for any education program or activity, but nothing herein shall be construed to require any such institution to provide any special services to such person because of his blindness or visual impairment.

Public Law 92–318, Title IX, § 904, June 23, 1972, 86 Stat. 375.

§ 1685. Authorty under other laws unaffected

Nothing in this chapter shall add to or detract from any existing authority with respect to any program or activity under which Federal financial assistance is extended by way of a contract of insurance or guaranty.

Public Law 92–318, Title IX, § 905, June 23, 1972, 86 Stat. 375.

§ 1686. Interpretation with respect to living facilities

Notwithstanding anything to the contrary contained in this chapter, nothing contained herein shall be construed to prohibit any educational institution receiving funds under this Act, from maintaining separate living facilities for the different sexes.

Public Law 92–318, Title IX, § 907, June 23, 1972, 86 Stat. 375.

8. Title VI of the Civil Rights Act of 1964 (Publ. L. 88–352, as amended), (42 U.S.C. 2000d through d–6).

SUBCHAPTER V.—FEDERALLY ASSISTED PROGRAMS

§ 2000d. Prohibition against exclusion from participation in, denial of benefits of, and discrimination under Federally assisted programs on ground of race, color, or national origin

No person in the United States shall, on the ground of race, color, or national origin, be excluded from participation in, be denied the benefits of, or be subjected to discrimination under any program or activity receiving Federal financial assistance. (Pub. L. 88–352, title VI, § 601, July 2, 1964, 78 Stat. 252.)

21

§ 2000d–1. Federal authority and financial assistance to programs or activities by way of grant, loan, or contract other than contract of insurance or guaranty; rules and regulations; approval by President; compliance with requirements; reports to congressional committees; effective date of administrative action

Each Federal department and agency which is empowered to extend Federal financial assistance to any program or activity, by way of grant, loan, or contract other than a contract of insurance or guaranty, is authorized and directed to effectuate the provisions of section 2000d of this title with respect to such program or activity by issuing rules, regulations, or orders of general applicability which shall be consistent with achievement of the objectives of the statute authorizing the financial assistance in connection with which the action is taken. No such rule, regulation, or order shall become effective unless and until approved by the President. Compliance with any requirement adopted pursuant to this section may be effected (1) by the termination of or refusal to grant or to continue assistance under such program or activity to any recipient as to whom there has been an express finding on the record, after opportunity for hearing, of a failure to comply with such requirement, but such termination or refusal shall be limited to the particular political entity, or part thereof, or other recipient as to whom such a finding has been made and, shall be limited in its effect to the particular program, or part thereof, in which such noncompliance has been so found, or (2) by any other means authorized by law: *Provided, however*, That no such action shall be taken until the department or agency concerned has advised the appropriate person or persons of the failure to comply with the requirement and has determined that compliance cannot be secured by voluntary means. In the case of any action terminating, or refusing to grant or continue, assistance because of failure to comply with a requirement imposed pursuant to this section, the head of the Federal department or agency shall file with the committees of the House and Senate having legislative jurisdiction over the program or activity involved a full written report of the circumstances and the grounds for such action. No such action shall become effective until thirty days have elapsed after the filing of such report. (Pub. L. 88–352, title VI, § 602, July 2, 1964, 78 Stat. 252.)

§ 2000d–2. Judicial review; Administrative Procedure Act.

Any department or agency action taken pursuant to section 2000d–1 of this title shall be subject to such judicial review as may otherwise be provided by law for similar action taken by such department or agency on other grounds. In the case of action, not otherwise subject to judicial review, terminating or refusing to grant or to continue financial assistance upon a finding of failure to comply with any requirement imposed pursuant to section 2000d–1 of this title, any person aggrieved (including any State or political subdivision thereof and any agency of either) may obtain judicial review of such action in accordance with section 1009 of Title 5, and such action shall not be deemed committed to unreviewable agency discretion within the meaning of that section. (Pub. L. 88–352, title VI, § 603, July 2, 1964, 78 Stat. 253.)

22

§ 2000d–3. Construction of provisions not to authorize administrative action with respect to employment practices except where primary objective of Federal financial assistance is to provide employment

Nothing contained in this subchapter shall be construed to authorize action under this subchapter by any department or agency with respect to any employment practice of any employer, employment agency or labor organization except where a primary objective of the Federal financial assistance is to provide employment. (Pub. L. 88–352, title VI, § 604, July 2, 1964, 78 Stat. 253.)

§ 2000d–4. Federal authority and financial assistance to programs or activities by way of contract of insurance or guaranty

Nothing in this subchapter shall add to or detract from any existing authority with respect to any program or activity under which Federal financial assistance is extended by way of a contract of insurance or guaranty. (Pub. L. 88–352, title VI, § 605, July 2, 1964, 78 Stat. 253.)

§ 2000–5. Prohibited deferral of action on applications by local educational agencies seeking federal funds for alleged noncompliance with Civil Rights Act.

The Commissioner of Education shall not defer action or order action or order action deferred on any application by a local educational agency for funds authorized to be appropriated by this Act, by the Elementary and Secondary Education Act of 1965, by the Act of September 30, 1950 (Public Law 874, Eighty-first Congress), by the Act of September 23, 1950 (Public Law 815, Eighty-first Congress), or by the Cooperative Research Act, on the basis of alleged noncompliance with the provisions of this subchapter for more than sixty days after notice is given to such local agency of such deferral unless such local agency is given the opportunity for a hearing as provided in section 2000d–1 of this title, such hearing to be held within sixty days of such notice, unless the time for such hearing is extended by mutual consent of such local agency and the commissioner, and such deferral shall not continue for more than thirty days after the close of any such hearing unless there has been an express finding on the record of such hearing that such local educational agency has failed to comply with the provisions of this subchapter: *Provided*, That, for the purpose of determining whether a local educational agency is in compliance with this subchapter, compliance by such agency with a final order or judgment of a Federal court for the desegregation of the school or school system operated by such agency shall be deemed to be in compliance with this subchapter, insofar as the matters covered in the order or judgment are concerned. (Pub. L. 89–750, title I, § 182, Nov. 3, 1966, 80 Stat. 1209; Pub. L. 90–247, title I, § 112, Jan. 2, 1968, 81 Stat. 787).

§ 2000d–6. Policy of United States as to application of nondiscrimination provisions in schools of local educational agencies

(a) Declaration of uniform policy.

It is the policy of the United States that guidelines and criteria established pursuant to title VI of the Civil Rights Act of 1964 and

23

section 182 of the Elementary and Secondary Education Amendments of 1966 dealing with conditions of segregation by race, whether de jure or de facto, in the schools of the local educational agencies of any State shall be applied uniformly in all regions of the United States whatever the origin or cause of such segregation.

(b) Nature of uniformity

Such uniformity refers to one policy applied uniformly to de jure segregation wherever found and such other policy as may be provided pursuant to law applied uniformly to de facto segregation wherever found.

(c) Prohibition of construction for diminution of obligation for enforcement or compliance with nondiscrimination requirements

Nothing in this section shall be construed to diminish the obligation of responsible officials to enforce or comply with such guidelines and criteria in order to eliminate discrimination in federally assisted programs and activities as required by title VI of the Civil Rights Act of 1964.

(d) Additional funds

It is the sense of the Congress that the Department of Justice and the Department of Health, Education, and Welfare should request such additional funds as may be necessary to apply the policy set forth in this section throughout the United States. (Pub. L. 91–230, § 2, Apr. 13, 1970, 84 Stat. 121.)

O

Food and Drug Administration Requirements for Specific Nonstandardized Foods

21 C.F.R. § 102.33 (2015)

Beverages that contain fruit or vegetable juice.

(a) For a carbonated or noncarbonated beverage that contains less than 100 percent and more than 0 percent fruit or vegetable juice, the common or usual name shall be a descriptive name that meets the requirements of § 102.5(a) and, if the common or usual name uses the word "juice," shall include a qualifying term such as "beverage," "cocktail," or "drink" appropriate to advise the consumer that the product is less than 100 percent juice (e.g., "diluted grape juice beverage" or "grape juice drink").

(b) If the product is a diluted multiple-juice beverage or blend of single-strength juices and names, other than in the ingredient statement, more than one juice, then the names of those juices, except in the ingredient statement, must be in descending order of predominance by volume unless the name specifically shows that the juice with the represented flavor is used as a flavor (e.g., raspberry-flavored apple and pear juice drink). In accordance with § 101.22(i)(1)(iii) of this chapter, the presence of added natural flavors is not required to be declared in the name of the beverage unless the declared juices alone do not characterize the product before the addition of the added flavors.

(c) If a diluted multiple-juice beverage or blend of single-strength juices contains a juice that is named or implied on the label or labeling other than in the ingredient statement (represented juice), and also contains a juice other than the named or implied juice (nonrepresented juice), then the common or usual name for the product shall indicate that the represented juice is not the only juice present (e.g., "Apple blend; apple juice in a blend of two other fruit juices.")

(d) In a diluted multiple-juice beverage or blend of single-strength juices where one or more, but not all, of the juices are named on the label other than in the ingredient statement, and where the named juice is not the predominant juice, the common or usual name for the product shall:

(1) Indicate that the named juice is present as a flavor or flavoring (e.g., "Rasp-cranberry"; raspberry and cranberry flavored juice drink); or

(2) Include the amount of the named juice, declared in a 5- percent range (e.g., Raspcranberry; raspberry and cranberry juice beverage, 10- to 15-percent cranberry juice and 3- to 8-percent raspberry juice). The 5-percent range, when used, shall be declared in the manner set forth in § 102.5(b)(2).

(e) The common or usual name of a juice that has been modified shall include a description of the exact nature of the modification (e.g., "acid-reduced cranberry juice," "deflavored, decolored grape juice").

(f) If the product is a beverage that contains a juice whose color, taste, or other organoleptic properties have been modified to the extent that the original juice is no longer recognizable at the time processing is complete, or if its nutrient profile has been diminished to a level below the normal nutrient range for the juice, then the source fruits or vegetables from which the modified juice was derived may not be depicted on the label by vignette or other pictorial representation.

(g)

(1) If one or more juices in a juice beverage is made from concentrate, the name of the juice must include a term indicating that fact, such as "from concentrate," or "reconstituted." Such terms must be included in the name of each individual juice or it may be stated once adjacent to the product name so that it applies to all the juices, (e.g., "cherry juice (from concentrate) in a blend of two other juices" or "cherry juice in a blend of 2 other juices (from concentrate)"). The term shall be in a type size no less than one-half the height of the letters in the name of the juice.

(2) If the juice is 100 percent single species juice consisting of juice directly expressed from a fruit or vegetable whose Brix level has been raised by the addition of juice concentrate from the same fruit or vegetable, the name of the juice need not include a statement that the juice is from concentrate. However, if water is added to this 100 percent juice mixture to adjust the Brix level, the product shall be labeled with the term "from concentrate" or "reconstituted."

Selected Administrative Materials: Deferred Action for Parents of Americans and Lawful Permanent Residents (DAPA)

Secretary
U.S. Department of Homeland Security
Washington, DC 20528

 **Homeland Security**

November 20, 2014

MEMORANDUM FOR: Thomas S. Winkowski
Acting Director
U.S. Immigration and Customs Enforcement

R. Gil Kerlikowske
Commissioner
U.S. Customs and Border Protection

Leon Rodriguez
Director
U.S. Citizenship and Immigration Services

Alan D. Bersin
Acting Assistant Secretary for Policy

FROM: Jeh Charles Johnson
Secretary

SUBJECT: **Policies for the Apprehension, Detention and Removal of Undocumented Immigrants**

     This memorandum reflects new policies for the apprehension, detention, and removal of aliens in this country. This memorandum should be considered Department-wide guidance, applicable to the activities of U.S. Immigration and Customs Enforcement (ICE), U.S. Customs and Border Protection (CBP), and U.S. Citizenship and Immigration Services (USCIS). This memorandum should inform enforcement and removal activity, detention decisions, budget requests and execution, and strategic planning.

     In general, our enforcement and removal policies should continue to prioritize threats to national security, public safety, and border security. The intent of this new policy is to provide clearer and more effective guidance in the pursuit of those priorities. To promote public confidence in our enforcement activities, I am also directing herein greater transparency in the annual reporting of our removal statistics, to include data that tracks the priorities outlined below.

The Department of Homeland Security (DHS) and its immigration components-CBP, ICE, and USCIS-are responsible for enforcing the nation's immigration laws. Due to limited resources, DHS and its Components cannot respond to all immigration violations or remove all persons illegally in the United States. As is true of virtually every other law enforcement agency, DHS must exercise prosecutorial discretion in the enforcement of the law. And, in the exercise of that discretion, DHS can and should develop smart enforcement priorities, and ensure that use of its limited resources is devoted to the pursuit of those priorities. DHS's enforcement priorities are, have been, and will continue to be national security, border security, and public safety. DHS personnel are directed to prioritize the use of enforcement personnel, detention space, and removal assets accordingly.

In the immigration context, prosecutorial discretion should apply not only to the decision to issue, serve, file, or cancel a Notice to Appear, but also to a broad range of other discretionary enforcement decisions, including deciding: whom to stop, question, and arrest; whom to detain or release; whether to settle, dismiss, appeal, or join in a motion on a case; and whether to grant deferred action, parole, or a stay of removal instead of pursuing removal in a case. While DHS may exercise prosecutorial discretion at any stage of an enforcement proceeding, it is generally preferable to exercise such discretion as early in the case or proceeding as possible in order to preserve government resources that would otherwise be expended in pursuing enforcement and removal of higher priority cases. Thus, DHS personnel are expected to exercise discretion and pursue these priorities at all stages of the enforcement process-from the earliest investigative stage to enforcing final orders of removal-subject to their chains of command and to the particular responsibilities and authorities applicable to their specific position.

Except as noted below, the following memoranda are hereby rescinded and superseded: John Morton, *Civil Immigration Enforcement: Priorities for the Apprehension, Detention, and Removal of Aliens*, March 2, 2011; John Morton, *Exercising Prosecutorial Discretion Consistent with the Civil Enforcement Priorities of the Agency for the Apprehension, Detention and Removal of Aliens*, June 17, 2011; Peter Vincent, *Case-by-Case Review of Incoming and Certain Pending Cases*, November 17, 2011; *Civil Immigration Enforcement: Guidance on the Use of Detainers in the Federal, State, Local, and Tribal Criminal Justice Systems*, December 21, 2012; *National Fugitive Operations Program: Priorities, Goals, and Expectations*, December 8, 2009.

2

A. Civil Immigration Enforcement Priorities

The following shall constitute the Department's civil immigration enforcement priorities:

Priority 1 (threats to national security, border security, and public safety)

Aliens described in this priority represent the highest priority to which enforcement resources should be directed:

(a) aliens engaged in or suspected of terrorism or espionage, or who otherwise pose a danger to national security;

(b) aliens apprehended at the border or ports of entry while attempting to unlawfully enter the United States;

(c) aliens convicted of an offense for which an element was active participation in a criminal street gang, as defined in 18 U.S.C. § 521(a), or aliens not younger than 16 years of age who intentionally participated in an organized criminal gang to further the illegal activity of the gang;

(d) aliens convicted of an offense classified as a felony in the convicting jurisdiction, other than a state or local offense for which an essential element was the alien's immigration status; and

(e) aliens convicted of an "aggravated felony," as that term is defined in section 101(a)(43) of the *Immigration and Nationality Act* at the time of the conviction.

The removal of these aliens must be prioritized unless they qualify for asylum or another form of relief under our laws, or unless, in the judgment of an ICE Field Office Director, CBP Sector Chief or CBP Director of Field Operations, there are compelling and exceptional factors that clearly indicate the alien is not a threat to national security, border security, or public safety and should not therefore be an enforcement priority.

Priority 2 (misdemeanants and new immigration violators)

Aliens described in this priority , who are also not described in Priority 1, represent the second-highest priority for apprehension and removal. Resources should be dedicated accordingly to the removal of the following:

(a) aliens convicted of three or more misdemeanor offenses, other than minor traffic offenses or state or local offenses for which an essential element

3

was the alien's immigration status, provided the offenses arise out of three separate incidents;

(b)   aliens convicted of a "significant misdemeanor," which for these purposes is an offense of domestic violence;[1] sexual abuse or exploitation; burglary; unlawful possession or use of a firearm; drug distribution or trafficking; or driving under the influence; or if not an offense listed above, one for which the individual was sentenced to time in custody of 90 days or more (the sentence must involve time to be served in custody, and does not include a suspended sentence);

(c)   aliens apprehended anywhere in the United States after unlawfully entering or re-entering the United States and who cannot establish to the satisfaction of an immigration officer that they have been physically present in the United States continuously since January 1, 2014; and

(d)   aliens who, in the judgment of an ICE Field Office Director, USCIS District Director, or USCIS Service Center Director, have significantly abused the visa or visa waiver programs.

These aliens should be removed unless they qualify for asylum or another form of relief under our laws or, unless, in the judgment of an ICE Field Office Director, CBP Sector Chief, CBP Director of Field Operations, USCIS District Director, or users Service Center Director, there are factors indicating the alien is not a threat to national security, border security, or public safety, and should not therefore be an enforcement priority.

Priority 3 (other immigration violations)

Priority 3 aliens are those who have been issued a final order of removal[2] on or after January 1, 2014. Aliens described in this priority, who are not also described in Priority 1 or 2, represent the third and lowest priority for apprehension and removal. Resources should be dedicated accordingly to aliens in this priority. Priority 3 aliens should generally be removed unless they qualify for asylum or another form of relief under our laws or, unless, in the judgment of an immigration officer, the alien is not a threat to the integrity of the immigration system or there are factors suggesting the alien should not be an enforcement priority.

---

[1] In evaluating whether the offense is a significant misdemeanor involving ..domestic violence," careful consideration should be given to whether the convicted alien was also the <u>victim</u> of domestic violence; if so, this should be a mitigating factor. *See generally,* John Morton, *Prosecutorial Discretion: Certain Victims, Witnesses, and Plaintiffs,* June 17, 2011.

[2] For present purposes, "final order" is defined as it is in 8 C.F.R. § 1241.1.

4

B.   Apprehension, Detention, and Removal of Other Aliens Unlawfully in the   United States

Nothing in this memorandum should be construed to prohibit or discourage the apprehension, detention, or removal of aliens unlawfully in the United States who are not identified as priorities herein. However, resources should be dedicated, to the greatest degree possible, to the removal of aliens described in the priorities set forth above, commensurate with the level of prioritization identified. Immigration officers and attorneys may pursue removal of an alien not identified as a priority herein, provided, in the judgment of an ICE Field Office Director, removing such an alien would serve an important federal interest.

C.   Detention

As a general rule, DHS detention resources should be used to support the enforcement priorities noted above or for aliens subject to mandatory detention by law. Absent extraordinary circumstances or the requirement of mandatory detention, field office directors should not expend detention resources on aliens who are known to be suffering from serious physical or mental illness, who are disabled, elderly, pregnant, or nursing, who demonstrate that they are primary caretakers of children or an infirm person, or whose detention is otherwise not in the public interest. To detain aliens in those categories who are not subject to mandatory detention, DHS officers or special agents must obtain approval from the ICE Field Office Director. If an alien falls within the above categories and is subject to mandatory detention, field office directors are encouraged to contact their local Office of Chief Counsel for guidance.

D.   Exercising Prosecutorial Discretion

Section A, above, requires DHS personnel to exercise discretion based on individual circumstances. As noted above, aliens in Priority 1 must be prioritized for removal unless they qualify for asylum or other form of relief under our laws, or unless, in the judgment of an ICE Field Office Director, CBP Sector Chief, or CBP Director of Field Operations, there are compelling and exceptional factors that clearly indicate the alien is not a threat to national security, border security, or public safety and should not therefore be an enforcement priority. Likewise, aliens in Priority 2 should be removed unless they qualify for asylum or other forms of relief under our laws, or unless, in the judgment of an ICE Field Office Director, CBP Sector Chief, CBP Director of Field Operations, USCIS District Director, or USCIS Service Center Director, there are factors indicating the alien is not a threat to national security, border security, or public safety and should not therefore be an enforcement priority. Similarly, aliens in Priority 3 should generally be removed unless they qualify for asylum or another form of relief under our laws or, unless, in the judgment of an immigration officer, the alien is not a threat to the integrity of the immigration system or there are factors suggesting the alien should not be an enforcement priority.

In making such judgments, DHS personnel should consider factors such as: extenuating circumstances involving the offense of conviction; extended length of time since the offense of conviction; length of time in the United States; military service; family or community ties in the United States; status as a victim, witness or plaintiff in civil or criminal proceedings; or compelling humanitarian factors such as poor health, age, pregnancy, a young child, or a seriously ill relative. These factors are not intended to be dispositive nor is this list intended to be exhaustive. Decisions should be based on the totality of the circumstances.

E.   Implementation

The revised guidance shall be effective on January 5, 2015. Implementing training and guidance will be provided to the workforce prior to the effective date. The revised guidance in this memorandum applies only to aliens encountered or apprehended on or after the effective date, and aliens detained, in removal proceedings, or subject to removal orders who have not been removed from the United States as of the effective date. Nothing in this guidance is intended to modify USCIS Notice to Appear policies, which remain in force and effect to the extent they are not inconsistent with this memorandum.

F.   Data

By this memorandum I am directing the Office of Immigration Statistics to create the capability to collect, maintain, and report to the Secretary data reflecting the numbers of those apprehended, removed, returned, or otherwise repatriated by any component of DHS and to report that data in accordance with the priorities set forth above. I direct CBP, ICE, and USCIS to cooperate in this effort. I intend for this data to be part of the package of data released by DHS to the public annually.

G.   No Private Right Statement

These guidelines and priorities are not intended to, do not, and may not be relied upon to create any right or benefit, substantive or procedural, enforceable at law by any party in any administrative, civil, or criminal matter.

6

Secretary
U.S. Department of Homeland Security
Washington, DC 20528

November 20, 2014

MEMORANDUM FOR: León Rodríguez
                 Director
                 U.S. Citizenship and Immigration Services

                 Thomas S. Winkowski
                 Acting Director
                 U.S. Immigration and Customs Enforcement

                 R. Gil Kerlikowske
                 Commissioner
                 U.S. Customs and Border Protection

FROM: Jeh Charles Johnson
                 Secretary

SUBJECT: **Exercising Prosecutorial Discretion with Respect to**
                 Individuals Who Came to the United States as
                 Children and with Respect to Certain Individuals
                 Who Are the Parents of U.S. Citizens or Permanent
                 Residents

This memorandum is intended to reflect new policies for the use of deferred action. By memorandum dated June 15, 2012, Secretary Napolitano issued guidance entitled *Exercising Prosecutorial Discretion with Respect to Individuals Who Came to the United States as Children.* The following supplements and amends that guidance.

The Department of Homeland Security (DHS) and its immigration components are responsible for enforcing the Nation's immigration laws. Due to limited resources, DHS and its Components cannot respond to all immigration violations or remove all persons illegally in the United States. As is true of virtually every other law enforcement agency, DHS must exercise prosecutorial discretion in the enforcement of the law. Secretary Napolitano noted two years ago, when she issued her prosecutorial discretion guidance regarding children, that "[o]ur Nation's immigration laws must be enforced in a strong and sensible manner. They are not designed to be blindly enforced without consideration given to the individual circumstances of each case."

1

Deferred action is a long-standing administrative mechanism dating back decades, by which the Secretary of Homeland Security may defer the removal of an undocumented immigrant for a period of time.[1] A form of administrative relief similar to deferred action, known then as "indefinite voluntary departure," was originally authorized by the Reagan and Bush Administrations to defer the deportations of an estimated 1.5 million undocumented spouses and minor children who did not qualify for legalization under the *Immigration Reform and Control Act* of 1986. Known as the "Family Fairness" program, the policy was specifically implemented to promote the humane enforcement of the law and ensure family unity.

Deferred action is a form of prosecutorial discretion by which the Secretary deprioritizes an individual's case for humanitarian reasons, administrative convenience, or in the interest of the Department's overall enforcement mission. As an act of prosecutorial discretion, deferred action is legally available so long as it is granted on a case-by-case basis, and it may be terminated at any time at the agency's discretion. Deferred action does not confer any form of legal status in this country, much less citizenship; it simply means that, for a specified period of time, an individual is permitted to be lawfully present in the United States. Nor can deferred action itself lead to a green card. Although deferred action is not expressly conferred by statute, the practice is referenced and therefore endorsed by implication in several federal statutes.[2]

Historically, deferred action has been used on behalf of particular individuals, and on a case-by-case basis, for classes of unlawfully present individuals, such as the spouses and minor children of certain legalized immigrants, widows of U.S. citizens, or victims of trafficking and domestic violence.[3] Most recently, beginning in 2012, Secretary Napolitano issued guidance for case-by-case deferred action with respect to those who came to the United States as children, commonly referred to as "DACA."

---

[1] Deferred action, in one form or another, dates back to at least the 1960s. "Deferred action" per se dates back at least as far as 1975. *See*, Immigration and Naturalization Service, Operation Instructions § 103.1(a)(1)(ii) (1975).

[2] INA § 204(a)(1)(D)(i)(II), (IV) *(Violence Against Women Act (VAWA) self-petitioners not in removal proceedings are "eligible for deferred action and employment authorization");* INA § 237(d)(2) *(DHS may grant stay of removal to applicants for T or U visas but that denial of a stay request "shall not preclude the alien from applying for . . . deferred action");* REAL ID Act of 2005 § 202(c)(2)(B)(viii), Pub. L. 109-13 *(requiring states to examine documentary evidence of lawful status for driver's license eligibility purposes, including "approved deferred action status");* National Defense Authorization Act for Fiscal Year 2004 § 1703(c) (d) Pub. L. 108-136 *(spouse, parent or child of certain U.S. citizen who died as a result of honorable service may self-petition for permanent residence and "shall be eligible for deferred action, advance parole, and work authorization").*

[3] In August 2001, the former-Immigration and Naturalization Service issued guidance providing deferred action to individuals who were eligible for the recently created U and T visas. Two years later, USCIS issued subsequent guidance, instructing its officers to use existing mechanisms like deferred action for certain U visa applicants facing potential removal. More recently, in June 2009, USCIS issued a memorandum providing deferred action to certain surviving spouses of deceased U.S. citizens and their children while Congress considered legislation to allow these individuals to qualify for permanent residence status.

By this memorandum, I am now expanding certain parameters of DACA and issuing guidance for case-by-case use of deferred action for those adults who have been in this country since January 1, 2010, are the parents of U.S. citizens or lawful permanent residents, and who are otherwise not enforcement priorities, as set forth in the November 20, 2014 Policies for the Apprehension, Detention and Removal of Undocumented Immigrants Memorandum.

The reality is that most individuals in the categories set forth below are hard-working people who have become integrated members of American society. Provided they do not commit serious crimes or otherwise become enforcement priorities, these people are extremely unlikely to be deported given this Department's limited enforcement resources—which must continue to be focused on those who represent threats to national security, public safety, and border security. Case-by-case exercises of deferred action for children and long-standing members of American society who are not enforcement priorities are in this Nation's security and economic interests and make common sense, because they encourage these people to come out of the shadows, submit to background checks, pay fees, apply for work authorization (which by separate authority I may grant), and be counted.

A.   Expanding DACA

DACA provides that those who were under the age of 31 on June 15, 2012, who entered the United States before June 15, 2007 (5 years prior) as children under the age of 16, and who meet specific educational and public safety criteria, are eligible for deferred action on a case-by-case basis. The initial DACA announcement of June 15, 2012 provided deferred action for a period of two years. On June 5, 2014, U.S. Citizenship and Immigration Services (USCIS) announced that DACA recipients could request to renew their deferred action for an additional two years.

In order to further effectuate this program, I hereby direct USCIS to expand DACA as follows:

Remove the age cap. DACA will apply to all otherwise eligible immigrants who entered the United States by the requisite adjusted entry date before the age of sixteen (16), regardless of how old they were in June 2012 or are today. The current age restriction excludes those who were older than 31 on the date of announcement (*i.e.*, those who were born before June 15, 1981). That restriction will no longer apply.

Extend DACA renewal and work authorization to three-years. The period for which DACA and the accompanying employment authorization is granted will be extended to three-year increments, rather than the current two-year increments. This change shall apply to all first-time applications as well as all applications for renewal effective November 24, 2014. Beginning on that date, USCIS should issue all work

3

authorization documents valid for three years, including to those individuals who have applied and are awaiting two-year work authorization documents based on the renewal of their DACA grants. USCIS should also consider means to extend those two-year renewals already issued to three years.

Adjust the date-of-entry requirement. In order to align the DACA program more closely with the other deferred action authorization outlined below, the eligibility cut-off date by which a DACA applicant must have been in the United States should be adjusted from June 15, 2007 to January 1, 2010.

USCIS should begin accepting applications under the new criteria from applicants no later than ninety (90) days from the date of this announcement. .

B.   Expanding Deferred Action

I hereby direct USCIS to establish a process, similar to DACA, for exercising prosecutorial discretion through the use of deferred action, on a case-by-case basis, to those individuals who:

- have, on the date of this memorandum, a son or daughter who is a U.S. citizen or lawful permanent resident;

- have continuously resided in the United States since before January 1, 2010;

- are physically present in the United States on the date of this memorandum, *and* at the time of making a request for consideration of deferred action with USCIS;

- have no lawful status on the date of this memorandum;

- are not an enforcement priority as reflected in the November 20, 2014 Policies for the Apprehension, Detention and Removal of Undocumented Immigrants Memorandum; and

- present no other factors that, in the exercise of discretion, makes the grant of deferred action inappropriate.

Applicants must file the requisite applications for deferred action pursuant to the new criteria described above. Applicants must also submit biometrics for USCIS to conduct background checks similar to the background check that is required for DACA applicants. Each person who applies for deferred action pursuant to the criteria above shall also be eligible to apply for work authorization for the period of deferred action, pursuant to my authority to grant such authorization reflected in section 274A(h)(3) of the Immigration and Nationality Act.[4] Deferred action granted pursuant to the program shall be for a period of three years. Applicants will pay the work authorization and biometrics fees, which currently amount to $465. There will be no fee waivers and, like DACA, very limited fee exemptions.

USCIS should begin accepting applications from eligible applicants no later than one hundred and eighty (180) days after the date of this announcement. As with DACA, the above criteria are to be considered for all individuals encountered by U.S. Immigration and Customs Enforcement (ICE), U.S. Customs and Border Protection (CBP), or USCIS, whether or not the individual is already in removal proceedings or subject to a final order of removal. Specifically:

- ICE and CBP are instructed to immediately begin identifying persons in their custody, as well as newly encountered individuals, who meet the above criteria and may thus be eligible for deferred action to prevent the further expenditure of enforcement resources with regard to these individuals.

- ICE is further instructed to review pending removal cases, and seek administrative closure or termination of the cases of individuals identified who meet the above criteria, and to refer such individuals to USCIS for case-by-case determinations. ICE should also establish a process to allow individuals in removal proceedings to identify themselves as candidates for deferred action.

- USCIS is instructed to implement this memorandum consistent with its existing guidance regarding the issuance of notices to appear. The USCIS process shall also be available to individuals subject to final orders of removal who otherwise meet the above criteria.

Under any of the proposals outlined above, immigration officers will be provided with specific eligibility criteria for deferred action, but the ultimate judgment as to whether an immigrant is granted deferred action will be determined on a case-by-case basis.

This memorandum confers no substantive right, immigration status or pathway to citizenship. Only an Act of Congress can confer these rights. It remains within the authority of the Executive Branch, however, to set forth policy for the exercise of prosecutorial discretion and deferred action within the framework of existing law. This memorandum is an exercise of that authority.

---

[4] INA § 274A(h)(3), 8 U.S.C. § 1324a(h)(3) ("As used in this section, the term 'unauthorized alien' means, with respect to the employment of an alien at a particular time, that the alien is not at that time either (A) an alien lawfully admitted for permanent residence, or (B) authorized to be so employed by this chapter or by the[Secretary]."); 8 C.F.R. § 274a.12 (regulations establishing classes of aliens eligible for work authorization).

U.S. Department of Justice
Executive Office for Immigration Review

Office of the Chief Immigration Judge

---

*5107 Leesburg Pike, Suite 2500
Falls Church, Virginia 22041*

April 6, 2015

MEMORANDUM

TO: All Immigration Judges
          All Court Administrators
          All Attorney Advisors and Judicial Law Clerks
          All Immigration Court Staff

FROM: Brian M. O'Leary
          Chief Immigration Judge

SUBJECT: Operating Policies and Procedures Memorandum 15-01:
          Hearing Procedures for Cases Covered by new DHS Priorities and Initiatives

I.   Introduction

This Operating Policies and Procedures Memorandum (OPPM) provides background and guidance on hearings for aliens who might be covered by new immigration-related enforcement priorities and initiatives established by the Department of Homeland Security (DHS). This OPPM supplements OPPM 13-01, entitled *Continuances and Administrative Closure*, issued on March 7, 2013.

II.   Authority

On November 20, 2014, the Secretary of Homeland Security (Secretary) announced several immigration policy initiatives affecting a number of DHS programs. Most notably for purposes of this OPPM, the Secretary announced revised civil immigration enforcement priorities for all of DHS, emphasizing priorities on removing national security threats, convicted felons, gang members and aliens apprehended at the border or ports of entry while attempting to unlawfully enter the United States, and setting other second and third-tier enforcement priorities for DHS. *See "Policies for the Apprehension, Detention, and Removal of Undocumented Immigrants,"* available at *http://www.dhs.gov/sites/default/files/publications.*[1]

---

[1]   On November 20, 2014, the Secretary also announced an expansion of the 2012 Deferred Action for Childhood Arrivals (DACA) program, which offered deferred action to certain

The Secretary's memorandum makes clear that DHS personnel are expected to exercise discretion based on individual circumstances and pursue these priorities at all stages of the enforcement process, from the earliest investigative stages to enforcing final orders of removal. The memorandum also emphasized the importance of exercising prosecutorial discretion as early in the case or proceeding as possible in order to preserve government resources that would otherwise be expended in pursuing enforcement and removal of higher priority cases. This memorandum is therefore likely to affect some of the cases currently pending on immigration court dockets. Through individualized review of pending cases, Immigration and Customs Enforcement (ICE) attorneys will be determining which cases are enforcement priorities and which are not. Cases that DHS determines through the exercise of prosecutorial discretion are not enforcement priorities are subject to requests for administrative closure or dismissal.

III.   Role of the Immigration Court

A central requirement of due process is "the opportunity to be heard at 'a meaningful time and in a meaningful manner.'" *Mathews v. Eldridge*, 424 U.S. 319, 333 (1976), *citing Armstrong v. Manzo*, 380 U.S. 545, 552 (1965). Further, immigration hearings must be "fundamentally fair." *See Matter of Sibrun*, 18 I&N Dec. 354, 356 (BIA 1983); *Constanza-Martinez v. Holder*, 739 F.3d 1100, 1102 (8th Cir. 2014). As we strive to adjudicate cases in our courts as efficiently as possible, these central due process principles must remain paramount. Likewise, while DHS' revised priorities may impact a number of cases in our courts over the coming years, our courts' responsibility to protect due process and the opportunity to be heard remains unchanged.

As noted in OPPM 13-01, the role of the immigration court, like any other tribunal, is to resolve disputes. At the present time, there are over 428,000 pending proceedings on our dockets, and some of these may be affected by the memorandum. In light of the memorandum it is imperative that we apply our limited adjudication resources to resolve actual cases in dispute.

To that end, one mechanism for DHS to identify pending cases in the removal system that are not enforcement priorities and communicate that to the court is to use already scheduled hearings on court dockets, particularly upcoming master calendar hearings. On April 6, 2015, ICE instructed its attorneys to exercise prosecutorial discretion as early in the case or

---

individuals who are unlawfully in the United States after having entered the country as children, and a new program for certain undocumented parents of U.S. citizens and lawful permanent residents, the Deferred Action for Parental Accountability (DAPA) policy. On February 16, 2015, the U.S. District Court for the Southern District of Texas temporarily enjoined DHS from implementing the DAPA and expanded DACA policies. *See Texas v. United States*, 2015 WL 648579 (S.D. Tex. Feb. 16, 2015). DHS has therefore instructed its officers, agents and attorneys to not consider the DAPA and expanded DACA policies as a basis for exercising prosecutorial discretion or for determining whether deferred action is appropriate, unless and until further guidance is given.   Therefore, this OPPM only pertains to DHS's exercise of prosecutorial discretion with regard to its revised enforcement priorities – which are not enjoined by the temporary injunction – and not the DAPA and expanded DACA policies.

proceedings as possible in order to preserve government resources that would otherwise be expended in pursuing enforcement and removal of high priority cases. Consequently, ICE attorneys have been directed to (1) review their cases and any requests for prosecutorial discretion *prior* to hearings, including master calendar hearings before Immigration Judges; and (2) be prepared at the next hearing to respond to questions from the Immigration Judge, and requests by respondents, about whether the ICE attorney believes that the case should: (i) remain on the court docket because it is a removal priority or (ii) be administratively closed or dismissed because the case is not a removal priority or appears eligible for some form of prosecutorial discretion.

Therefore, Immigration Judges should be prepared to ask ICE attorneys appearing before them at master calendar hearings, on the record, whether the case remains a removal priority for ICE and whether ICE is seeking dismissal or administrative closure. Before deciding whether to close or dismiss the matter, the judge should of course ask the respondent or his or her representative for the respondent's position on these matters.

Judges are encouraged to use the docketing tools available to them to ensure the fair and timely resolution of cases before them.   That includes continuances, termination and administrative closure in appropriate cases. *See* OPPM 13-01 and *Matter of Avetisyan*, 25 I&N Dec. 688 (BIA 2012). The process outlined herein is not intended to be the only mechanism for ICE to exercise prosecutorial discretion for cases pending in the immigration courts.

Note that this OPPM does not change EOIR's current adjudication priorities. Rather it provides guidance and information concerning cases of aliens who might be covered by DHS' new immigration-related enforcement priorities and memorandum.

IV. Conclusion

It is our expectation that the parameters of the new DHS memorandum will focus DHS resources on cases that meet the stated priorities. Judges are encouraged to use docketing practices that ensure respondents receive fair and timely adjudications, and act consistently with the role of the immigration courts in resolving disputes. That includes closing cases that ICE has determined do not fit within the Secretary's enforcement priorities. If you have any questions, please contact your Assistant Chief Immigration Judge.

Nothing in this OPPM is intended to replace independent research, the application of case law and regulations to individual cases or the decisional independence of Immigration Judges as defined in 8 C.F.R. § 1003.10.

Executive Actions and Orders of the 45th President

Presidential Executive Order on a Comprehensive Plan for Reorganizing the Executive Branch

EXECUTIVE ORDER

- - - - - - -

COMPREHENSIVE PLAN FOR REORGANIZING THE EXECUTIVE BRANCH

By the authority vested in me as President by the Constitution and the laws of the United States of America, it is hereby ordered as follows:

Section 1. Purpose. This order is intended to improve the efficiency, effectiveness, and accountability of the executive branch by directing the Director of the Office of Management and Budget (Director) to propose a plan to reorganize governmental functions and eliminate unnecessary agencies (as defined in section 551(1) of title 5, United States Code), components of agencies, and agency programs.

Sec. 2. Proposed Plan to Improve the Efficiency, Effectiveness, and Accountability of Federal Agencies, Including, as Appropriate, to Eliminate or Reorganize Unnecessary or Redundant Federal Agencies. (a) Within 180 days of the date of this order, the head of each agency shall submit to the Director a proposed plan to reorganize the agency, if appropriate, in order to improve the efficiency, effectiveness, and account-ability of that agency.

(b) The Director shall publish a notice in the Federal Register inviting the public to suggest improvements in the organization and functioning of the executive branch and shall consider the suggestions when formulating the proposed plan described in subsection (c) of this section.

(c) Within 180 days after the closing date for the submission of suggestions pursuant to subsection (b) of this section, the Director shall submit to the President a pro-posed plan to reorganize the executive branch in order to improve the efficiency, effectiveness, and accountability of agencies. The proposed plan shall include, as appropriate, recommendations to eliminate unnecessary agencies, components of agencies, and agency programs, and to merge functions. The proposed plan shall include recommendations for any legislation or administrative measures necessary to achieve the proposed reorganization.

(d) In developing the proposed plan described in subsection (c) of this section, the Director shall consider, in addition to any other relevant factors:

(i) whether some or all of the functions of an agency, a component, or a program are appropriate for the Federal Government or would be better left to State or local governments or to the private sector through free enterprise;

(ii) whether some or all of the functions of an agency, a component, or a program are redundant, including with those of another agency, component, or program;

(iii) whether certain administrative capabilities necessary for operating an agency, a component, or a program are redundant with those of another agency, component, or program;

(iv) whether the costs of continuing to operate an agency, a component, or a program are justified by the public benefits it provides; and

(v) the costs of shutting down or merging agencies, components, or programs, including the costs of addressing the equities of affected agency staff.

(e) In developing the proposed plan described in subsection (c) of this section, the Director shall consult with the head of each agency and, consistent with applicable law, with persons or entities outside the Federal Government with relevant expertise in organizational structure and management.

Sec. 3. General Provisions.

(a) Nothing in this order shall be construed to impair or otherwise affect:

(i) the authority granted by law to an executive department or agency, or the head thereof; or

(ii) the functions of the Director relating to budgetary, administrative, or legislative proposals.

(b) This order shall be implemented consistent with applicable law and subject to the availability of appropriations.

(c) This order is not intended to, and does not, create any right or benefit, substantive or procedural, enforceable at law or in equity by any party against the United States, its departments, agencies, or entities, its officers, employees, or agents, or any other person.

DONALD J. TRUMP

THE WHITE HOUSE,
March 13, 2017.

Presidential Executive Order on Enforcing the Regulatory Reform Agenda

EXECUTIVE ORDER

- - - - - - -

ENFORCING THE REGULATORY REFORM AGENDA

By the authority vested in me as President by the Constitution and the laws of the United States of America, and in order to lower regulatory burdens on the American people by implementing and enforcing regulatory reform, it is hereby ordered as follows:

Section 1. Policy. It is the policy of the United States to alleviate unnecessary regulatory burdens placed on the American people.

Sec. 2. Regulatory Reform Officers. (a) Within 60 days of the date of this order, the head of each agency, except the heads of agencies receiving waivers under section 5 of this order, shall designate an agency official as its Regulatory Reform Officer (RRO). Each RRO shall oversee the implementation of regulatory reform initiatives and policies to ensure that agencies effectively carry out regulatory reforms, consistent with applicable law. These initiatives and policies include:

(i) Executive Order 13771 of January 30, 2017 (Reducing Regulation and Controlling Regulatory Costs), regarding offsetting the number and cost of new regulations;

(ii) Executive Order 12866 of September 30, 1993 (Regulatory Planning and Review), as amended, regarding regulatory planning and review;

(iii) section 6 of Executive Order 13563 of January 18, 2011 (Improving Regulation and Regulatory Review), regarding retrospective review; and

(iv) the termination, consistent with applicable law, of programs and activities that derive from or implement Executive Orders, guidance documents, policy memoranda, rule interpretations, and similar documents, or relevant portions thereof, that have been rescinded.

(b) Each agency RRO shall periodically report to the agency head and regularly consult with agency leadership.

Sec. 3. Regulatory Reform Task Forces. (a) Each agency shall establish a Regulatory Reform Task Force composed of:

(i) the agency RRO;

(ii) the agency Regulatory Policy Officer designated under section 6(a)(2) of Executive Order 12866;

(iii) a representative from the agency's central policy office or equivalent central office; and

(iv) for agencies listed in section 901(b)(1) of title 31, United States Code, at least three additional senior agency officials as determined by the agency head.

(b) Unless otherwise designated by the agency head, the agency RRO shall chair the agency's Regulatory Reform Task Force.

(c) Each entity staffed by officials of multiple agencies, such as the Chief Acquisition Officers Council, shall form a joint Regulatory Reform Task Force composed of at least one official described in subsection (a) of this section from each constituent agency's Regulatory Reform Task Force. Joint Regulatory Reform Task Forces shall implement this order in coordination with the Regulatory Reform Task Forces of their members' respective agencies.

(d) Each Regulatory Reform Task Force shall evaluate existing regulations (as defined in section 4 of Executive Order 13771) and make recommendations to the agency head regarding their repeal, replacement, or modification, consistent with applicable law. At a minimum, each Regulatory Reform Task Force shall attempt to identify regulations that:

(i) eliminate jobs, or inhibit job creation;

(ii) are outdated, unnecessary, or ineffective;

(iii) impose costs that exceed benefits;

(iv) create a serious inconsistency or otherwise interfere with regulatory reform initiatives and policies;

(v) are inconsistent with the requirements of section 515 of the Treasury and General Government Appropriations Act, 2001 (44 U.S.C. 3516 note), or the guidance issued pursuant to that provision, in particular those regulations that rely in whole or in part on data, information, or methods that are not publicly available or that are insufficiently transparent to meet the standard for reproducibility; or

(vi) derive from or implement Executive Orders or other Presidential directives that have been subsequently rescinded or substantially modified.

(e) In performing the evaluation described in subsection (d) of this section, each Regulatory Reform Task Force shall seek input and other assistance, as permitted by law, from entities significantly affected by Federal regulations, including State, local, and tribal governments, small businesses, consumers, non-governmental organizations, and trade associations.

(f) When implementing the regulatory offsets required by Executive Order 13771, each agency head should prioritize, to the extent permitted by law, those regulations that the agency's Regulatory Reform Task Force has identified as being outdated, unnecessary, or ineffective pursuant to subsection (d)(ii) of this section.

(g) Within 90 days of the date of this order, and on a schedule determined by the agency head thereafter, each Regulatory Reform Task Force shall provide a report to the agency head detailing the agency's progress toward the following goals:

(i) improving implementation of regulatory reform initiatives and policies pursuant to section 2 of this order; and

(ii) identifying regulations for repeal, replacement, or modification.

Sec. 4. Accountability. Consistent with the policy set forth in section 1 of this order, each agency should measure its progress in performing the tasks outlined in section 3 of this order.

(a) Agencies listed in section 901(b)(1) of title 31, United States Code, shall incorporate in their annual performance plans (required under the Government Performance and Results Act, as amended (see 31 U.S.C. 1115(b))), performance indicators that measure progress toward the two goals listed in section 3(g) of this order. Within 60 days of the date of this order, the Director of the Office of Management and Budget (Director) shall issue guidance regarding the implementation of this subsection. Such guidance may also address how agencies not otherwise covered under this subsection should be held accountable for compliance with this order.

(b) The head of each agency shall consider the progress toward the two goals listed in section 3(g) of this order in assessing the performance of the Regulatory Reform Task Force and, to the extent permitted by law, those individuals responsible for developing and issuing agency regulations.

Sec. 5. Waiver. Upon the request of an agency head, the Director may waive compliance with this order if the Director determines that the agency generally issues very few or no regulations (as defined in section 4 of Executive Order 13771). The Director may revoke a waiver at any time. The Director shall publish, at least once every 3 months, a list of agencies with current waivers.

Sec. 6. General Provisions. (a) Nothing in this order shall be construed to impair or otherwise affect:

(i) the authority granted by law to an executive department or agency, or the head thereof; or

(ii) the functions of the Director relating to budgetary, administrative, or legislative proposals.

(b) This order shall be implemented consistent with applicable law and subject to the availability of appropriations.

(c) This order is not intended to, and does not, create any right or benefit, substantive or procedural, enforceable at law or in equity by any party against the United States, its departments, agencies, or entities, its officers, employees, or agents, or any other person.

DONALD J. TRUMP

THE WHITE HOUSE,

February 24, 2017

Presidential Executive Order on Reducing Regulation and Controlling Regulatory Costs

EXECUTIVE ORDER

- - - - - - -

REDUCING REGULATION AND CONTROLLING REGULATORY COSTS

By the authority vested in me as President by the Constitution and the laws of the United States of America, including the Budget and Accounting Act of 1921, as amended (31 U.S.C. 1101 et seq.), section 1105 of title 31, United States Code, and section 301 of title 3, United States Code, it is hereby ordered as follows:

Section 1. Purpose. It is the policy of the executive branch to be prudent and financially responsible in the expenditure of funds, from both public and private sources. In addition to the management of the direct expenditure of taxpayer dollars through the budgeting process, it is essential to manage the costs associated with the governmental imposition of private expenditures required to comply with Federal regulations. Toward that end, it is important that for every one new regulation issued, at least two prior regulations be identified for elimination, and that the cost of planned regulations be prudently managed and controlled through a budgeting process.

Sec. 2. Regulatory Cap for Fiscal Year 2017. (a) Unless prohibited by law, whenever an executive department or agency (agency) publicly proposes for notice and comment or otherwise promulgates a new regulation, it shall identify at least two existing regulations to be repealed.

(b) For fiscal year 2017, which is in progress, the heads of all agencies are directed that the total incremental cost of all new regulations, including repealed regulations, to be finalized this year shall be no greater than zero, unless otherwise required by law or consistent with advice provided in writing by the Director of the Office of Management and Budget (Director).

(c) In furtherance of the requirement of subsection (a) of this section, any new incremental costs associated with new regulations shall, to the extent permitted by law, be offset by the elimination of existing costs associated with at least two prior regulations. Any agency eliminating existing costs associated with prior regulations under this subsection shall do so in accordance with the Administrative Procedure Act and other applicable law.

(d) The Director shall provide the heads of agencies with guidance on the implementation of this section. Such guidance shall address, among other things, processes for standardizing the measurement and estimation of regulatory costs; standards for determining what qualifies as new and offsetting regulations; standards for determining the costs of existing regulations that are considered for elimination; processes for accounting for costs in different fiscal years; methods to oversee the issuance of rules with costs offset by savings at different times or different agencies; and emergencies and other circumstances that might justify individual waivers of the requirements of this section. The Director shall consider phasing in and updating these requirements.

Sec. 3. Annual Regulatory Cost Submissions to the Office of Management and Budget. (a) Beginning with the Regulatory Plans (required under Executive Order 12866 of September 30, 1993, as amended, or any successor order) for fiscal year 2018, and for each fiscal year thereafter, the head of each agency shall identify, for each regulation that increases incremental cost, the offsetting regulations described in section 2(c) of this order, and provide the agency's best approximation of the total costs or savings associated with each new regulation or repealed regulation.

(b) Each regulation approved by the Director during the Presidential budget process shall be included in the Unified Regulatory Agenda required under Executive Order 12866, as amended, or any successor order.

(c) Unless otherwise required by law, no regulation shall be issued by an agency if it was not included on the most recent version or update of the published Unified Regulatory Agenda as required under Executive Order 12866, as amended, or any successor order, unless the issuance of such regulation was approved in advance in writing by the Director.

(d) During the Presidential budget process, the Director shall identify to agencies a total amount of incremental costs that will be allowed for each agency in issuing new regulations and repealing regulations for the next fiscal year. No regulations exceeding the agency's total incremental cost allowance will be permitted in that fiscal year, unless required by law or approved in writing by the Director. The total incremental cost allowance may allow an increase or require a reduction in total regulatory cost.

(e) The Director shall provide the heads of agencies with guidance on the implementation of the requirements in this section.

Sec. 4. Definition. For purposes of this order the term "regulation" or "rule" means an agency statement of general or particular applicability and future effect designed to implement, interpret, or prescribe law or policy or to describe the procedure or practice requirements of an agency, but does not include:

(a) regulations issued with respect to a military, national security, or foreign affairs function of the United States;

(b) regulations related to agency organization, management, or personnel; or

(c) any other category of regulations exempted by the Director.

Sec. 5. General Provisions. (a) Nothing in this order shall be construed to impair or otherwise affect:

> (i) the authority granted by law to an executive department or agency, or the head thereof; or

> (ii) the functions of the Director relating to budgetary, administrative, or legislative proposals.

(b) This order shall be implemented consistent with applicable law and subject to the availability of appropriations.

(c) This order is not intended to, and does not, create any right or benefit, substantive or procedural, enforceable at law or in equity by any party against the United States, its departments, agencies, or entities, its officers, employees, or agents, or any other person.

DONALD J. TRUMP

THE WHITE HOUSE,

January 30, 2017.

Memorandum: Implementing Executive Order 13771, Titled "Reducing Regulation and Controlling Regulatory Costs"

MEMORANDUM FOR: REGULATORY POLICY OFFICERS AT EXECUTIVE DEPARTMENTS AND AGENCIES AND MANAGING AND EXECUTIVE DIRECTORS OF CERTAIN AGENCIES AND COMMISSIONS

FROM: Dominic J. Mancini, Acting Administrator Office of Information and Regulatory Affairs

SUBJECT: Guidance Implementing Executive Order 13771, Titled "Reducing Regulation and Controlling Regulatory Costs"

I. Introduction

This guidance, in the form of Questions and Answers (Q&As), addresses the requirements of Executive Order (EO) 13771, titled "Reducing Regulation and Controlling Regulatory Costs." It applies to Fiscal Years (FY) 2017 and beyond. This guidance supplements the Office of Management and Budget (OMB) interim guidance issued on February 2, 2017, titled "Interim Guidance Implementing Section 2 of the EO of January 30, 2017, Titled 'Reducing Regulation and Controlling Regulatory Costs.'" While OMB's Office of Information and Regulatory Affairs (OIRA) believes this guidance largely treats the subjects covered in the February 2, 2017 interim guidance in a consistent manner, where these two memoranda are in conflict, this guidance supersedes the previous guidance. It reflects OIRA's consideration of the comments received in response to the February 2, 2017, interim guidance. Comments sent by members of the public are available on Regulations.gov in docket ID OMB-2017-0002.

II. General Requirements

The guidance explains, for purposes of implementing Section 2, the following requirements:

- "Unless prohibited by law, whenever an executive department or agency . . . publicly proposes for notice and comment or otherwise promulgates a new regulation, it shall identify at least two existing regulations to be repealed." Sec. 2 (a).

- "For fiscal year 2017 . . . the heads of all agencies are directed that the total incremental cost of all new regulations, including repealed regulations, to be finalized this year shall be no greater than zero, unless otherwise required by law or consistent with advice provided in writing by the Director of the Office of Management and Budget . . . ." Sec. 2 (b).

- "In furtherance of the requirement of subsection (a) of this section, any new incremental costs associated with new regulations shall, to the extent permitted by law, be offset by the elimination of existing costs associated with at least two prior regulations." Sec. 2 (c).

In general, executive departments or agencies ("agencies") may comply with those requirements by issuing two EO 13771 deregulatory actions (described below) for each EO 13771 regulatory action (described below). The incremental costs associated with EO 13771 regulatory actions must be fully offset by the savings of EO 13771 deregulatory actions.

In addition, agencies planning to issue one or more EO 13771 regulatory actions on or before September 30, 2017, should for each such EO 13771 regulatory action:

- Identify two existing regulatory actions the agency plans to eliminate or propose for elimination on or before September 30, 2017 in a reasonable period of time before the agency issues the EO 13771 regulatory action; and

- Fully offset the total incremental cost of such EO 13771 regulatory action as of September 30, 2017.

Guidance on the requirements of Section 3(a) is forthcoming.

Beginning with FY 2018, Section 3(d) requires the Director of OMB to identify to agencies a total amount of incremental costs (or "regulatory cap" as stated in Section 2) for all EO 13771 deregulatory and EO 13771 regulatory actions finalized during the fiscal year. The total incremental cost imposed by each agency should not exceed the agency's allowance for that fiscal year, unless required by law or approved by the Director. The total incremental cost allowance may be an increase or reduction in total regulatory cost, and will be informed by agencies' draft submissions for the Regulatory Plan.

Please consult with OIRA if you have any particular questions regarding the applicability or interpretation of EO 13771 not addressed in these Q&As.

Agencies should continue to comply with all applicable laws and requirements. In addition, EO 12866 remains the primary governing EO regarding regulatory planning and review. Accordingly, among other requirements, except where prohibited by law, agencies must continue to assess and consider both the benefits and costs of regulatory actions, including deregulatory actions, when making regulatory decisions, and issue regulations only upon a reasoned determination that benefits justify costs.

III. Definitions

This section provides definitions for terms used in this guidance. The definitions should not necessarily be applied to other sections of EO 13771 that this guidance does not cover, and do not replace definitions used in other EOs or statutes.

Q1. What is an "agency"?

A: An "agency," unless otherwise indicated, means any authority of the United States that is an "agency" under 44 U.S.C. 3502(1), other than those considered to be

independent regulatory agencies, as defined in 44 U.S.C. 3502(5). A cabinet department is considered a single agency for purposes of EO 13771 compliance.

Q2. What is an "EO 13771 regulatory action"?

A: An "EO 13771 regulatory action" is:

> i. A significant regulatory action as defined in Section 3(f) of EO 12866 that
> has been finalized and that imposes total costs greater than zero; or

> ii. A significant guidance document (e.g., significant interpretive guidance)
> reviewed by OIRA under the procedures of EO 12866 that has been finalized
> and that imposes total costs greater than zero.

For example, EO 13771 regulatory actions include negotiated rulemakings that are
significant as defined in Section 3(f) of EO 12866, that have been finalized, and that
impose total costs greater than zero.

Q3. What is a "significant guidance document"?

A: As defined in OMB's Final Bulletin for Agency Good Guidance Practices , a "significant guidance document" is a guidance document disseminated to regulated
entities or the general public that may reasonably be anticipated to:

> i. Lead to an annual effect on the economy of $100 million or more or adversely
> affect in a material way the economy, a sector of the economy, productivity,
> competition, jobs, the environment, public health or safety, or State, local, or
> tribal governments or communities;

> ii. Create a serious inconsistency or otherwise interfere with an action taken or
> planned by another agency;

> iii. Materially alter the budgetary impact of entitlements, grants, user fees, or
> loan programs or the rights and obligations of recipients thereof; or

> iv. Raise novel legal or policy issues arising out of legal mandates, the Presi-
> dent's priorities, or the principles set forth in EO 12866, as further amended.

A significant guidance document does not include legal advisory opinions for internal Executive Branch use and not for release (such as Department of Justice Office of
Legal Counsel opinions); briefs and other positions taken by agencies in investigations, pre-litigation, litigation, or other enforcement proceedings; speeches; editori-
als; media interviews; press materials; Congressional correspondence; guidance
documents that pertain to a military or foreign affairs function of the United States
(other than guidance on procurement or the import or export of non-defense articles and services); grant solicitations; warning letters; case or investigatory letters
responding to complaints involving fact-specific determinations; purely internal
agency policies guidance documents that pertain to the use, operation or control of
a government facility; internal guidance documents directed solely to other Federal
agencies; and any other category of significant guidance documents exempted by an
agency in consultation and concurrence with the OIRA Administrator. In the list
above, "internal" policies and guidance documents do not include those that

materially affect an agency's interactions with non-Federal entities, even if nominally directed only to agency personnel. For example, an internal directive to field staff on how to implement a regulatory requirement could be a significant guidance document if it satisfied any of (i) through (iv) above.

If they satisfy the definition above, modifications to existing guidance and interpretative documents would be considered significant guidance documents.

Q4. What is an "EO 13771 deregulatory action"?

A: An "EO 13771 deregulatory action" is an action that has been finalized and has total costs less than zero. An EO 13771 deregulatory action qualifies as both: (1) one of the actions used to satisfy the provision to repeal or revise at least two existing regulations for each regulation issued, and (2) a cost savings for purposes of the total incremental cost allowance. EO 13771 deregulatory actions are not limited to those defined as significant under EO 12866 or OMB's Final Bulletin on Good Guidance Practices.

An EO 13771 deregulatory action may be issued in the form of an action in a wide range of categories of actions, including, but not limited to:

- Informal, formal, and negotiated rulemaking;
- Guidance and interpretative documents;
- Some actions related to international regulatory cooperation; and
- Information collection requests that repeal or streamline recordkeeping, reporting, or disclosure requirements.

Significant proposed rules issued before noon on January 20, 2017, that are formally withdrawn by notice in the Federal Register and removed from the Unified Agenda of Regulatory and Deregulatory Actions may qualify as repeal actions, but do not qualify for cost savings.

Please consult with OIRA regarding other actions your agency believes should qualify as an EO 13771 deregulatory action.

Q5. What does "offset" mean?

A: The term "offset" means at least two EO 13771 deregulatory actions have been taken per EO 13771 regulatory action and that the incremental cost of the EO 13771 regulatory action has been appropriately counterbalanced by incremental cost savings from EO 13771 deregulatory actions, consistent with the agency's total incremental cost allowance.

Q6. What is a "statutorily or judicially required" rulemaking?

A: A statutorily required rulemaking is one for which Congress has provided by statute an explicit requirement and explicit timeframe for rulemaking. For example, a statute that states, an agency "shall issue nutrition labeling requirements within 10 years" of the statute's enactment date would be considered a statutorily required rule.

A judicially required rulemaking is one for which there is a judicially established binding deadline for rulemaking, including deadlines established by settlement agreement or consent decree.

Agencies should consult with OIRA to determine whether a rule falls within the definition of a statutorily or judicially required rulemaking.

Q7. What is a rule issued with respect to a "national security function" of the United States?

A: For the purposes of EO 13771, a regulation issued with respect to a national security function is a regulation that satisfies the two following requirements:

1. The benefit-cost analysis demonstrates that the regulation is anticipated to improve national security as its primary direct benefit; and

2. (A) For regulations the agency considers legislative rules: OIRA and the agency agree the regulation qualifies for a "good cause" exception under 5 U.S.C. 553(b)(3)(B); or (B) For other regulations (including significant guidance) the agency and OIRA agree that applying the requirements of EO 13771 to the regulation would be impracticable or contrary to public interest.

Q8. What is "total incremental cost"?

A: The term "total incremental cost" means the sum of all costs from EO 13771 regulatory actions minus the cost savings from EO 13771 deregulatory actions.

IV. Scope Questions

Q9. Which new regulations as defined in EO 13771 must be offset?

A: Agencies are required to offset EO 13771 regulatory actions issued after noon on January 20, 2017. This includes those EO 13771 regulatory actions that are rules finalizing a Notice of Proposed Rulemaking (or in certain instances an interim final rule; see Question 11 for a further discussion) issued before noon on January 20, 2017.

Agencies should use the existing significance determination process outlined in EO 12866 for determining whether an action is an EO 13771 regulatory action. Agencies should not assume that actions that appear, or have appeared, in the Unified Agenda of Regulatory and Deregulatory Actions as nonsignificant have been determined by OIRA to be nonsignificant. Agencies should obtain an affirmative significance determination from OIRA before publishing regulatory actions.

Q10. How are interim and direct final rules treated?

A: In general, significant interim and direct final rules must be offset. However, a significant interim final rule or direct final rule may qualify for an exemption with respect to the timing for identifying and issuing the EO 13771 deregulatory actions.

Q11. How are significant rules that finalize interim final rules (IFR) treated?

A: If the final rule neither increases nor decreases the cost of the IFR, then the action does not need to be offset nor does it qualify as an EO 13771 deregulatory action. If the final rule includes changes that increase the cost of the IFR, then the final rule must be offset (however, if the final rule imposes only de minimis costs relative to the IFR, the final rule may qualify for an exemption). If the final rule reduces the cost of the IFR, then the rule and the cost savings relative to the IFR may qualify as an EO 13771 deregulatory action.

Q12. Must agencies identify EO 13771 deregulatory actions for significant advance notices of proposed rulemaking (ANPRM)?

A: No. With respect to rulemaking, the requirements of EO 13771 do not apply to pre-notice of proposed rulemaking activities such as ANPRMs.

Q 13. How are regulatory actions that implement Federal spending programs or establish fees and penalties treated?

A: In general, Federal spending regulatory actions that cause only income transfers between taxpayers and program beneficiaries (e.g., regulations associated with Pell grants and Medicare spending) are considered "transfer rules" and are not covered by EO 13771. Additionally, an action that establishes a new fee or changes the existing fee for a service, without imposing any new costs, does not need to be offset; nor does an action that establishes new penalties or fines or changes those already in existence.

However, in some cases, such regulatory actions may impose requirements apart from transfers, or transfers may distort markets causing inefficiencies. In those cases, the actions would need to be offset to the extent they impose more than de minimis costs. Examples of ancillary requirements that may require offsets include new reporting or recordkeeping requirements or new conditions, other than user fees, for receiving a grant, a loan, or a permit. Analogously, if an action reduces the stringency of requirements or conditions for transfer recipients or permit holders, the action may qualify as an EO 13771 deregulatory action. Also, an action that causes transfers that, for example, induce moral hazard or other inefficient behavior may need to be offset and an action that reduces such transfers may qualify as an EO 13771 deregulatory action.

Please consult with OIRA on these actions, especially with regards to potential distortionary costs due to transfers. See OMB Circular A-4 for a discussion of the distinction between transfers and costs generally.

Q14. How are activities treated that are associated with regulatory cooperation or international standards?

A: Regulatory activities associated with regulatory cooperation with foreign governments that reduce costs to entities or individuals within the United States, including at the border, or otherwise lower the cost of regulations on the United States economy, may qualify as EO 13771 deregulatory actions. Activities associated with standard-setting that reduce costs to entities or individuals within the United States may also qualify as EO 13771 deregulatory actions. However, agency actions to harmonize with the standards of an international body or foreign government that increase costs on United States entities or individuals may need to be offset. OIRA recognizes such harmonization could also lead to operating efficiencies for businesses that agencies may be able to capture in their analysis of the benefits and costs of EO 13771 actions.

Agencies should consult OIRA on how to treat specific regulatory activities related to regulatory cooperation or international standard-setting.

Q15. Do regulatory actions overturned by subsequently enacted laws qualify for savings?

A: Generally, yes. OIRA considers Acts of Congress that overturn final regulatory actions, such as disapprovals of rules under the Congressional Review Act, to operate in a similar manner as agency EO 13771 deregulatory actions.

Q16. Do regulatory actions that are vacated or remanded by a court qualify as EO 13771 deregulatory actions?

A: If a regulatory action issued before noon on January 20, 2017, is vacated by a judicial order for which all appeals have been resolved, OIRA will consider on a case-by-case basis whether the regulatory action being vacated qualifies as an EO 13771 deregulatory action.

If an EO 13771 regulatory action was issued on or after noon on January 20, 2017, any judicial order for which all appeals have been resolved vacating the regulatory action, and any related subsequent agency action (such as a withdrawal of a vacated regulation from the Code of Federal Regulations in order to comply with the order), will not qualify as an EO 13771 deregulatory action. Any EO 13771 deregulatory actions used to offset a vacated EO 13771 regulatory action, however, would be available to offset other EO 13771 regulatory actions (after accounting for any sunk costs incurred in complying with the vacated action).

If a court permits a regulatory action to remain in effect after a judicial remand for further agency proceedings, such as through remand without vacatur, the remanded action remains in effect. Therefore, there is no action at the time of remand that could qualify as an EO 13771 deregulatory action. In the same way that an agency complies with EO 12866 when issuing a subsequent agency action to revise a remanded regulatory action, an agency will similarly need to comply with EO 13771. A subsequent agency action may qualify as an EO 13771 deregulatory action if the subsequent agency action is deregulatory in nature, or may need to be offset if the action is a significant regulatory action that is final and that imposes costs (i.e., an EO 13771 regulatory action).

Agencies should notify OIRA of any judicial decisions that affect regulatory actions subject to EO 13771.

Q17. What happens if an EO 13771 deregulatory action is remanded or vacated by a court?

A: As in the answer to the previous question, OIRA recognizes the inherent case-by-case nature of the issues raised by the potential remand or vacatur of an EO 13771 deregulatory action. For example, such decisions may happen years after a rule is finalized, and may affect compliance with both the cost allowances and the repeal provisions established pursuant to EO 13771. The agency should contact OIRA to determine how a remand or vacatur of an EO 13771 deregulatory action affects the agency's obligations under EO 13771.

Q18. Does EO 13771 apply to significant regulatory actions in which the law prohibits the consideration of costs in determining a statutorily required standard?

A: Because EO 13771 applies only to the extent permitted by law, agencies are still required to comply with their statutory obligations. Accordingly, if a statute prohibits consideration of cost in taking a particular regulatory action, EO 13771 does not change the agency's obligations under that statute. However, agencies will generally be required to offset the costs of such regulatory actions through other deregulatory actions taken pursuant to statutes that do not prohibit consideration of costs. Because each agency's obligations will differ depending on the particular statutory language at issue, these issues must be addressed on a case-by-case basis.

Please consult with OIRA regarding questions about particular statutory language and its relationship to EO 13771.

Q19. How do the requirements of EO 13771 apply to significant regulatory actions issued by one agency that do not have the force and effect of law until adopted, with or without change, by another agency?

A: Because the agency authorities that establish such sequential or otherwise overlapping regulatory responsibilities differ by program, these actions will need to be handled on a case-by-case basis. However, agencies in these circumstances should always work together to avoid double-counting costs and cost savings; they should also work together as closely as possible when developing regulatory approaches for such programs. In cases where one agency's action does not qualify as an EO 13771 regulatory action because it is not a significant regulatory action under EO 12866, associated actions by other agencies may still be covered by EO 13771.

Q20. Does EO 13771 apply to regulatory actions of independent regulatory agencies?

A: No. EO 13771 applies only to those agencies that meet the definition of "agency" in this guidance. Nevertheless, independent regulatory agencies are encouraged to identify existing regulations that, if repealed or revised, would achieve cost savings that would fully offset the costs of significant regulatory actions while continuing to meet the agency's statutory obligations.

IV. Accounting Questions

Q21. How should costs and cost savings be measured?

A: Except where noted in other portions of this guidance, costs should be estimated using the methods and concepts appearing in OMB Circular A-4. There are several types of impacts that, under OMB Circular A-4, could be reasonably categorized as either benefits or costs, with the only difference being the sign (positive or negative) on the estimates. In most cases where there is ambiguity in the categorization of impacts, agencies should conform to the accounting conventions they have followed in past analyses. For example, if medical cost savings due to safety regulations have historically been categorized as benefits rather than reduced costs, they should continue to be categorized as benefits for EO 13771 regulatory actions. Identifying cost savings, such as fuel savings associated with energy efficiency investments, as benefits is a common accounting convention followed in OIRA's reports to Congress on the benefits and costs of Federal regulations.

Cost savings estimates for EO 13771 deregulatory actions should follow the same conventions, but in reverse. Only those impacts that have been traditionally estimated as costs when taking a regulatory action should be counted as cost savings when taking an EO 13771 deregulatory action. For example, the medical cost savings described above as historically being counted as benefits when regulating should not then be counted as "negative cost savings" when deregulating.

An agency that has used different accounting conventions across different past analyses should consult with OIRA regarding the categorization of ambiguous impacts. In general, when faced with ambiguity, OIRA will attempt to achieve greater consistency in the categorization of similar types of costs and benefits across different agencies.

OIRA notes that rules that cause an increase in the resources used by Federal agencies to accomplish their programmatic goals may need to be offset, and rules that reduce the real resources used by Federal agencies to accomplish their goals may qualify as EO 13771 deregulatory actions. These types of impacts have long been considered regulatory costs under OMB Circular A-4, and are a component of the costs OIRA includes in its reports to Congress on the benefits and costs of Federal regulations.

For EO 13771 deregulatory actions that revise or repeal recently issued rules, agencies generally should not estimate cost savings that exceed the costs previously projected for the relevant requirements, unless credible new evidence show that costs were previously underestimated. On the other hand, a less recent regulatory impact analysis (RIA) may need revision to reflect, among other things, the fact that only costs occurring after the effective date of the regulatory repeal should be the basis for the cost savings estimate (i.e., agencies should not count sunk costs). Where an agency believes it can significantly improve upon a prior cost estimate, especially a recent one, through methodological enhancements, the agency should first discuss those methodologies with OIRA.

Q22. How should cost savings be determined for regulatory actions that expand consumption and/or production options?

A: For regulatory actions that expand consumption and/or production options-sometimes referred to as "enabling" regulatory actions or regulations--cost savings should include the full opportunity costs of the previously forgone activities. Opportunity cost in this context would equal the sum of consumer and producer surplus, minus any fixed costs. See OMB Circular A-4 for a more detailed discussion of these concepts.

Generally, "one-time" regulatory actions (i.e., those actions that are not periodic in nature) that expand consumption and/or production options would qualify as EO 13771 deregulatory actions.

There may be situations where this approach for determining the cost offsets generated by an enabling regulatory action is inappropriate. For instance, this approach may not be appropriate in certain circumstances where, if an agency were to fail to issue a regulatory action, a significant existing and ongoing economic activity would be prohibited. See Question 26. Cost offsets for such regulatory actions will be determined on a case-by-case basis.

Please consult with OIRA on all such non-routine regulations.

Q23. How does Executive Order 13771 apply to routine hunting and fishing regulatory actions?

A. Routine hunting and fishing regulatory actions that establish annual harvest limits are not required to be offset, and are not eligible to be used as cost savings. This includes migratory bird hunting frameworks under the Migratory Bird Treaty Act and fishery management plans and amendments under the Magnuson-Stevens Fishery Conservation and Management Act. This exemption does not apply to regulatory actions that affect hunting and fishing activity that are not routine regulatory actions.

Q24. What base year should agencies use?

A: Agencies should adjust all estimates to 2016 dollars using the GDP deflator, as released on March 30, 2017, until further guidance is provided by OIRA.

Q25. How should agencies calculate cost and cost savings for the purpose of EO 13771 accounting?

A: Agencies should calculate the present value (as of 2016) of costs for EO 13771 regulatory actions and cost savings for EO 13771 deregulatory actions over the full duration of the expected effects of the actions using both 7 percent and 3 percent end-of-period discount rates.

Q26. In determining costs and cost savings under EO 13771, how should regulatory baselines be determined?

A: For the most part, agencies should follow the guidance about regulatory baselines provided in OMB Circular A-4. However, there can be uncertainty, which is recognized in OMB Circular A-4, regarding how best to capture the directive to assess impacts against the state of the world in the absence of the regulation. Provided below are two cases in which this uncertainty, or other challenges arising in the context of OMB Circular A-4, have often been addressed by performing analyses with multiple baselines. In each of these cases, OIRA has also provided guidance about how to determine costs or cost savings for the purposes of EO 13771:

1. When a regulatory action: finalizes an interim final rule (IFR), agencies are typically encouraged to present two sets of estimates: the overall regulatory impacts and the incremental impacts relative to the IFR. For purposes of determining costs or available cost savings under EO 13771, agencies finalizing an IFR should include only the incremental impacts of the final rule, relative to the IFR.

2. There are multiple Federal programs and policies-such as discharge general permitting under the Clean Water Act or Medicare quality performance tracking¬-that are updated or renewed at regular intervals via rulemaking. Because these updates reliably occur, an assessment of the incremental changes between the previous and updated programs is often much more informative than a comparison of the updated programs against hypothetical discontinuance. Although multiple-baseline analysis is likely to continue to be encouraged in such cases for analysis conducted under EO 12866, for purposes of EO 13771, costs or cost savings should be determined by the incremental changes between previous and updated programs. For example, if an agency is statutorily or judicially required to issue a regulation every five years to permit or prohibit an activity, and the agency previously issued a regulation to address the requirement, the appropriate baseline to use for estimating the costs or cost savings of the new regulation under EO 13771 is likely the existing regulation (or interim operating conditions if there is temporarily no regulation in effect).

Please consult with OIRA if you have questions regarding the appropriate baseline upon which to calculate costs or cost savings.

Q27. How should agencies treat unquantified costs and cost savings?

A: As stated in OMB Circular A-4, agencies should use their best efforts to monetize the effects of both regulatory actions and deregulatory actions and, in some cases, significant guidance documents. Depending on the likely magnitude of the effects, such efforts may include conducting or sponsoring studies to develop monetized estimates. In proposed/draft regulatory actions expected to lead to EO 13771 regulatory actions or EO 13771 deregulatory actions agencies should, at a minimum, clearly identify any non-monetized costs or cost savings, explain the key reason(s) why monetization is not possible, discuss any information the agency has that is relevant to estimating such costs, and request information from the public to monetize such costs at the final stage.

The weight assigned to unquantified effects will depend on their significance and degree of certainty, and will be handled on a case-by-case basis. See OMB Circular A-4 for more information on unquantified costs.

Q28. How should agencies treat EO 13771 regulatory actions and EO 13771 deregulatory actions published by multiple agencies?

A: These will be handled on a case-by-case basis. Agencies should consult OIRA as early as possible to determine the appropriate treatment of the action.

Q29. Can agencies "bank" cost savings and deregulatory actions?

A: Yes. Agencies may bank both EO 13771 deregulatory actions and the associated cost savings for use in the same or a subsequent fiscal year towards EO 13771's requirement to identify at least two existing regulations to be repealed (unless prohibited by law) and, separately, to comply with the total incremental cost allowance. Surplus EO 13771 deregulatory actions and cost savings do not expire at the end of a fiscal year and can be used in subsequent fiscal years.

For example, if an agency issues four EO 13771 deregulatory actions, the agency may apply them to up to two subsequent EO 13771 regulatory actions, including those occurring in a future fiscal year. Regardless, at the end of each fiscal year, an agency must be able to identify, and should have finalized, twice as many EO 13771 deregulatory actions as EO 13771 regulatory actions.

Similarly, if an agency issues two EO 13771 deregulatory actions with total cost savings of $200 million to offset the cost of an EO 13771 regulatory action with a cost of $150 million, the agency may bank the surplus cost savings of $50 million to offset the cost of another EO 13771 regulatory action, regardless of when the latter action is issued. See Questions 24 and 25 for accounting conventions that allow for appropriate comparison of costs and cost savings experienced at different time periods.

Q30. Can EO 13771 deregulatory actions (and associated cost savings) be transferred within an agency?

A: Yes. The requirements of EO 13771 apply agency-wide. An EO 13771 deregulatory action issued by a component in one agency can be used to offset an EO 13771 regulatory action issued by a different component in that same agency.

Q31. Can EO 13771 deregulatory actions (and associated cost savings) be transferred between agencies?

A: An agency that is not able to identify sufficient EO 13771 deregulatory actions for an EO 13771 regulatory action it intends to issue may submit a written request to the Director of OMB to assess whether the transfer of EO 13771 deregulatory action credits (after consultation with the supplying agency) would be appropriate before submitting the EO 13771 regulatory action to OMB for review under EO 12866. However, if the transfer is not appropriate, the agency must identify adequate offsets absent an exemption.

VI. Process Questions

Q32. How does EO 13771 affect the consideration of regulatory benefits or other requirements under EO 12866?

A: EO 13771 does not change the requirements of EO 12866, which remains the primary governing EO regarding regulatory review and planning. In particular, EO 13771 has no effect on the consideration of benefits in informing any regulatory decisions. For all EO 13771 regulatory actions and EO 13771 deregulatory actions, except where prohibited by law, agencies must continue to assess and consider both benefits and costs and comply with all existing requirements and guidance, including but not limited to those in EO 12866 and OMB Circular A-4 .

Q33. Which EO 13771 regulatory actions might qualify for a full or partial exemption from EO 13771 requirements?

A: The following categories of EO 13771 regulatory actions may qualify for a full or partial exemption from EO 13771's requirements: 1) expressly exempt actions; 2) emergency actions; 3) statutorily or judicially required actions; and 4) de minimis actions. These categories are not exhaustive. For any EO 13771 regulatory action an agency believes qualifies for an exemption under any of the circumstances provided below, agencies should submit exemption requests to OIRA prior to submitting the action to OMB for review under EO 12866 or prior to publication of the EO 13771 regulatory action if it was not subject to EO 12866 review.

- Expressly exempt -EO 13771 expressly exempts regulations issued with respect to a military, national security (see Question 7 above), or foreign affairs function, and regulations related to agency organization, management, or personnel. These actions qualify for a full exemption. See 5 USC 553.

- Emergencies -EO 13771 regulatory actions addressing emergencies such as critical health, safety, financial, non-exempt national security matters, or for some other compelling reason, may qualify for an exemption. In most cases, exemptions for such rules will be granted with respect to the timing of required offsets, allowing the agency to address the emergency before identifying and issuing EO 13771 deregulatory actions. Agencies will generally still be required to offset such actions. If necessary, the costs of such actions, and the requirement to identify for repeal at least two existing regulations, will be moved to the subsequent fiscal year for purposes of determining EO 13771 compliance.

- Statutorily or judicially required - EO 13771 does not prevent agencies from issuing regulatory actions in order to comply with an imminent statutory or judicial deadline, even if they are not able to satisfy EO 13771's requirements by the time of issuance. However, agencies will be required to offset any such EO 13771 regulatory actions as soon as practicable thereafter. In addition, this flexibility may not apply to discretionary provisions attached to EO 13771 regulatory actions required to comply with statutory or judicial deadlines.

- De minimis - EO 13771 regulatory actions with de minimis costs may qualify for an exemption. For example, if OIRA designates a proposed rule as significant under

EO 12866 because it raises novel legal or policy issues, and the agency estimates the action would have present value costs of $50,000 spread over a large number of persons and/or entities, OIRA may exempt the action from some or all of the requirements of EO 13771.

Q34. Is a significant final regulatory action exempt from the requirements of EO 13771 if the action was designated not significant at a prior stage?

A: Generally, no. Any regulatory action that is identified as significant at the final rule stage that imposes total costs greater than zero would need to be offset to comply with EO 13771, regardless of the determination in an earlier phase. Therefore, the agency should consult OIRA as soon as possible if it believes an action that was not determined to be significant at the draft or proposed rule stage may now be determined to be significant, perhaps due to substantive issues identified through public comment or further agency analysis.

Q35. How should agencies prioritize existing requirements to repeal or revise?

A: Agencies should follow the requirements in EO 13777 for prioritizing existing requirements to repeal or revise. EO 13777 establishes Regulatory Reform Task Forces in agencies, and directs those task forces to evaluate existing regulations and make recommendations to the agency head regarding their repeal, replacement, or modification, consistent with applicable law. EO 13777 directs each Regulatory Reform Task Force to identify regulations that:

- Eliminate jobs, or inhibit job creation;

- Are outdated, unnecessary, or ineffective;

- Impose costs that exceed benefits;

- Create a serious inconsistency or otherwise interfere with regulatory reform initiatives and policies;

- Are inconsistent with the requirements of section 515 of the Treasury and General Government Appropriations Act, 2001 (44 U.S.C. 3516 note), or the guidance issued pursuant to that provision, in particular those regulations that rely in whole or in part on data, information, or methods that are not publicly available or that are insufficiently transparent to meet the standard for reproducibility; or

- Derive from or implement EOs or other Presidential directives that have been subsequently rescinded or substantially modified.

EO 13777 further directs each Regulatory Reform Task Force to seek input and other assistance, as permitted by law, from entities significantly affected by Federal regulations, including State, local, and tribal governments, small businesses, consumers, non-governmental organizations, and trade associations. Input from such public engagement may be used to prioritize recommendations to repeal or revise. Finally, where the costs of an EO 13771 regulatory action will be incurred entirely or to a large degree by a certain sector or geographic area, the agency should prioritize EO 13771 deregulatory actions that affect the same sector or geographic area, to the extent feasible and permitted by law.

Q36. Can regulatory and deregulatory actions be bundled in the same action?

A: Yes, under certain circumstances. Many actions submitted to OIRA for review under EO 12866 consist of logically connected changes to multiple but related sections of the Code of Federal Regulations. For example, a rule exempting some categories of regulated entities from compliance with a previously issued regulation may also require eligible entities to submit additional documentation to demonstrate eligibility for the exemption. In these cases, it may be legitimate and appropriate to pursue such changes through a single "bundled" action, and this guidance is not meant to materially change agency decision making in this area. Where an agency combines such provisions, the cost impact (the difference between costs imposed and cost savings, per Question 21) of such rules will generally determine whether such actions are EO 13771 regulatory actions that need to be offset, or EO 13771 deregulatory actions. Agencies, however, should avoid artificially bundling provisions that are not logically connected in a single regulatory action. OIRA may determine that the regulatory and deregulatory portions of the rule should be considered separately for purposes of EO 13771 compliance.

Agencies should consult with OIRA when considering bundling regulatory and deregulatory actions.

Q37. When and how should agencies identify EO 13771 deregulatory actions?

A: The agency's Unified Agenda of Regulatory and Deregulatory Actions should reflect compliance with the requirements of EO 13771, and should include, to the extent practicable, EO 13771 deregulatory actions that, when combined with EO 13771 deregulatory actions that are not regulations (such as Paperwork Reduction Act information collection reforms), are sufficient to offset those actions appearing in the Agenda that are or are expected to resultin EO 13771 regulatory actions. At a minimum, the agency should identify all EO 13771 deregulatory actions, along with cost savings estimates, by the time it submits to OMB for review under EO 12866 the corresponding EO 13771 regulatory action. In the rare event that an agency is unable to identify sufficient EO 13771 deregulatory actions, OIRA will address such a situation on a case-by-case basis.

While each Federal Register notice should identify whether the regulation is an EO 13771 regulatory action, there is no need to discuss specific offsetting EO 13771 deregulatory actions within the same Federal Register entry. Additionally, offsetting the costs of regulatory actions to comply with the requirements of EO 13771 should not serve as the basisor rationale, in whole or in part, for issuing an EO 13771 deregulatory action.

Q38. When must identified EO 13771 deregulatory actions be finalized?

A: To the extent practicable, agencies should issue EO 13771 deregulatory actions before or concurrently with the EO 13771 regulatory actions they are intended to offset. By the end of each fiscal year, including any carryover from previous fiscal years, agencies should have:(1) issued at least twice the number of EO 13771 deregulatory actions as EO 13771 regulatory actions; and (2) appropriately offset the cost of all final EO 13771 regulatory actions issued. The offsets should be consistent with their respective total incremental cost allowance for future fiscal years, and agencies are, expected to maintain compliance, to the extent practicable, throughout the year. These requirements exclude those EO 13771 regulatory actions issued during the year for which either law prohibits compliance with EO 13771 or the agency received an exemption from OIRA. When an agency receives a partial exemption from OIRA (e.g., with respect to the timing of EO 13771 deregulatory actions), the requirements should be addressed as soon as practicable. Agencies should plan in advance and leave sufficient time, if necessary, for OIRA to complete its review under EO 12866 or the Paperwork Reduction Act, and for agencies to publish in the Federal Register any EO 13771 deregulatory actions needed to comply with EO 13771 before the end of each fiscal year.

Q39. What happens if an agency is not in full compliance with the requirements of EO 13771 at the end of a fiscal year?

A: If, by the end of a fiscal year, an agency does not finalize at least twice as many EO 13771 deregulatory actions as EO 13771 regulatory actions issued during the fiscal year, or has not met its total incremental cost allowance for that fiscal year, the agency must, within 30 days of the end of the fiscal year, submit for the OMB Director's approval, a plan for coming into full compliance with EO 13771 that addresses each of the following:

1. The reasons for, and magnitude of, non-compliance;

2. How and when the agency will come into full compliance; and

3. Any other relevwant information requested by the Director.

This excludes EO 13771 regulatory actions that are exempt or where compliance with EO 13771 is prohibited by law.

OMB may recommend that an agency take additional steps to achieve compliance, such as publishing a notice in the Federal Register requesting ideas from the public on EO 13771 deregulatory actions to pursue. OMB may also request that agencies post plans approved by the Director.

This guidance is not intended to, and does not, create any right or benefit, substantive or procedural, enforceable at law or in equity by any party against the United States, its departments, agencies, or entities, its officers, employees, or agents, or any other person.

Presidential Memorandum Regarding the Hiring Freeze

MEMORANDUM FOR THE HEADS OF EXECUTIVE DEPARTMENTS AND AGENCIES

SUBJECT: Hiring Freeze

By the authority vested in me as President by the Constitution and the laws of the United States of America, I hereby order a freeze on the hiring of Federal civilian employees to be applied across the board in the executive branch. As part of this freeze, no vacant positions existing at noon on January 22, 2017, may be filled and no new positions may be created, except in limited circumstances. This order does not include or apply to military personnel. The head of any executive department or agency may exempt from the hiring freeze any positions that it deems necessary to meet national security or public safety responsibilities. In addition, the Director of the Office of Personnel Management (OPM) may grant exemptions from this freeze where those exemptions are otherwise necessary.

Within 90 days of the date of this memorandum, the Director of the Office of Management and Budget (OMB), in consultation with the Director of OPM, shall recommend a long-term plan to reduce the size of the Federal Government's workforce through attrition. This order shall expire upon implementation of the OMB plan.

Contracting outside the Government to circumvent the intent of this memorandum shall not be permitted.

This hiring freeze applies to all executive departments and agencies regardless of the sources of their operational and programmatic funding, excepting military personnel.

In carrying out this memorandum, I ask that you seek efficient use of existing personnel and funds to improve public services and the delivery of these services. Accordingly, this memorandum does not prohibit making reallocations to meet the highest priority needs and to ensure that essential services are not interrupted and national security is not affected.

This memorandum does not limit the nomination and appointment of officials to positions requiring Presidential appointment or Senate confirmation, the appointment of officials to non-career positions in the Senior Executive Service or to Schedule C positions in the Excepted Service, or the appointment of any other officials who serve at the pleasure of the appointing authority. Moreover, it does not limit the hiring of personnel where such a limit would conflict with applicable law. This memorandum does not revoke any appointment to Federal service made prior to January 22, 2017.

This memorandum does not abrogate any collective bargaining agreement in effect on the date of this memorandum.

DONALD J. TRUMP

Executive Order Minimizing the Economic Burden of the Patient Protection and Affordable Care Act Pending Repeal

EXECUTIVE ORDER

- - - - - - -

MINIMIZING THE ECONOMIC BURDEN OF THE PATIENT PROTECTION AND AFFORDABLE CARE ACT PENDING REPEAL

By the authority vested in me as President by the Constitution and the laws of the United States of America, it is hereby ordered as follows:

Section 1. It is the policy of my Administration to seek the prompt repeal of the Patient Protection and Affordable Care Act (Public Law 111-148), as amended (the "Act"). In the meantime, pending such repeal, it is imperative for the executive branch to ensure that the law is being efficiently implemented, take all actions consistent with law to minimize the unwarranted economic and regulatory burdens of the Act, and prepare to afford the States more flexibility and control to create a more free and open healthcare market.

Sec. 2. To the maximum extent permitted by law, the Secretary of Health and Human Services (Secretary) and the heads of all other executive departments and agencies (agencies) with authorities and responsibilities under the Act shall exercise all authority and discretion available to them to waive, defer, grant exemptions from, or delay the implementation of any provision or requirement of the Act that would impose a fiscal burden on any State or a cost, fee, tax, penalty, or regulatory burden on individuals, families, healthcare providers, health insurers, patients, recipients of healthcare services, purchasers of health insurance, or makers of medical devices, products, or medications.

Sec. 3. To the maximum extent permitted by law, the Secretary and the heads of all other executive departments and agencies with authorities and responsibilities under the Act, shall exercise all authority and discretion available to them to provide greater flexibility to States and cooperate with them in implementing healthcare programs.

Sec. 4. To the maximum extent permitted by law, the head of each department or agency with responsibilities relating to healthcare or health insurance shall encourage the development of a free and open market in interstate commerce for the offering of healthcare services and health insurance, with the goal of achieving and preserving maximum options for patients and consumers.

Sec. 5. To the extent that carrying out the directives in this order would require revision of regulations issued through notice-and-comment rulemaking, the heads of agencies shall comply with the Administrative Procedure Act and other applicable statutes in considering or promulgating such regulatory revisions.

Sec. 6. (a) Nothing in this order shall be construed to impair or otherwise affect:

(i) the authority granted by law to an executive department or agency, or the head thereof; or

(ii) the functions of the Director of the Office of Management and Budget relating to budgetary, administrative, or legislative proposals.

(b) This order shall be implemented consistent with applicable law and subject to the availability of appropriations.

(c) This order is not intended to, and does not, create any right or benefit, substantive or procedural, enforceable at law or in equity by any party against the United States, its departments, agencies, or entities, its officers, employees, or agents, or any other person.

DONALD J. TRUMP

THE WHITE HOUSE,

January 20, 2017.